Advance Praise for *Too Small to Fail*

'An idea whose time has come.'
Steven Pinker, Johnstone Family Professor of Psychology,
Harvard University

'If you are happy with your country, don't read this book. But if you think your country could do significantly better, this book will show you how.'
Lars Kolind, Chairman, The World Scout Foundation

'With global governance being challenged, this book offers provoking thoughts and ideas from the smaller nations as to what redefining success looks like.'
Paul Polman, Co-founder & Chair IMAGINE,
former CEO, Unilever

'James Breiding's new book reveals the growing importance of social cohesion and trust for a nation's prosperity. Society is a boat and if it sinks, the next big start-up like Google won't save it.'
Yossi Vardi, Israeli Innovator and Serial Entrepreneur

'With the world receding, *Too Small to Fail* is a valuable reminder of the importance of openness and connectivity.'

Laurent Freixe, CEO, Zone Americas, Nestlé

'An excellent portrayal of how lack of entitlement drives small nations' success: they expect to have to adapt to outside forces, so they do.'

Janan Ganesh, Columnist, *The Financial Times*

'Policy makers and investors have for too long paid too little attention to the importance of responsible, long-term ownership for company performance and the wealth of nations. Breiding's chapter 'Towards More Responsible Ownership' in *Too Small to Fail* is a loud and necessary wake-up call.'

Steen Thomsen, Professor, Center for Corporate Governance, Copenhagen Business School

'Learn from Finland. It has the most effective schools because it does just about the opposite of what we are doing in the United States.'

Howard Gardner, John H. and Elisabeth A. Hobbs Research Professor of Cognition and Education, Harvard Graduate School of Education

'This important book shows how small countries make globalization work successfully.'

Harold James, Professor of History and International Affairs, Claude and Lore Kelly Professor of European Studies, Princeton University

'This is a story everyone interested in country competitiveness needs to hear. Scale is simply not enough. Small is often beautiful and there are many lessons larger countries can learn from their success.'

Kristine Braden Chief of Staff, Office of the CEO, Citigroup

TOO SMALL TO FAIL

WHY SOME SMALL NATIONS OUTPERFORM LARGER ONES AND HOW THEY ARE RESHAPING THE WORLD

R. JAMES BREIDING

HARPER
BUSINESS

An Imprint of HarperCollins Publishers

First published in India in 2019 by Harper Business
An imprint of HarperCollins *Publishers*
A-75, Sector 57, Noida, Uttar Pradesh 201301, India
www.harpercollins.co.in

2 4 6 8 10 9 7 5 3 1

P-ISBN: 978-93-5302-357-7
E-ISBN: 978-93-5302-358-4

Typeset in 10.5/14.2 Sabon LT Std at
Manipal Technologies Limited, Manipal

Printed and bound at
Thomson Press (India) Ltd

To Mineko, Johanna, Joshua, Nicholas, Liv and Morris.

If we want to improve, we must be content to be thought foolish and stupid.

—Epictetus

Contents

Foreword

Too Small to Fail challenges us to question and rethink many of our assumptions about the world.

Since the Peace of Westphalia in 1648, we have been living in a world of nation states. Our understanding of the world has been guided by scholars such as Hans Morgenthau.

In his magnum opus, *Politics Among Nations*, Morgenthau theorized that the power of the state is derived from the size of its territory, population, military, economy, natural resource endowment, national character, morale, government and diplomacy. This view of the power of states was valid when national boundaries were sacrosanct, when economies were relatively self-reliant and self-contained, and before the advent of multinational corporations, information technology, a global capital market and revolution in military affairs.

The world we live in today is radically different from the world fifty years ago. It has been transformed by international trade, global business, world money, information technology, the internet, mobility of talent and knowledge as a country's most important natural resource.

I would argue that Hans Morgenthau's concept of the Territorial State has been replaced by Philip Bobbitt's concept of the Market State. What is a Market State? It is a state which has taken advantage of the new opportunities of international trade, open borders, globalization, information technology and human mobility. Such a state would therefore be a major player in international trade, be a large recipient and provider of foreign direct investment, act as an important financial centre and communications hub and host a big family of multinational corporations and foreign talent. The nations Breiding has chosen to feature in his book are exemplar of a Market State, including my own, Singapore.

Breiding's book forces us to question the conventional wisdom about countries. For example, we tend to equate bigness with success. This is clearly wrong. Not all big countries are successful, and not all successful countries are big. In fact, some of the most successful countries in the world are small countries.

Other countries could have qualified for inclusion such as Liechtenstein, New Zealand and Norway, and there is a growing list of aspirational nations with promising trajectories such as Estonia, Chile, Costa Rica, Mauritius and others.

Breiding's book contains the following revelations about small countries which would surprise most people. First, some of the richest countries in the world are small countries. Second, some of the most competitive economies in the world are small economies. Third, some of the highest-ranking countries in the UN Human Development Index are small countries. Fourth, some of the top twenty trading entities of the world are small countries. Fifth, some of the world's largest exporters of capital are small countries. Sixth, some of the least corrupt countries are small countries. Seventh, some of the countries with the best scores for adherences to the rule of law are small countries. Eighth, some of the countries with the best education systems are small countries. Ninth, some of the countries with the best gender equality are small countries. Tenth, some of the highest ranking countries with regard to ease of doing business are small countries.

Breiding also argues that several factors which are most determinant of a nation's success in this day and age are not yet measured by institutions such as the World Bank and World Economic Forum: adaptability, modesty, social cohesion and a sustainable attitude towards ownership and the environment. These factors feature prominently in successful small nations and are destined to take on greater importance.

We should not, however, equate smallness with success. There are many small countries which are not successful. The truth is that size is only one factor influencing a country's success or failure. What matters most is the policies it pursues and the values it upholds.

Small countries have a better chance of success if their economies are open and they practise free trade. Domestically, they should uphold the rule of law, combat corruption and empower women and children. Investment in quality education and training are essential. They should uphold the values of hard work, honesty, transparency and accountability. They should support international cooperation and multilateralism.

This is an important book because most authors focus on the big countries. Very few have focused on the smaller countries. I thank James Breiding for writing this very important and path-breaking book. He has drawn the world's attention to this class of eight small super-achievers. It is a book which questions conventional wisdom about countries and the nature of the world we live in today and will live in tomorrow. There are big lessons which the world can learn from these small countries.

Tommy Koh
Professor of Law, National University of Singapore
Ambassador-at-Large, Ministry of Foreign Affairs,
Singapore

Prologue

A small nation is usually stronger in proportion than a large one.

A thousand arguments could be advanced in favour of this principle. First, management becomes more difficult because of the great distances, the way weight becomes heavier at the edge of a larger lever.

It also becomes a heavier burden with the increasing number of steps involved in the exercise of power. The needs of the subjects are not better handled by this multiplicity of authorities. They would have been comfortable if only one person had overseen them.

That is not all. Not only is the government not strong and quick, but the people also have little affection for their leaders who never see them. It is impossible for the same laws to fit so many different communities, sectors and customs.

The leaders, who are overly preoccupied, do not see anything but for themselves. Talent is buried, virtue unknown and vice unpunished among such a multitude of men who do not know one another.

Thus, a body falls too large in proportion to its structure and is lost under its weight. On the other hand, the state must secure a solid foundation for itself so that it can withstand the inevitable shocks.

From here, we see that there are reasons for expansion and preferences for reduction. In every body politic, there is a maximum strength which it cannot exceed and which it only loses by increasing in size. It is better to count on the vigour that comes of good government than on the resources a great territory furnishes. It is best to establish limits that will make a nation's size neither too large for good governance, nor too small for self-maintenance. The statesman's ability to find the relationship between them is of great importance.

Jean-Jacques Rousseau, *The Social Contract and Discourses* (1762), abridged

In a large republic, there are large fortunes, and consequently little moderation of spirit. The common good is sacrificed to a thousand considerations; it is subordinated to various exceptions; it depends on accidents. In a small republic, the public good is more strongly felt, better known, and closer to each citizen.

Montesquieu, C.L. *The Spirit of Laws*

Kings and princes can indeed create professors and privy-councillors, and confer titles and decorations, but they cannot make great men – spirits that soar above the base turmoil of this world.

Beethoven, L.v. *Selected Letters*

Introduction

Warren Buffett, probably the world's most successful investor, has attributed much of his good fortune to the lottery of life, tracing it to being born 'in the right country, at the right time' – namely, America in 1930 (Crippen 2010). Some six decades later, in 1988, the *Economist* wholeheartedly agreed with a study that the US was the most desirable place to spend a lifetime. But as with all lotteries, odds change. Redoing the analysis in 2012, the magazine put the US in the humble sixteenth spot in the global order, below Taiwan and just above the United Arab Emirates (*Economist* 2012). Surging into the top ranks this time around were small countries with populations of less than twenty-five million people, such as Switzerland, Singapore and Ireland.

Small countries now make up eleven of the top fifteen advanced economies in terms of per capita income. They took nine out of the top ten spots in IMD's most recent Global Competitiveness Report (Jamrisko 2019). And in 2018, they took fifteen of the top twenty positions in the United Nations Human Development Index.

What explains their remarkable ascendance?

Much of the current debate on global economic performance focuses not on success but on failure. There is a shelf load of books discussing flawed states, foremost among them is *Why Nations Fail* by Daron Acemoglu and James Robinson published in 2012. In part, this is because of the elephantine case of the US, which is often the inspiration for studies of all kinds. But as Harvard University's Steven Pinker reminds us, 'There are so many more ways for things to go wrong than to go right,' making success far more valuable to explain than failure (Pinker 2017).

1

Have we not heard enough about failure? After all, history shows that unlike lotteries, progress is usually a matter of finding something which works and reverse-engineering it. Nations do not spontaneously organize themselves to achieve higher PISA (Programme for International Student Assessment) rankings, file more patents and export more goods. Food does not fall on our plates, clothes on our backs or roofs over our heads. Wealth, not poverty, is what begs a better explanation.

Given the rising concern in large nations over wealth disparities, dwindling job opportunities, stagnating growth and waning confidence in political systems, now may be a good time to peek over the garden hedge and see what we can learn from the success of small countries on all these fronts. As many large nations struggle with the trade-offs between sovereignty and globalization – as signalled by Donald Trump's election in America, the vote for Brexit in Britain and rising right-wing populism elsewhere in the world – could smaller economies provide some helpful guidance?

For centuries, a country's status has been measured by the size of its territorial reach, its military might and its natural resource endowment. These were the foundations for the Treaty of Westphalia in 1648, the blueprint of the modern system of nation states. While still important to the global balance of power, these physical metrics are waning today in relevance in the face of increasing global economic interdependence, driven largely by rapid developments in information technology, telecommunication and transportation. Gaining sway over the world's treasures is no longer a matter of giant armies and navies, but of winning trade battles and global contests for professional talent. And, in a surprisingly large number of cases, the smaller, nimbler countries are winning.

This shift from the mega-states to the minnows reflects the changing structure of global commerce. In the past, enterprises sprang up parochially and grew organically before morphing into international and sometimes multinational businesses. But their strengths could still be traced to their industrial-age origins in places like Manchester, St. Louis and Stuttgart. Today, the location of a company matters much less. Products cross borders multiple times, reaching customers from all around the world. Technology, manufacturing, customers, competition and financing can come from anywhere in the world and at any time, often leaving traditional behemoths behind.

Big Lessons from Small Countries

Too Small to Fail analyses several successful countries which have created strengths out of their physical limitations. It tries to understand what they do differently and why they seem to do it better. What is their secret recipe for a better educated, more egalitarian and wealthier population?

The book looks first at the forest and then the trees. The first section surveys small countries such as Denmark, Ireland and Switzerland to uncover common patterns behind their success, besides having made a virtue out of their smallness. Some are fairly obvious, such as outstanding education systems and openness towards trade, talent and ideas. Others are more counter-intuitive, such as humility, vulnerability, adaptability and their attitude towards ownership. We then do a deeper dive into concrete examples of public policies which have enabled these results. We study how Singapore's healthcare system achieved superior outcomes at a quarter of the American cost and at 40 per cent of Britain's, and how Ireland transformed itself from a state of impoverishment and neglect into the rising star of Europe. We look at how Israel managed to create its own indigenous form of Silicon Valley and why Finnish schoolchildren outperform their peers elsewhere in the world. We then ask whether these lessons are relevant to other countries and if they can be replicated, in whole or in part.

Finally, we consider the future of the nation state, asking what these emerging patterns mean for the rest of the world, including the super-sized countries which have until now dominated its governance and economics. We conclude that the world is marching towards smaller states, rewarding their approaches and amplifying their strengths in ways which might ultimately force larger states to pay attention. I also believe that at the level of the individual, citizenship will be more mobile and fungible in the future, as people are able to move more freely and nations increasingly compete in a slower growth environment for the world's brightest minds and wealthiest people.

Crawling between the Toes of the Elephants

Karl Marx once said, 'Men make their own history, but they do not make it as they please; they do not make it under self-selected circumstances, but under circumstances existing already' (Marx 1852, cited in Thompson 2011). *Too Small to Fail* is a story about successful adaptation to circumstances which already existed. However, given that they have made considerable progress with regard to global challenges, they are worth studying.

Though there are almost an infinite type of small nations in the world, the most successful share certain common attributes. They conduct their economies more openly and rely heavily on foreign trade for their survival. Their economies are more exposed and thus sensitive to new opportunities and threats, making them more alert and willing to adapt. Their consumers are exposed to a greater variety of new products and services and their societies are more likely to attract talented immigrants. With this openness comes greater tolerance, enabling a more level playing field, often irrespective of gender, religion or sexual preference, and thus, creating larger pools of talent.

Since it is their human rather than natural resources which determine their competitiveness, smaller states tend to maintain education systems which reflect the needs of industry better. Teachers enjoy public respect, higher pay and work in tandem with parents to develop skills of the students. Children grow up embracing meritocracy and egalitarianism, not privilege and elitism. They learn at an early age to place more value on the community than the individual, on collaboration rather than rivalry and on social norms rather than regulations. Not just the universities but also the vocational schools and apprenticeship systems equip them with the skills they need for a solid foundation of a successful career.

Small countries also draw strength from their historical status as underdogs bullied by larger neighbours. Fifty years ago, newly independent Singapore lost its mandate to host port facilities for Britain's Royal Navy at a time when its industrial base was weak to non-existent. Switzerland faced neighbouring imperialist giants through most of its modern history, devising survival strategies such as neutrality to head off invasions. Denmark is just a shadow of its former imperial self, having lost vast swaths of territory through diplomatic mishaps and military defeats, but it has learned how to do more with less. Finland was jostled between the Swedish monarchy and the Russian Czar for seven hundred years until it emerged as a staunchly independent nation. The Dutch have crossed swords with the French, Germans, Spanish and others, and still found within themselves the ingenuity to deter the encroaching North Sea and applied it to building a global mercantile empire. Each have turned their vulnerability into a source of vigilance, flexibility and renewal.

Along with resilience, these histories have instilled a sense of modesty. A history lesson in Great Britain rarely passes without children being reminded, for good or bad, of the glory of the past empire and the exploits of Admiral Nelson or Winston Churchill. France cherishes its legacy as La Grande Nation. The Chinese characters for the word 'China' mean 'middle or centre country', reflecting their belief that the world revolves around Beijing and that countries like Korea and Japan are provincial satellites. In the US, Donald Trump's potent battle cry, 'make America great again', helped pave the way to his election. But there is a fine line between pride and arrogance. In an increasingly competitive world, modesty often provides a distinct advantage. After all, people prefer counterparts whom they can like and trust – hard to do if your prospective partner is chauvinistic.

Large countries tend to approach competition – be it in sport, war or business – with a winner-take-all mindset. Yet, mutuality brings greater rewards. Small countries have realized the value of mutual respect and collaboration in a changing world compared with hard-nosed rivalry. To take just the most obvious example, reciprocity is fundamental to trade, allowing both sides to benefit from their dealings. Too-small-to-fail (*TSTF*) countries have realized that cooperation rather than domination is the key to success, and they are adept at achieving their goals not by aggression and coercion but through negotiation.

Counter-intuitively, smaller countries often shun the perceived advantages of centralization, opting instead for more decentralized systems which instil a greater sense of self-reliance and empower people at the community level where costs and benefits of government services are more readily ascertainable. These systems give voice to their citizens, foster a sense of shared community and even spur domestic competition among government agencies. Swiss voters, for instance, are increasingly asked to take a position on concrete issues such as climate change, or the amount of debt its parliament can impose on its citizens, thus dispersing power to individuals and providing a check on elected representatives.

There is an even more fundamental grassroots advantage to those living in a smaller state. Notwithstanding their propensity for earning higher incomes, citizens of these countries tend to be less avaricious. In fact, the qualities of greed and self-interest are currently undergoing a major re-evaluation by economists. Since as early as the mid-eighteenth century, thinkers, most notably David Hume, have argued that such impulses drive economic progress. But new evidence shows that citizens of smaller nations place less value on money for its own sake than their counterparts do in larger nations. This strengthens the societies and economies of the smaller nations, on the whole.

People in smaller countries also seem to be more willing to make sacrifices for the sake of the future. Rather than kick the can down the road, smaller countries have shown more willingness to embrace long-term problems in the present in order to prevent mortgaging their children's futures. Government debt levels tend to be substantially lower and the concern for the environment stronger. Switzerland leads the world in clean energy production and Denmark is working towards becoming CO_2 neutral by 2025.[1]

Altogether, these trends offer powerful clues about what our world will look like a century from now. *Too Small to Fail* argues that smaller and nimbler nations will be more successful in the future, and consequently, there are likely to be more of them.

Historically, the sizes of countries have been determined as a trade-off between the advantages of scale and the costs of increasing heterogeneity, as the economists Alberto Alesina and Enrico Spolaore argued in *The Size of Nations* (2003). Benefits of scale derive from several factors. A large population, for example, allows defence costs to be amortized over more taxpayers, thus lowering the per capita expense. A richer resource endowment fuels industrial growth and a bigger domestic market propels the economy by generating local demand.

---

1. 'Denmark aims to be the world's first CO_2 neutral capital city by 2025' (Københavns Kommune).

But even at the time Alesina and Spolaore published their book a decade and a half ago, all these advantages were beginning to erode. Lower transportation costs, access to cheaper goods and information through the internet reduced the benefits of having a large domestic market or natural resources. Customer demand was no longer limited to national borders and free trade enabled access to vastly larger markets and productivity gains.

Greater humility breeds fewer conflicts. Smaller countries have learned the advantages of avoiding geopolitical rivalry on the global stage, thus sparing themselves the hefty costs of military spending and the temptation to demonstrate its results. Given the growing disparity in strength between a few major powers and the rest of the world, 'realpolitik' means that smaller countries are increasingly forced to form allegiances with one of the superpowers (America or China) and effectively pay rent in exchange for their protection, rather than build their own costly defence systems.

While the benefits of size have decreased, the costs of heterogeneity have increased. Recent political upheavals, such as Brexit, the election of Trump and the surging right-wing movements in France, the Netherlands and Germany suggest that homogeneity is now elbowing diversity off the agenda in many societies. In a time of polarization, each side takes actions which please its most passionate members, but in doing so, alienate many potential supporters.

'Me' Vs 'We' Societies

Since the 1960s, traditionally cohesive institutions such as family, marriage, military and religion have weakened. Harvard political scientist Robert Putnam argued in *Bowling Alone* (2000) that we have become increasingly disconnected from one another and our social structures – whether that means the family, church, employers or neighbours. These loosened or, in many cases, broken bonds have been accompanied by a proliferation of new identities with regard to gender, generation, race, sexual preference and ideology. It has been popular during the past few decades to celebrate diversity with the steady beat of the old slogan – 'E pluribus unum', or 'out of many, one' – with the stress on individual identity, as though its benefits were infinitely linear.

But recent trends suggest that identity has been relatively blurred, which ultimately begs the question: Who exactly are 'we the people'?

The countries included in *Too Small to Fail* have managed to maintain their cohesiveness without restricting their ability to adapt and reinvent. They have achieved a greater sense of belonging and avoided the kind of stratification of communities which push common people out of sight, and thus, out of mind. With regard to gender, for example, Nordic countries have found ways to be equal without being the same. They remind us that throughout human history, social norms, rather than the rules and laws which are characteristic of larger states, have regulated much of our behaviour. The Nobel Prize-winning economist Kenneth Arrow argued that smaller, more homogenous societies are easier to govern and that democracy can grow dysfunctional when electorates become substantially more diverse and polarized.

Towards Smaller, Nimbler Nation States

Too Small to Fail argues that these models will only grow in relevance. For most of the past century, many nations enjoyed a win–win environment and grew wealthier from regular productivity gains and the easing of trade barriers. Now, according to Gideon Rachman, the foreign affairs commentator at the *Financial Times*, nations face a more zero-sum world where self-interest assumes far greater importance (Rachman 2010). Pankaj Mishra argues similarly in *Age of Anger* that the world will become more divided and disorderly as economies slow down and inequalities increasingly reveal themselves.

Societies will have to cope with slower growth and learn to do more with less. The haves will come under greater scrutiny and criticism from the have-nots. Studies show that we are far more likely to feel empathy towards those with whom we feel an affinity. In empathetic societies, policies which redistribute wealth find more ready acceptance, as Scandinavia demonstrates. The Danes, for example, believe that taxes are a necessary investment for a better society. Yes, individuals have rights, but in order for the collective to be cohesive, individuals also have duties. When the sense of affinity wanes, individuals begin to view taxes as an annual punishment for creating wealth and thus something to be avoided – or at least minimized through exploiting loopholes.

Citizens may polarize themselves between 'those who do work' and 'those who mooch off those who do work', undermining the acceptance of redistribution policies aimed at reducing inequality.

Supranational governance structures like the European Union led by appointed rather than elected officials, as well as societies which feel uncomfortably placed in regional groupings which are legacies of an obsolete epoch, may find it more difficult to stay together under these circumstances.

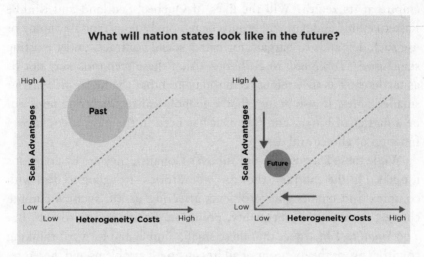

Figure 0.1: Changing Dynamics of State Formation

This graph shows how scale will take on less importance and social cohesion more for state formation in the future.

Source: Lambais and Breiding 2019; Alesina and Spolaore 2005

Too Small to Fail is not an attempt to find a 'one size fits all' benchmark to evaluate the relative success of nations, nor does it seek to concoct a 'paint by numbers' manual on how to do it with a false sense of precision and legitimacy. Each of the countries under study have experienced unique and complex trajectories which are irreproducible and, in any many cases, not comparable to other countries.

Countries discussed in *Too Small to Fail* could, however, be the main beneficiaries from this fragmentation. If smaller, nimbler and less heterogeneous societies confer competitive advantages, then it is likely for there to be more of them in the future. Figure 0.1 represents this trend. Legacy nation groupings burdened with incompatible ethnicity, language and traditions could experience deepening fault lines. Recent monetary crises in the EU already provide a hint of things to come.

It is tempting to speculate on what new national structure could emerge. Political movements for independence are gaining ground across the world from Catalan to California. Why couldn't the six million people living in the Miami conurbation join forces with Cubans and Puerto Ricans to create a Novo Havana as a proud vestige of the Spanish empire at its zenith? Will the likes of Quebec, Scotland and Middle Eastern ethnic and national groups be tempted to push for autonomy or use such demands to bargain for better social contracts under existing structures?[2] *Too Small to Fail* argues that these scenarios may not be as far-fetched as they might seem today and that the future will favour smaller states. It also argues that a geopolitical restructuring need not be a matter of lottery and fate as it has been in the past; it could be a function of choice and design.

While these Davids may prevail over Goliaths, they are by no means utopias. On the contrary, they are laboratories struggling to deal with complex and challenging problems affecting us all, such as climate change, immigration, inequality, pollution, health and terrorism. But *Too Small to Fail* argues that these small, nimble and forward-thinking countries are at the forefront of addressing these problems and therefore, in Hegel's words, are 'the land of the future, where, in the ages that lie before us, the burden of the world's history shall reveal itself'.

References and Further Reading

Acemoglu, D. and J.A. Robinson. *Why Nations Fail: The Origins of Power, Prosperity and Poverty* (London: Profile Books, 2013).

Alesina, A. and E. Spolaore. *The Size of Nations* (Cambridge, MA: MIT Press, 2003).

Crippen, A. 'CNBC Transcript: Warren Buffet & Bill Gates – Keeping America Great'. *CNBC*, 2010. https://www.cnbc.com/id/33901003.

---

2. A social contract is an actual or implied agreement between a government and its citizens that defines the obligations and duties of both parties.

Human Development Report Office. '2018 Statistical Update'. *Human Development Index (HDI)*, 2018. http://hdr.undp.org/en/2018-update.

Jamrisko, M. 'Singapore Dethrones U.S. as World's Most Competitive Economy'. *Bloomberg*, 2019. https://www.bloomberg.com/news/articles/2019-05-28/singapore-dethrones-u-s-to-top-world-competitiveness-rankings.

Københavns Kommune. 'The CPH 2025 Climate Plan', no date. https://urbandevelopmentcph.kk.dk/artikel/cph-2025-climate-plan.

Mishra, Pankaj. *Age of Anger: A History of the Present* (New York: Farrar, Straus and Giroux, 2017)

Pinker, S. '2017: What scientific term or concept ought to be more widely known?' *Edge*, 2017. https://www.edge.org/response-detail/27023.

Putnam, R. *Bowling Alone: The Collapse and Revival of American Community*. (New York: Simon & Schuster, 2001).

Rachman, G. 'Zero-Sum World'. *The Financial Times*, 2010. https://www.ft.com/content/bcfb2d80-dd62-11df-beb7-00144feabdc0.

Schwab, K. et al. *The Global Competitiveness Report 2018*. World Economic Forum. http://reports.weforum.org/global-competitiveness-report-2018/.

'The lottery of life: Where to be born in 2013'. *The Economist*, 2012. https://www.economist.com/news/2012/11/21/the-lottery-of-life.

Part A
Secret Sauces

1

The Fallacy of Scale

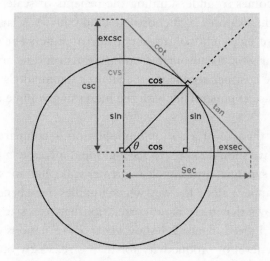

Fallacy of Scale suggests that we may place too much value on exact forms of measurement.

Source: Wikimedia Commons

Any intelligent fool can make things bigger, more complex and more violent. It takes a touch of genius – and a lot of courage – to move in the opposite direction.

—E.F. Schumacher, *Small Is Beautiful*

What gravity is to physics, 'π' is to geometry or entropy is to chemistry, 'economies of scale' is meant to be for prosperity. The 'bigger is better' mantra has driven nation formation throughout history. Nations strived to achieve vaster territories, larger natural resource endowments and bigger swaths of new citizens. Larger populations mean larger consumer markets and the cost per citizen across a wide range of common benefits declines considerably. Hence, amenities such as hospitals, roads, airports, schools, sewage treatment plants and police protection should be much cheaper per person in the US than, for example, in Singapore. The cost of defence becomes exponentially lower with the size of population as conscripted forces can be called upon in the time of war and the cost of professional armies can be shared across more people at a fraction of the cost.

When it comes to understanding the benefits of scale, it may help to consider the example of a chocolate chip cookie. A large company can purchase eggs, chocolate and flour at much cheaper prices. Much of their work is automated and production runs are larger and longer, so the cost per cookie is less. Hence, a company's profitability should increase exponentially with the increasing volume of its cookie production.

So, when the size of a nation's population is compared to its per capita GDP, we should expect to see a gradual increase in productivity reflecting the synergies attributable to greater scale. But, for some reason, something happens along the way which nullifies these benefits of scale. Research shows that there is no correlation between size and relative productivity. Indeed, figure 1.1 shows that *TSTF* nations demonstrate a remarkable level of productivity for their size, vastly outperforming larger nations.

The lack of a straight-line relationship is not limited to productivity per person. 75 per cent of the twenty most competitive countries in the world have populations of under twenty-five million people (IMD 2018). The US has the second highest per capita spending on health care in the world and the world's most sophisticated healthcare industry (Miller and Lu 2018). Far from achieving benefits of scale, the US ranks fifty-fourth, together with Azerbaijan, with regard to effectiveness. Singapore, a country with less than six million people, has the second-most effective healthcare system in the world, with per capita healthcare costs which are a quarter of those in the US.

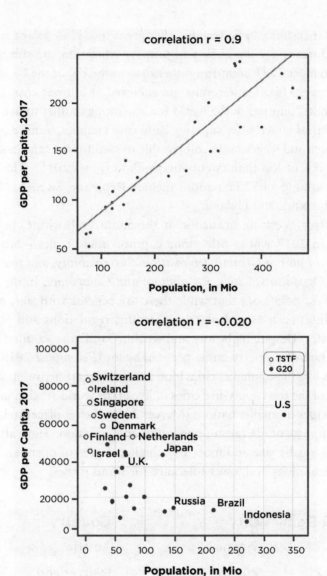

Figure 1.1: Bigger Doesn't Mean Better among Nations

The top graph demonstrates what close correlation between a nation's size and its GDP per capita would look like theoretically. The bottom graph shows that, in reality, there is effectively no correlation (r = 0 means random). It also shows that a clutch of smaller nations (TSTF) have a considerably higher GDP per capita relative to their size.

Source: World Bank, NZZ; R. J. Breiding

Similar results can be seen in other areas too. PISA scores, a widely accepted metric for the quality of primary education, are substantially higher in most *TSTF* countries rather than in the UK or the US (Jackson and Kiersz 2016). These results are achieved at a lower cost. Eight of the ten best countries in the world for a working mother to live in (i.e., the countries which offer superior child care facilities, a more inclusive work force and wages more comparable to men for the same task) have populations of less than twenty-five million (Jones 2015). The highest ranking among all *TSTF* nations include Denmark, Sweden, Norway, the Netherlands and Finland.

Geoffrey West, an academic at the Santa Fe Institute, published a book in 2017 whose title alone captures these issues – *Scale: The Universal Laws of Growth, Innovation, Sustainability, and the Pace of Life, in Organisms, Cities, Economies, and Companies.* In the case of cities, West points out that while there are benefits with size, negative externalities such as violent crimes, traffic, regulations and pollution grow faster. Despite its beauty and wealth, San Francisco now has the highest rate of property crime per inhabitant (*Economist* 2019). With statistics like these, smaller cities look increasingly attractive. Indeed, the ranking of the top twenty-five cities to live in the world are dominated by smaller cities in smaller nations (Mercer 2019). Better places to live tend to be outposts of liberalism, possibility and ambition. Their attraction is fueled less by size and more by a higher degree of openness to new ideas, technology and lower tolerance for status games.

2019 Rank	City	Country
1	Vienna	Austria
2	Zürich	Switzerland
3	Munich	Germany
3	Auckland	New Zealand
3	Vancouver	Canada
6	Düsseldorf	Germany
7	Frankfurt	Germany

9	Geneva	Switzerland
8	Copenhagen	Denmark
10	Basel	Switzerland
11	Sydney	Australia
11	Amsterdam	Netherlands
13	Berlin	Germany
14	Bern	Switzerland
15	Wellington	New Zealand
16	Toronto	Canada
17	Melbourne	Australia
18	Luxembourg	Luxembourg
19	Ottawa	Canada
19	Hamburg	Germany
21	Perth	Australia
21	Montreal	Canada
23	Stockholm	Sweden
23	Nuremberg	Germany
25	Singapore	Singapore
25	Oslo	Norway

Figure 1.2: The World's Most Liveable Cities

Smaller cities in smaller countries dominate the Mercer rankings of the world's most liveable cities.

Source: Mercer 2019

With regard to companies, and after studying the records of 23,000 businesses, West concludes that corporate productivity is significantly sublinear. This means that after an initial period of flourishing, profit per employee shrinks as the number of employees grows. In his words, 'it is the bleak reality of corporate growth that efficiencies of scale are almost always outweighed by the burdens of bureaucracy.'

Figure 1.3: Size and Productivity

Source: Banx

There are plenty of examples throughout *TSTF* nations where smallness prevails against the apparent advantages of size. New Zealand's All Blacks have dominated rugby for two decades even though the team draws from less than five million people to field its fifteen-person team, a ratio that dwarfs its larger peers. Alinghi, a team led by Ernesto Bertarelli, won the America Cup, a coveted sailing race historically reserved for the world's great naval powers. Alinghi hailed from a land-locked country with a population of around eight million. A joke in Hebrew is that the Soviet Union was a disastrous scale up of the Kibbutz, the small collective communities in Israel. Switzerland, Singapore, Sweden and Israel have considerably more billionaires per capita than larger nations such as the US, Britain, China or India (Brinded 2015). Sweden and Switzerland are staunchly egalitarian, but still manage to generate opportunities for exceptional wealth creation; think of the Kamprads (IKEA), the Rausings (Tetrapack) or the Schindlers. There are lots of possible explanations for their success, but advantages of scale are not among them. These are just some of the examples that demonstrate how power has decoupled from size.

Given that technology is causing the speed of change to accelerate at an unprecedented rate, adaptability has supplanted scale in importance for the preservation of power (Our World in Data 2016). Organisms as species or organizations as entities tend to perish when the rate of external change exceeds the rate of internal change. It took nearly a century for 90 per cent of people in America to drive a car while it only took five years to reach a 90 per cent penetration rate for smart phones (Rieder 2015). Products which now feel habitual such as Airbnb, Google Maps or WhatsApp did not exist a decade ago. As Tancredi Falconeri wrote ironically in *The Leopard*, a famous Italian novel, 'Everything must change so that everything can stay the same.'

'Adaptability', notwithstanding its decisive contribution to a nation's competitiveness, does not feature prominently in any of the metrics included in the complex calculations performed by the World Economic Forum, World Bank or IMF.

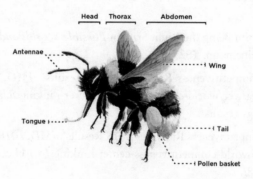

Figure 1.4: Bumble bee Anatomy

The anatomy of a bumble bee implies that it should not be able to fly – but it does.

Source: *Blooms for Bees*, no date

I'll close with an amusing story. Henrik Tvarnø, the former director of the Danish Parliament, who looks after the A.P. Møller Foundation in Denmark, once explained to me the so-called 'bumble bee' metaphor. It went something like this – The world's greatest scientists once gathered at the Royal Society to study the aerodynamics of a bumble bee. The group included world renowned aerospace engineers, physicists, mechanical engineers and even zoologists. They concluded unanimously that the bumble bee could not physically fly because its wings were too small relative to its wing span to support its weight.

Denmark has expensive social contracts and high taxes. It has highly flexible labour laws combined with generous unemployment benefits. But the Danish bumble bee flies. And it scores very well across a variety of performance metrics, not the least of which is the happiness and prosperity of its citizens.

Too Small to Fail is also a story about bumble bees which shouldn't fly – but do.

References and Further Reading

Brinded, L. 'The 15 most billionaire-dense countries'. *Business Insider*, 2015. https://www.businessinsider.com/countries-ranked-by-billionaires-in-proportion-to-population-2015-7?r=US&IR=T.

'Bumblebee Anatomy'. *Blooms for Bees*, no date. http://www.bloomsforbees. co.uk/guide/.

Haldane, J.B.S. 'On Being the Right Size' in *Possible Worlds and Other Essays* (London: Heinemann, 1927).

'IMD World Competitiveness Rankings 2017 Results'. *IMD*, 2017. https:// www.imd.org/wcc/world-competitiveness-center-rankings/competitiveness-2017-rankings-results/.

'IMD World Competitiveness Rankings 2018 Results'. *IMD*, 2018. https://www. imd.org/wcc/world-competitiveness-center-rankings/world-competitiveness-ranking-2018/.

Jackson, A. and A. Kiersz. 'The latest ranking of top countries in math, reading and science is out – and the US didn't crack the top 10'. *Business Insider*, 2016. https://www.businessinsider.com/pisa-worldwide-ranking-of-math-science-reading-skills-2016-12?r=US&IR=T.

Jones, R. 'The best and worst places in the world to be a mother'. *The Telegraph*, 2015. https://www.telegraph.co.uk/women/womens-life/11576970/The-best-and-worst-places-in-the-world-to-be-a-mother.html.

Lampedusa, Giuseppe Tomasi di. *The Leopard* (New York: Pantheon, 1958).

Lane, S. 'Former fed chief Volcker warns of US decent into "plutocracy" '. *The Hill*, 2018. https://thehill.com/policy/finance/412756-volcker-warns-of-us-descent-into-plutocracy.

'Quality of Living City Rankings'. *Mercer*, 2018. https://mobilityexchange. mercer.com/Insights/quality-of-living-rankings.

Miller, L.J. and W. Lu. 'These are the economies with the most (and least) efficient health care'. *Bloomberg*, 2018. https://www.bloomberg.com/news/articles/2018-09-19/u-s-near-bottom-of-health-index-hong-kong-and-singapore-at-top.

'Property crime rates test San Franciscans' values'. *The Economist*, 16 February 2019. https://www.economist.com/united-states/2019/02/16/property-crime-rates-test-san-franciscans-values.

Rieder, R. 'The topic we should all be paying attention to (in 3 charts)'. *BlackRock*, 2015. https://www.blackrockblog.com/2015/12/11/economic-trends-in-charts/.

Schumacher, E.F. *Small Is Beautiful: A Study of Economics As If People Mattered* (London: Vintage, 1933).

Schwab, K. et al. *The Global Competitiveness Report 2017-2018*. World Economic Forum. http://www3.weforum.org/docs/GCR2017-2018/05FullReport/TheGlobalCompetitivenessReport2017–2018.pdf.

———*The Global Competitiveness Report 2018*. World Economic Forum. http://reports.weforum.org/global-competitiveness-report-2018/.

'Technology adoption in US households'. *Our World in Data*, 2016. https://ourworldindata.org/grapher/technology-adoption-by-households-in-the-united-states?time=1903..2016.

Thompson, P. 'Karl Marx, part 3: Men make their own history'. *The Guardian*, 2011. https://www.theguardian.com/commentisfree/belief/2011/apr/18/karl-marx-men-make-history.

West, G. *Scale: The Universal Laws of Growth, Innovation, Sustainability, and the Pace of Life, in Organisms, Cities, Economies, and Companies* (New York: Penguin Press, 2017).

Conversations and Interviews
Henrik Tvarnø and Oswald Gruebel.

2

Openness

How a Steel Box Opened Up the World

A Shipping Container

Source: A.P. Møller-Mærsk

> It is the long history of humankind (and animal-kind, too) that those who learned to collaborate and improvise most effectively with others have prevailed.
>
> —*Charles Darwin*

I'm sitting in Søren Skou's office with a panoramic view of Copenhagen's Øresund (Sound), historically the bastion port on the Baltic sea. Streams of cargo ships, each long enough to fit the Empire State building, methodically weave in and out of the narrow strait separating Denmark and Sweden. Most ships plying between the Baltic Sea and the Atlantic pass through here, making it one of the world's busiest ports and a fitting home for A.P. Møller-Mærsk, the world's leading shipping company. Over coffee, I hope to learn from Skou, the soft-spoken CEO of Maersk, how a country with only 0.1 per cent of the world's population is responsible for shipping 25 per cent of its trade.

The story begins in Newark, New Jersey. On a drizzly April morning in 1956, *Ideal X*, a converted World War II tanker on the verge of being scrapped, sailed from Port Newark to Houston with fifty-eight large, identical metal boxes on board. It was the start of containerization, a technology which would soon transform the global shipping industry and, more importantly, the nature of global trade.

For centuries, shipping had depended on a vast labour force stationed at every port to handle goods. A typical transatlantic cargo ship might contain 200,000 separate items, bound for dozens of destinations. Loading this cargo from the dockside to the tightest corners of the hull, and then gradually unloading it again, was painstaking, clumsy and time-consuming.

In the 1950s, Malcolm McLean, a truck driver from rural North Carolina, thought of a better way. 'I watched them take each crate off a truck and slip it into a sling, which would then lift the crate into the hull of the ship. Once there, every sling had to be unloaded and the cargo stowed properly. The thought occurred to me that it would be easier to simply lift the trailer of my truck up and, without any of its contents being touched, put it on the ship' (Levinson 2006).

McLean pursued his idea through the purchase and relaunch of *Ideal X*, and it had spectacular consequences. Today, some 90 per cent of world trade moves on ships specially designed to carry standard-size containers (IMO, n.d.). The time is long gone when docks were corrupt, complex political ghettoes made famous by Marlon Brando in *On the Waterfront*. Instead, computers orchestrate a perfectly timed choreography of giant cranes which run on slick rails along the dockside. Thousands of containers destined for hundreds of destinations are meticulously directed and tracked by global computer networks.

The first and most obvious benefit of containerization was a huge improvement in shipping productivity. The average cost of shipping a cubic metre of cargo has fallen 80 per cent since 1930 (Our World in Data 2007). This had many more benefits. With shippers able to offer lower unit costs, shipping volumes soared, leading to the development of ever larger ships with still more efficiencies (Kremer 2013). And then, the most important gain – ships were built to go faster, which resulted in shorter turn-around times for shippers.

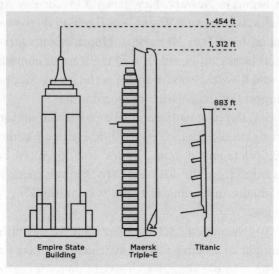

Figure 2.1: Risk Ahoy

This particular Maersk ship is almost as tall as the Empire State Building, which demonstrates the increasing size of container ships.

Source: A.P. Møller-Mærsk

Skou points outside his window towards A.P. Møller-Mærsk's logistic hub, which is located a few hundred metres away. He says, 'It no longer makes a difference in most instances whether a company produces in Tianjin or St Louis because the cost of distance has been reduced to a minor fraction of the production price.'

McLean, the unassuming truck driver of Scottish decent from the outback of North Carolina, was to globalization what René Descartes was to the Enlightenment, and Luther to the Reformation. For centuries, the cost of distance has been a major determining factor for the prosperity of countries. New Zealanders famously lamented their moribund economic development to 'the tyranny of distance.' Even in the 1950s, the world was still largely characterized by local, provincial and national manufacturers and distributors because proximity to consumers was needed to avoid expensive shipping costs. Since natural resources were bulky and expensive to transport, factories benefited by being close to the source of raw material. This meant that having natural resources mattered to a country. For example, in places such as Pittsburgh, Essen and Sheffield, steelworks were sited close to coal and iron ore deposits.

Distances also determined lifestyle. Cities are monuments paying tribute to spatial socio-economics with their dense urban hubs designed to minimize the cost of moving raw materials, labour and finished goods. Distance to water, energy, suppliers and customers, all influenced where businesses produced and sold, where rail tracks were laid, streets were built, employers located jobs and where families chose to live, work, shop and play.

It is probably coincidental that the great political drive in the second half of the twentieth century to reduce international trading barriers came at the same time as the revolution in shipping. But the two forces working together undermined national borders to an extent that few predicted and many are now ruing.

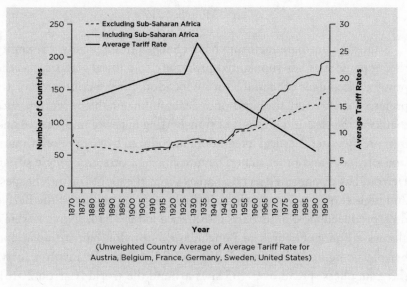

Figure 2.2: Average Tariff Rates and Number of Countries

This graph shows that a marked increase in the number of nations has coincided with a substantial reduction in trade barriers.

Source: Alesina, Spolaore and Wacziarg, 2000

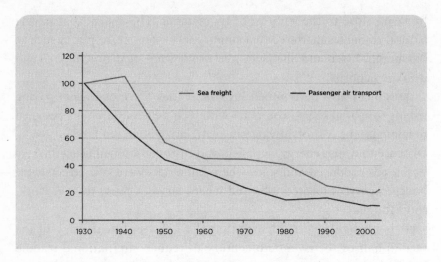

Figure 2.3: Declining Cost of Distance

*This figure demonstrates how the cost of shipping sea freight
and travelling by plane has declined over time.*

Source: Minsch, 2019

Strategies for manufacturing have changed dramatically. Proximity to shipping lanes has supplanted proximity to natural resources as the prime determinant of manufacturing location. Steel factories today are preferred on coastal sites and on a scale unimaginable a century ago, thanks to the ease and low cost of transporting huge volumes of coal and iron ore by water. Vertical integration, introduced by Henry Ford to turn iron ore, coal and other materials into finished cars on a single site in Detroit, has disappeared as companies scour the globe for the cheapest and highest quality components. Mattel Corp, the maker of the Barbie doll, produced most of its parts in America in the 1950s. Now, Barbie's clothes are manufactured in Bangladesh, her nylon hair in Japan and her plastic figure in Taiwan. A Boeing 787 Dreamliner involves forty-three suppliers spread over 135 sites around the world (Carroll 2016). Only a minor part of the iPhone is produced or assembled in the US; the battery, chassis, display, camera and memory are all produced abroad.

In another example of the trend, the vast majority of container ships moving around the world today are not filled with finished products such as microwave ovens or iPhones. Instead, intermediate components, which can be densely packed, fill the containers. Over half of all exports, measured by value, cross a border at least twice before reaching their end users (*Economist* 2017). This is the new reality of international trade, which makes it difficult for national governments to assert their authority over trade issues. It has also affected Britain's drive to leave the European Union. Component assemblies for vehicles assembled in British factories cross the English Channel up to five times before the final installation. Thanks to the customs union and single market of the EU, this huge trade is without border controls or tariffs. What will happen if Britain leaves the customs union and single market, as the current government is determined to do?

Figure 2.4: Globalization

Source: Banx

Throughout history, the exchange of goods has been decisive to rising prosperity. The Phoenicians of the Levant coast were among the most prosperous races on the Mediterranean. The Dutch and East India Trading companies were precursors to modern day multinational companies. At one point, the international sugar trade was so valuable that England considered exchanging their holdings in Canada for the tiny French colony of Guadeloupe, an important exporter of sugar at the time.

Today, few people in the US, Europe or Japan sew their own clothes, grow their own food, build their own houses or exclusively buy products made in their own countries. It would cost too much and take too much time. For most of us, it makes economic sense to buy a product from another who specializes in such production or for whom it is easier to make or for less.

This was also the vision of the nineteenth century British economist, David Ricardo, who said that resources should be free to flow to their most efficient use and that trade can be a 'positive sum' game if nations pursue their natural 'comparative advantages' (Ricardo 2001). Adam Smith took this reasoning one step further, arguing that further gains from trade arise when nations specialize so that they can get better at what they do.

But McLean's 'steel box' epiphany of globalization differed significantly in degree, kind and consequence. The cost of transportation declined to such an extent that it unleashed a tsunami of global trade of unprecedented speed and scale. Since the 1970s, the volume of global trade has increased at about 2–3 times the rate of GDP growth, a rate normally reserved for Silicon Valley unicorns (Ortiz-Ospina, Beltekian and Roser 2018). Paul Samuelson of MIT said that in the West, 30 per cent of the gain in real income per capita since 1980 has been due to increasing global trade (Samuelson and Barnett 2006).

The freeing of global trade has been particularly beneficial to small countries. Traditionally, they were at a disadvantage in the negotiation of bilateral or multilateral trade agreements and often had to align themselves with a bigger country. As trade became a more level playing field, many small countries exploited their new opportunities well. Harvard's Professor Robert Barro was the first to point out that small size tends to encourage openness because small states must trade to survive (Barro 2012).

The countries featured in *TSTF* have done more than survive – they have flourished as export champions. Singapore has exports of 173 per cent of its GDP, Ireland 120 per cent, the Netherlands 87 per cent, Switzerland 66 per cent and Denmark 55 per cent (World Bank 2017). On average, *TSTF* countries export nearly three times the proportion of their economies compared with the Organization for Economic Cooperation and Development (OECD) average and more than six times compared with the US (Germany is the only large country featuring in the list of leading exporters).

Many powerful and omnipresent multinational conglomerates, such as General Electric, Hitachi, Siemens and United Technologies, were caught on the wrong foot as the world's ecosystem shifted away from national borders and towards competition in an increasingly borderless world along specific parts of the value chain. Hermann Simon, the author of *Hidden Champions of the Twenty-First Century*, points out that the emergence of medium-sized and B2B companies quietly working under the radar have become world market leaders in their respective industries.[3]

Many of these stealth companies constitute the vertebrate of the economies of *TSTF* countries. They are often unheard of because end users are not their target customers. Most of us are only familiar with Facebook, M&M's, Barbie or other products we use as consumers. How many of us know that Givaudan as well as Firmenich, based in Switzerland, control a large portion of the flavours and fragrances industry? Chances are that the fragrances in your laundry detergent, lavender scented shampoo or vanilla flavoured yoghurt come from one of these companies. Franke in Switzerland produces all the kitchen equipment for McDonalds. Kone (Finland) and Schindler (Switzerland) dominate the global market for elevators and escalators. They have helped verticalize the world, especially in Asia, similar to how trains horizontalized our lives a century ago. Universo SA, founded in 1909 by a group of small, individual watch hand producers, now manufacture most of the world's tiny watch hands. Sweden's Höganäs AB is the world's largest producer of powdered metals for use in metallurgical industries. GN ReSound is a Danish hearing aid designed especially for iPhones. There are countless others (See appendix).

Hermann Simon, who has been studying these hidden champions for over twenty years, told me that these companies succeed because 'they want to become and stay number one in the world'. His studies show that these companies file five times the number of patents per employee at one-fourth of the average cost per patent. Moreover, their employee attrition rates run an average of 3 per cent (vs more than 20 per cent for conglomerates) and they spend twice the level on R&D (Simon 2009). Despite this, they are substantially more profitable than average companies.

---

3. B2B stands for business to business. They are companies which focus on
   selling products and services to other companies rather than end customers.

Conclusion

A simple steel box vastly expanded the volume and degrees of freedom of international trade. In this volatile and competitive world, global trade continues to grow faster than domestic output. Nations with an outward focus are increasingly winning the export battle. They are, in turn, rewarded with more jobs and greater wealth creation. They are rewarded not out of generosity, but because through the contest of competition, they emerge with products that ultimately benefit the consumer. The winning products must be better, cheaper or more convenient.

Yes, there are opponents of free trade and we will continue to hear the call for greater degrees of protectionism, especially during downward cycles, or from those who are losing out. But the inexorable tendency which has prevailed since David Ricardo defined the theory of the 'comparative advantage' of trade in 1817 has been simple and compelling – 'It can hurt but it's worth it.'

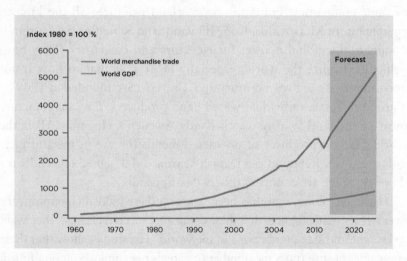

Figure 2.5: World GDP and Global Trade

This graph shows the dramatic growth in international trade against world GDP.

Source: WTO, Oxford Economics, no date

This is an immensely different and more competitive environment than we have ever experienced, creating considerable opportunities for risk and reward. Nations of any size, large or small, which can recalibrate their industrial ecosystems to adapt to the new rules of the game, stand to reap the benefits. In addition to profiting from growing trade, the world's most open economies have also become more open with respect to ideas, talent, innovation and connectivity. With the increasing use of the internet, more products based on knowledge are available rather than on material and decreasing transportation costs have blurred the traditional national boundaries.

It feels like the genie is out of the bottle.

References and Further Reading

Alesina, A., E. Spolaore and R. Wacziarg. 'Economic Integration and Political Disintegration'. *American Economic Review*, vol. 90, no. 5 (2000): pp. 1276–1296.

Barro, R.J. 'Small is beautiful'. *Wilson Initiative*, 2000. http://wilson.cat/en/mitjans-escrits/lectures-recomanades/item/191-lo-pequeño-es-hermoso.html.

Carroll, J. 'From job losses to security threats: five myths about global trade'. *City A.M.*, 2016. http://www.cityam.com/250602/job-losses-security-threats-five-myths-global-trade.

'Exports of Goods and Services (% of GDP)'. *The World Bank* (2017) https://data.worldbank.org/indicator/NE.EXP.GNFS.ZS.

Hummels, D. 'Have international transportation costs declined?'. *University of Chicago*, 1999. http://citeseerx.ist.psu.edu/viewdoc/download?doi=10.1.1.458.9651&rep=rep1&type=pdf.

Hummels, D. (2007). 'Transportation Costs and International Trade in the Second Era of Globalization'. *Journal of Economic Perspectives*, 21(3), (2007): pp. 131–154.

'IMO profile'. *Business.un.org*, no date. https://business.un.org/en/entities/13.

Jensen, L. *Culture Shock in Maersk Line: From Entrepreneurs and Kings to Modern Efficiency*. 3rd edition (Denmark: Vespucci Maritime Publishing, 2014).

Kremer, W. 'How much bigger can container ships get?'. *BBC News,* 2013. https://www.bbc.co.uk/news/magazine-21432226.

Krugman, P. 'Increasing returns and economic geography'. *Journal of Political Economy*, vol. 99, no. 3 (1991): pp. 483–99. https://pr.princeton.edu/pictures/g-k/krugman/krugman-increasing_returns_1991.pdf.

Krugman, P. 'Growing world trade: causes and consequences'. *Brookings Papers on Economic Activity*, 1995. https://www.brookings.edu/wp-content/uploads/1995/01/1995a_bpea_krugman_cooper_srinivasan.pdf.

Levinson, M. *The Box: How the Shipping Container Made the World Smaller and the World Economy Bigger* (Princeton; London: Princeton University Press, 2006).

Lukas, P. and M. Overfelt. 'Mattel: how a stylish doll became a head-turning classic and put a pair of fledgling entrepreneurs in play'. *CNN*, 2003. https://money.cnn.com/magazines/fsb/fsb_archive/2003/04/01/341015.

Maersk. 'Risk Ahoy'. Pinterest, 2013. https://www.pinterest.dk/pin/44726380 6715332878/?autologin=true.

Minsch, R. 'Declining Cost of Distance'. *Economie Suisse*, 2019.

Ortiz-Ospina, E., D. Beltekian and M. Roser. 'Trade and Globalization'. *Our World in Data*, 2018. https://ourworldindata.org/trade-and-globalization.

Ricardo, D. *On the Principles of Political Economy and Taxation* (Kitchener: Batoche Books, 2001). https://socialsciences.mcmaster.ca/econ/ugcm/3ll3/ricardo/Principles.pd.

Samuelson, P.A. and W.A. Barnett. *Inside the Economist's Mind: Conversations with Eminent Economists* (Malden, MA: Wiley-Blackwell, 2007).

Simon, H. *Hidden Champions of the Twenty-first Century: The Success Strategies of Unknown World Market Leaders.* (New York; London: Springer, 2009).

Solow, R.M. 'Technical Change and the Aggregate Production Function'. *The Review of Economics and Statistics*, vol. 39, no. 3 (1957): pp. 312–20. http://www.jstor.org/stable/1926047.

'The decline of transport and communication costs relative to 1930'. *Our World in Data*, 2007. https://ourworldindata.org/grapher/real-transport-and-communication-costs?time=1930..2005.

'The retreat of the global company'. *The Economist*, 2017. https://www.economist.com/briefing/2017/01/28/the-retreat-of-the-global-company.

'World Trade and GDP'. The European Express Association, no date. http://www.euroexpress.org/the-express-industry/trade-competitiveness.

Conversations and Interviews

Hermann Simon, Robert Barro and Søren Skou.

3

Innovation

The Sexiness of Ideas

The Light Bulb Moment

Source: Wikimedia Commons

> The beauty of ideas is that they have sex with each other and, if mutually beneficial, propagate.
>
> —Matt Ridley, *The Rational Optimist*

Innovation is a journey from possibilities into realities.

The journey can sometimes be a marathon, at other times brief. The word 'innovation' itself comes from the Latin 'innovare', meaning to 'make new'. 'Innovation' can even be synonymous with 'capitalism'. Robert Solow, the Nobel laureate, stated that technical innovations explain the majority of prosperity today. Historically, prosperity was achieved through conquest, land ownership, cheap labour and, at its most extreme and diabolical, slavery. Today, a nation's prosperity is increasingly a function of its ability to innovate. And herein lies one of the fundamental propositions of *Too Small to Fail* – economic power

35

has decoupled from size, a radical difference from the Westphalian conception of nation states.

Ideas procreate, but some environments are more conducive to their germination and growth. According to the World Economic Forum, seven of the world's most innovative nations are *TSTF* countries. However, innovation is tricky to define and the road of the genesis and creation of an idea is often rocky. So how did the smaller nations get there? Why do they seem, in Ridley's words, to foster the procreation of ideas better? And can they retain their prowess? This chapter delves into the nature of innovation and then attempts to answer these questions.

Switzerland	1
United States	2
Israel	3
Finland	4
Germany	5
Netherlands	6
Sweden	7
Japan	8
Singapore	9
Denmark	10

* 2017-2018 rank out of 137 economies

Figure 3.1: Top Ten Most Innovative Economies

In the 2017-2018 Global Competitiveness Report, the World Economic Forum ranked 137 economies in terms of innovation. Seven of the top ten were TSTF countries.

Source: McKenna, 2018

* * *

The Nature of Innovation

Innovation is fickle and illusive. Friedrich Hayek, the Nobel Prize-winning economist, argued that the essence of competition is that outcomes are unpredictable. If all the facts were identified and outcomes known beforehand, there would be nothing worth striving for. He said, 'Imagine if we knew already the winners of prestigious prizes for science, sporting contests or poems, why would we enter the contest?' (Hayek 1968).

Hayek felt that free markets, like science, are based on experimentation. Left to their own devices, free markets propel discovery, provide rewards for success and punishments for failure. Competition for the prize grinds out improvements but it is the customer who is the final arbiter, coldly calculating the respective costs and benefits. Successful entrepreneurs, as well as scientists, are those who see the opportunities which others don't. Since innovations can also be taken advantage of by others, and there is less or even no reward for coming in second place, there is a decisive first mover advantage. This requires doing something no one has ever done before, so innovation is prone to considerable risk.

Innovation is costly because it is still fundamentally based on 'trial and error' and usually requires many attempts, meaning that there needs to be a disposition to take risks and a high tolerance for failure. Less than one of 10,000 molecules tested for active ingredients will ever result in an FDA (Food and Drug Administration) approved drug for companies like Novo Nordisk or Roche. The success rate for launching new consumer products at companies like Nestlé is less than 3 per cent (Breiding 2012).

Since innovation is a struggle between potential losers and potential winners, it is political. Niccolo Machiavelli said, 'There is nothing more difficult to take in hand, more perilous to conduct, or more uncertain in its success, than to take the lead in the introduction of a new order of things, because the innovator has for enemies all those who have done well under the old conditions, and lukewarm defenders in those who may do well under the new.' There are endless sources of resistance. Workers fear losing their jobs, governments fear losing tax income, suppliers fear losing an order, academics fear being discredited and investors fear losing money. Collectively, Machiavelli understood that these groups constitute a formidable and resistance. No one in Nestlé's senior management believed Nespresso would be a success and now it is their most profitable product.

To overcome this type of resistance, perseverance and stamina are important. An innovator must have enough kinetic energy from the outset to overcome such formidable obstacles. The status quo is full of naysayers. British geneticist J.B.S. Haldane described 'The four stages of acceptance' for an innovation (Haldane 1963):

1. This is worthless nonsense.
2. This is an interesting, but perverse, point of view.
3. This is true, but quite unimportant.
4. I always said so.

However, sometimes innovation is not strictly new. The media marvels at breakthroughs like Tesla, the Apple iPhone and Uber because they are radical and consumer solutions. Setting aside all their sex appeal, innovation is usually more about evolution than revolution. Most industries are characterized not by one big discovery, but by lots of little discoveries. Think of how often we are required to update our iTunes or Adobe software, and how little we notice it.

"AND I WASN'T EVEN REPLACED BY THE LATEST MODEL OF ROBOT."   BANX

Figure 3.2: Innovation

Source: Banx

Innovation increasingly likes relay teams. Luis M.A. Bettencourt et al. point out that while there has been continuous growth in the number of patents issued each year, the introduction of fundamentally new classes of technology seems rarer now than ever (Bettencourt et al. 2015). When examining the patent office's files, they found that nearly half the patents issued by the US during the nineteenth century were for single-code inventions, such as Thomas Edison inventing the light bulb, Schockley discovering the transistor or Goodyear inventing the rubber tyre. These days, 90 per cent of patents are for inventions which combine at least two patent codes, suggesting that invention now proceeds mainly by recombining multiple technologies.

TSTF Nations: Attributes of Innovation

Innovation is a path-dependent process and there are many aspects which coalesce to yield a positive outcome, so a standard recipe for success is difficult to identify. However, several attributes seem to help explain why *TSTF* countries are head-and-shoulders above most of their peers in innovation.

First, *TSTF* countries try harder. It is hardly surprising that nations with the highest innovation rates spend the most on research relative to their GDP. They have more rolls of the dice. Having the financial means to innovate is one thing, but *TSTF* countries also have a better sense of how to spend their research budget.

Second, they have finely tuned radars to detect threats and opportunities because they are more 'open', as discussed in the previous chapter. Singapore is not especially known for its innovation, but it has an outstanding surveillance system to spot and take them up when they arise. Several ministries have 'futures divisions' on the lookout for promising innovations.

A part of their financial alertness stems from their vulnerability. Exports are crucial for their economy and any decline in competitiveness will strike at the heart of the nation's prosperity. Exports for *TSTF* nations are three times the level of the OECD and seven times the level of the US. Exports of the US have only increased from 9 per cent of GDP in 1990 to 12.5 per cent recently, suggesting that the US economy has hardly profited from the massive increase in global trade (World Bank

Rank	Best Countries for Business (1)	Global Innovation Index (2)	R&D as % of GDP (3)	Researchers in R&D per million people (3)	Global Competitiveness Index (4)	Corruption Perceptions Index (5)
1	United Kingdom	Switzerland	Israel	Israel	Switzerland	Denmark
2	Sweden	Netherlands	Korea, Rep.	Denmark	Denmark	New Zealand
3	Hong Kong	Sweden	Switzerland	Sweden	Norway	Finland
4	Netherlands	United Kingdom	Sweden	Korea, Rep.	Austria	Sweden
5	New Zealand	Singapore	Japan	Singapore	Netherlands	Norway
6	Canada	United States	Austria	Iceland	Canada	Switzerland
7	Denmark	Finland	Germany	Finland	Finland	Singapore
8	Singapore	Denmark	Denmark	Norway	Sweden	Netherlands
9	Australia	Germany	Finland	Ireland	Luxembourg	Luxembourg
10	Switzerland	Ireland	United States	Switzerland	Germany	Canada

Large countries population >50 million
TSTF countries
Other Small Countries population < 50 Million

Figure 3.3: Smaller but More Competitive

TSTF nations consistently rank in the top ten across a range of important metrics globally.

Source: Forbes; INSEAD; World Bank; The World Economic Forum Competitiveness Report 2018; Transparency International CPI 2014

2017). Indeed, *TSTF* nations such as Denmark, Finland, Ireland, Israel and Switzerland have achieved annual gain in per capita GPD due to increasing trade between 1990 and 2016 of 2–3.5 times the level of Britain and the US. Brian Mikkelsen, CEO of the Danish Chamber of Commerce and former member of the Danish Parliament, told me, 'The gains arising from trade in Denmark since 1990 have exceeded, and thus effectively funded, the collective costs of Denmark's public health care, education and child-care services, which are among the most generous in the world.'

As technology becomes more cross disciplinary, knowledge needs to be shared, which requires reciprocity and trust. The likelihood of dealing with people multiple times increases with fair behaviour, as we address in a later chapter on the importance of social cohesion. Speaking additional languages amplifies this ability. Switzerland has the highest percentage of academic papers with a foreigner as a co-author, followed closely by Denmark and the Netherlands (Schneider and Sørensen 2015).[4] This means that their scientists are interacting with the best experts across the world, and there is less of a 'not invented here' inhibition. The aptitude in languages boosts trading across the globe, helping nations open themselves up for international trade. According to a Pew research report, more than 80 per cent of Danish, Finish, Swedish and Swiss students speak a second language, compared with only 20 per cent in the US (Devlin 2018).

Third, *TSTF* countries place more economic emphasis on products over services, and it is the manufacturing of products which provides a more fertile ground for innovation. Services tend to be linked to the number of hours worked and there are only a limited number of ways a tax return, call centre or legal contract can be done quicker or better. Products such as medical devices and computer software, on the other hand, offer endless possibilities to innovate and lend themselves to preserving competitive advantage via intellectual property.

---

4. Some 70 per cent of academic publications in Switzerland have a foreigner as a co-author compared to around 20 per cent for US. Other *TSTF* nations rank similarly high—Denmark (62 per cent), the Netherlands (60 per cent) and Sweden (62 per cent).

While manufacturing is in inexorable decline in the wake of globalization and technological advances, the most successful *TSTF* nations have steadfastly kept their manufacturing bases and research hubs, while larger, more short-sighted countries have let theirs wither away. Manufacturing as a portion of GDP in the US and the UK has declined 43 per cent and 52 per cent respectively since the 1980s, whilst manufacturing in Denmark, Singapore and Switzerland has declined by 13 per cent, 27 per cent and 25 per cent respectively (World Bank 2017).

When we look at patent filings, a proxy for innovation, it is again the *TSTF* countries which lead the pack. Switzerland, for example, has ten times more patents per capita compared to the UK and eight times more than the US. Ricardo Hausmann, a professor in the Harvard Kennedy School, and César Hidalgo, from the MIT Media Lab, assert that a nation's prosperity stems from having many competencies and an ability to produce products which few other countries can. They coined their measure of national vitality 'Economic Complexity'. Novo Nordisk, for example, the world's leading supplier of synthetic insulin, developed its competency by combining the expertise of Danish brewers in fermentation with pancreas from pigs (pig production was and remains central to Danish export). Phonak, one of the largest hearing aid companies, managed to design a hearing aid small enough to hide behind the ear, using battery technology from the Swiss watch industry. Nine of the fifteen highest scores for 'Economic Complexity' are for nations with populations which are less than twenty-five million.

Fourth, *TSTF* countries are more able to take risks and possess a longer-term orientation. At the individual level, citizens of *TSTF* nations benefit from having more robust social contracts, so they have greater security and freedom of choice. The thought of losing a job should a start-up not succeed or trying out a new career at middle age (which is common practice in places like Denmark, the Netherlands or Switzerland) is not as utterly frightening as in other countries. Clinging to an uninspiring job out of fear of hardship is hardly a recipe for innovation.

Thus, in *TSTF* countries, citizens are encouraged to take risks. They can go and work for or launch a start-up, testing the waters to see if it works out. In Sweden, all employees have a statutory right to take six months off work and start their own business (Fleming 2019). No wonder Sweden is dubbed 'Europe's start-up capital' and has produced more unicorns (successful start-ups worth more than $1 billion) such as Klarna, Spotify and Skype than anywhere outside of Silicon Valley (Fleming 2019).

At the corporate level, as we point out in our chapter on ownership, industry ownership is characterized by larger, more engaged and longer-term oriented owners, so the pressure to meet quarterly targets or the temptation to repurchase treasury shares to bump up the share price is less of a distraction to what is good for the company in the long run. Many of Denmark's most important export-oriented companies like Novo Nordisk and A.P. Møller-Mærsk are owned in perpetuity by foundations, so the mindset is framed for the long term rather than the short term. Contrast this with the US, where the average tenure of a CEO for an S&P 500 listed company is five years, meaning that any research initiative or new product launch undertaken will likely be credited to their successor. We can begin to understand which incentive systems are oriented towards greater innovation.

At the government level, our chapter on Denmark reveals how it became a global leader in renewable wind energy and more inexpensive and clean cloud storage by instituting policies which created incentives to develop these pioneer businesses. Singapore established as its top down target that 20 per cent of its economy should be in manufacturing and it has met this aim. Ireland's Industrial Development Authority (IDA) routinely leads the world in landing the highest amount of Foreign Direct Investments, weighted by high paying jobs. Dr. Ami Appelbaum, the energetic Chairman of the Israel Innovation Authority (IIA), the government's technology arm, seeks out and promotes cutting edge technological projects. In 2018, IIA invested $470 million in 920 startups on the condition that its investment was matched by the private sector.

At the university level, Professor Ralph Eichler, who ran the Swiss Federal Institute of Technology (ETH), the Swiss equivalent to MIT and the nation's most important source of research spending, feels that excessive time pressure and over-measurement discourage innovation. He told me that Asian countries 'gave KPIs [key performance indicators] for everything, so researchers chose lower risk projects so they don't look foolish. This discourages risk taking and breakthrough innovations.'

However, innovation is not just due to attitude and money. Eichler asserts, 'Research is 50 per cent planned and 50 per cent serendipitous.'

And this brings us to our next and perhaps the most important attribute of innovation among *TSTF* nations – their proclivity towards serendipity, which is the fifth factor in the success of *TSTF* nations.

Serendipity is the phenomenon of discovering something valuable without intentionally seeking it out. This is like finding the missing sock under the couch while looking for the TV remote. Our history is full of examples of serendipitous innovations like Fleming's chance discovery of penicillin or the accidental invention of chocolate chip cookies. This idea relates to Hayek's notion of 'competition by discovery' or Ridley's ideas about sexual intercourse – the final product comes as an after-result of something entirely different; it is a happy accident. *TSTF* countries embrace these happy accidents and actually go further to create and foster environments which make them more likely to happen.

Discovery entails both surprise and coincidence. Environments which encourage unexpected connections and associations make for more fertile, innovative ground in what is termed 'serendipity heuristics', which is the idea that loose and sporadic associations are superior to concrete and routine ones. Patrick Aebischer, the former head of the EPFL in Lausanne, told me that Pritzker Prize winning Japanese architects Kazuyo Sejima and Ryue Nishizawa won the competition to design the Rolex Learning Centre because it optimized the likelihood of unplanned, chance encounters. 'It was about the architecture of serendipity rather than the building that counted for us,' he explained.

Figure 3.4: Rolex Learning Centre

The Rolex Learning Centre was designed by Kazuyo Sejima and Ryue Nishizawa to increase the chances of unplanned encounters.

Source: Alain Herzog, EPFL

Jan Gehl, who helped design Copenhagen's comprehensive bike and pedestrian pathways, agreed, 'Life is more serendipitous at 3 km per hour compared to those who step into a car in the morning, walk across their underground parking lot and take the elevator to the twenty-first floor, only to repeat the same pattern twice each day.' Cycling encourages casual, unplanned public interactions whilst driving just gets you from one place to the next. 'Noticing is what is necessary to experience life and make new connections,' Gehl explained.

Similarly, Jane Jacobs, in *The Death and Life of Great American Cities*, argues, 'Serendipity and spontaneity is what makes a city alive.' Serendipity allows us to interact with society and create a 'a web of public familiarity, respect and trust without "entangling relationships" or needing to engage in intimacy'. Jacobs was an outspoken critic of 1950s urban planning policy, which was designed around the automobile. She asserted that big city living is often characterized by routine commutes – parking in the same underground lot, taking the same elevator to the same office every day – which preclude the chance encounters needed for serendipity to happen. Moreover, technology increasingly acts as a force at work to reduce the likelihood of chance encounters. As our lives become more digitally mediated, we are more likely to interact with those sharing similar views, creating pre-defined feedback loops and echo chambers where diversity of perspectives is squelched.

TSTF nations are prone to similar pressures and constraints but are arguably less vulnerable to their adverse impact. They are smaller, with shorter lines of communication, so the likelihood of signal distortion is less. I remember speaking at a conference in Copenhagen, hosted by Deloitte, and chatting to a participant afterwards. She told me, 'If we're dissatisfied with something politically, just about everyone in this audience knows a member of parliament personally or, if not, is one person away from someone who has a close relationship with one.'

In networking terms, this is called 'collaboration distance'. The idea that anyone in the world is six or fewer steps away from any other person is often referred as the 'six degrees of separation'. In *TSTF* nations, as the example above illustrates, most people are within two degrees of separation and deal with the same people more frequently. So, the opportunity for perpetuating 'fake news' and other forms of misrepresented information is lower, since it is more likely to be called out and rejected.

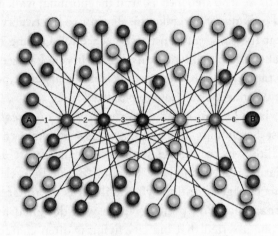

Figure 3.5: Six Degrees of Separation

The idea was coined by Frigyes Karinthy in 1929, and popularized in an eponymous play written by John Guare in 1990.

Source: Wikimedia Commons

Structure is the sixth factor which aids the success of *TSTF* nations. Niall Ferguson's book *The Square and the Tower* contrasts the relative strengths and weaknesses of networks versus hierarchies throughout history. He concludes that, while both forms of structure have their advantages, networks are superior to hierarchies with regard to innovation. *TSTF* nations have relatively flat social structures and externally centric nodes, offering more chances of encounters with the outside and thus a greater likelihood of ideas 'procreating'. Hierarchical structures are better at storing power and maintaining order by following the chain of command. They are designed to avoid surprises rather than stimulate new ideas.

As our chapter on Israel points out, subordinates in the Israeli military and start-up scene are encouraged to challenge and contradict their superiors, even to the point of insubordination, as long as it's genuinely meant to lead to better understanding or improvement. Dutch workers openly challenge directives which don't make sense and are considered argumentative by American, German or Japanese standards. In a rapidly changing and knowledge-based economy, innovation is more likely to occur when challenging the status quo than by blindly adhering to it.

 TSTF countries tend to be more egalitarian in structure, so new ideas can be produced by a broader spectrum of society. While this may sound unimportant, the University of Chicago's Deirdre McCloskey argued in her work *Bourgeois Equality: How Ideas, Not Capital or Institutions, Enriched The World* that far from capital, technology or institutions, it was the ability of merchants to engage in trade without the sneer of the aristocrat, the damning of the priest or the envy of the peasant which unleashed the industrial revolution. In a more contemporary context, we may think about the openness of *TSTF* countries to immigrants. Most of the best companies in Silicon Valley, Zurich or Tel Aviv are usually founded by at least one pivotal foreigner. Studies show that immigrants are inclined to take more risks, in part because they are out of their comfort zones. Of course, immigration has been the secret of success in London and Palo Alto – think of Sergey Brin, Elon Musk or Sigmund Warburg.

 Being open minded is vital. 'When is the last time you changed your mind?' Eichler asked me. He explained that a modest and open mind is a valuable catalyst to recognizing that 'aha!' opportunity, which most of us fail to see. We will deal with modesty as a common characteristic of small and successful countries in a later chapter. Modesty is helpful in many contexts, including the proclivity to innovate. An open and non-arrogant mind is better able to produce innovation than a know-all attitude.

 Open-mindedness can also be learned. I recently met Sabina Läderach, an aspiring diplomat working for the Swiss embassy in Cairo. She told me that in her service, the first assignment is intentionally designed to challenge established beliefs and stereotypes arising from the applicant's field of interest. In her case, having graduated with a degree in Arab studies, she was assigned to Israel.

 Perhaps most crucially, *TSTF* nations are innovative because they are rewarded for being so. The higher social mobility of *TSTF* nations means there is a higher chance of an individual rising in social stature. This offers a greater incentive to exert oneself. Socially immobile and rigid societies can cause individual resignation and discourage effort.

Ross Levine and Rona Rubenstein analysed the shared traits of US
entrepreneurs in a 2013 paper and found that most were white, male and
highly educated. 'If one does not have money in the form of an inherited
family wealth, the chances of becoming an entrepreneur drop quite a bit,'
Levine said. When a nation restricts its entrepreneurial talent based on
means rather than ability, this is a weakness, not a strength.

Figure 3.6: Serendipity

Source: Banx

The Future

The source of our prosperity has forever been, and continues to be,
technical innovation. Capitalism thrives on competition, which means
our products must be better, cheaper or more convenient to gain clients.
Innovation is the crucial rung in this ladder. Figure 3.7 shows the clear
correlation between a nation's prosperity and its ability to innovate. It
also shows how *TSTF* nations are punching above their weight.

There are a number of reasons why this is the case. Innovative nations
spend more, they are more aware of threats and opportunities (partially
due to vulnerability), they are more open-minded and adaptable

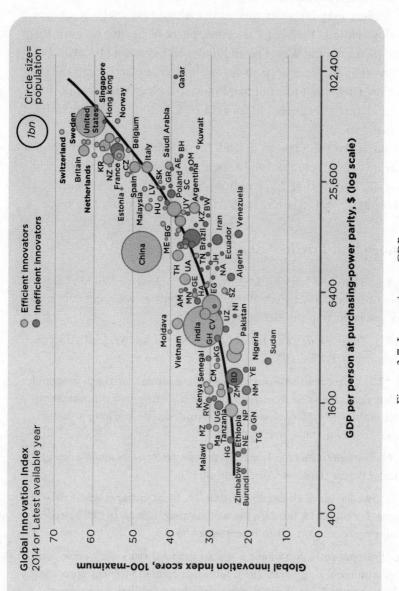

Figure 3.7: Innovation vs GDP

This graph shows a positive correlation between a nation's prosperity and its ability to innovate. TSTF nations outperform most other countries.

Source: Mazzarol, 2013

(partially due to their networking environment) and thus challenge the status quo, they opt for products over services which are economically preferable, they take more risks, encourage chance encounters and have the fall-back of strong social contracts. Most importantly, they are more inclusive and reward enterprise.

Some readers may consider this an oversimplified analysis. Others may say this reminds them of Palo Alto, parts of Seattle or even the hedge fund district in the West End of London. They would be right. But studies show that 80 per cent of all successful start-up activity in the US occurs within a 100 km radius of San Francisco, New York and Boston (Rachleff 2018); the same could be said of London. Is this inclusive enough? Is it enough?

Above all, innovation means to lead. Steve Jobs once said that those who innovate are leaders not followers; they must bravely try the new and uncertain. I argue that *TSTF* nations have in many respects arrived at the future first. And they have earned it one innovation at a time.

References and Further Reading

Bergquist, K., C. Fink and J. Raffo. 'Identifying and Ranking the World's Largest Clusters of Inventive Activity'. *WIPO*, 2017. https://www.wipo.int/edocs/pubdocs/en/wipo_pub_gii_2017-chapter12.pdf.

Breiding, R.J. *Swiss Made: The Untold Story behind Switzerland's Success* (London: Profile Books, 2013).

Devlin, K. 'Most European students are learning a foreign language in school while Americans lag'. *Pew Research Center*, 2018. https://www.pewresearch.org/fact-tank/2018/08/06/most-european-students-are-learning-a-foreign-language-in-school-while-americans-lag/.

Ferguson, N. *The Square and the Tower: Networks, Hierarchies and the Struggle for Global Power* (London: Allen Lane, 2017).

Fleming, S. 'Sweden gives all employees time off to be entrepreneurs'. *World Economic Forum*, 2019. https://www.weforum.org/agenda/2019/02/sweden-gives-all-employees-time-off-to-be-entrepreneurs/.

Groth, A. 'Entrepreneurs don't have a special gene for risk—they come from families with money'. *Quartz*, 2015. https://qz.com/455109/entrepreneurs-dont-have-a-special-gene-for-risk-they-come-from-families-with-money/.

Haldane, J.B.S. 'The Truth About Death' in *Journal of Genetics*, vol. 58 (1963): p. 464.

Hayek, F. 'Competition as a discovery procedure'. Translated by M.S. Snow. *The Quarterly Journal of Austrian Economics*, Vol. 5, No. 3 (2002): pp. 9–23. https://mises.org/sites/default/files/qjae5_3_3.pdf.

Hidalgo, C.A. and R. Hausmann. 'The building blocks of economic complexity'. *PNAS*, 2009. https://doi.org/10.1073/pnas.0900943106.

Jacobs, J. *The Death and Life of Great American Cities* (London: Pimlico, 2000).

Levine, R. and Y. Rubinstein. 'Smart and illicit: who becomes an entrepreneur and do they earn more?' *NBER Working Paper Series*, 2013. https://www.nber.org/papers/w19276.pdf?new_window=1.

Machiavelli, N. *The Prince*. Translated by N.H. Thomson (Campbell, CA: FastPencil, 2010).

Mazzarol, T. 'At the bottom of the top, Australia and the 2013 Global Innovation Index'. *The Conversation*, 2013. https://theconversation.com/at-the-bottom-of-the-top-australia-and-the-2013-global-innovation-index-16246.

McCloskey, D. *Bourgeois Equality: How Ideas, Not Capital or Institutions, Enriched the World*. (Chicago; London: University of Chicago Press, 2016).

McKenna, J. 'South Korea and Sweden are the most innovative countries in the world'. *World Economic Forum*, 2018. https://www.weforum.org/agenda/2018/02/south-korea-and-sweden-are-the-most-innovative-countries-in-the-world/.

Rachleff, A. 'The 2019 Wealthfront Career-Launching Companies List'. *Linkedin*, 2018. https://www.linkedin.com/pulse/2019-wealthfront-career-launching-companies-list-andy-rachleff/.

Schneider, J.W. and M.P. Sørensen. 'Measuring research performance of individual countries: the risk of methodological nationalism'. 2015. https://pure.au.dk/ws/files/90990388/1bcd2793_df8a_42bc_92b8_722449962a7e.pdf.

Weissmann, J. 'Entrepreneurship: the ultimate white privilege?'. *The Atlantic*, 2013. http://www.theatlantic.com/business/archive/2013/08/entrepreneurship-the-ultimate-white-privilege/278727/.

World Bank. 'Exports of goods and services (% of GDP)'. *World Bank Group*, 2017. https://data.worldbank.org/indicator/NE.EXP.GNFS.ZS.

World Bank. 'Manufacturing, value added (% of GDP)'. *World Bank Group*, 2017. https://data.worldbank.org/indicator/NV.IND.MANF.ZS.

Youn, H., D. Strumsky, L.M.A. Bettencourt and Jose Lobo. 'Invention as a combinatorial process: evidence from US patents'. *Journal of the Royal Society Interface*, vol. 12, no. 106 (2015). https://doi.org/10.1098/rsif.2015.0272.

Conversations and Interviews

Brian Mikkelsen, Jan Gehl, Patrick Aebischer, Ralph Eichler and Sabina Läderach.

4

The Merits of Modesty

A Contrast in Modesty

John McEnroe (left) and Roger Federer (right) – contrasting styles in tennis are shaped by social norms.

Source: Wikimedia Commons

'Make America great again', Donald Trump's all too familiar slogan, helped harness popular support and ultimately paved the way for his victory in the 2016 US presidential election. Trump is not alone in appealing to our deeply ingrained sense of patriotism. Examples of patriotism can be seen across the globe. But history reminds us that there is a fine line between pride and arrogance.

The advantages of *TSTF* nations have thus far been more conventional and intuitive – superior education systems, openness to trade, lower levels of debt and greater emphasis on manufacturing and innovation. Each of these are fairly obvious and measurable. But how do we quantify the value of something as soft and subtle as modesty? And can it provide a distinct advantage in an increasingly connected and competitive world?

In this chapter, we suggest that modesty is an inherent characteristic of small, successful nations. We then discuss the advantages which modesty confers at both the collective and individual level.

* * *

Our national identities, without exception, have been socially constructed. Each country is a composite of its unique evolution. Along the way, traditions are defined, achievements are recognized and deviations from social norms are punished. Each society propagates fairy tales and heroic models to aspire to.

National narratives have been composed throughout a history which has frequently been characterized by war. There have been long and repeated incidents of confrontation involving life, death and devastation which have ingrained a deep sense of 'us' versus 'them'. Charles Tilly, a reputed military historian, once said, 'War made the state and states made war'. Indeed, until recently, hardly a generation passed when nations were not at war with one another. Those who engaged and succeeded in this conquest game won boasting rights. Think of the Roman empire, Alexander the Great, the British empire or the USSR.

But war has become less frequent with the spread of democracy and increasing commercial trade. The incentive to resolve disputes diplomatically has increased, while confrontation has become costlier. In *The Remnants of War*, Cornell's John Mueller points out that war is on a dramatic decline and has been largely abandoned as a means of conquest. Harvard's Stephen Walt says, 'The US has spent approximately $30 trillion of taxpayers' funds on defence since the Second World War, but this has not resulted in any meaningful additions of territories, strategic ports or claims to valuable natural resources such as oil.'

TSTF countries never participated in these costly campaigns, or did so and then retracted. Harvard's Steven Pinker pointed out to me, 'Denmark, the Netherlands and Sweden imperialized and then got out of the conquest-for-greatness game, to their advantage.' During the Kalmar Union in the sixteenth century, Denmark controlled all of Scandinavia, Iceland and parts of Germany along the Baltic sea. Ove Kaj Pedersen, Professor Emeritus in Political Science at Copenhagen Business School, believes that the painful and humiliating feelings experienced by the vanquished after losing countless wars and relinquishing territory to the victor is what led to the Danish sense of modesty and humility. The Netherlands, Portugal and Sweden followed a similar trajectory of imperial conquest and then downsizing (or 'right-sizing' as is popularly touted in their current history books).

The Irish sense of humility has been cultivated through its own unique experience. For centuries, Ireland defined itself in terms of victimhood and inferiority in relation to Great Britain. When its much larger neighbour was not subjugating Ireland for physical domination, it was wounding the nation's fragile pride with arrogance and ridicule.

The Protestant Reformation which fermented in small countries such as the Netherlands, Switzerland and Scotland shunned ostentation and encouraged modesty. Jews have been persecuted over thousands of years, and while modesty is not a commonly attributed cultural trait, a sense of humility has nevertheless been deeply engrained in their psyche.

Irrespective of origins, the correlation between size and modesty seems obvious. Just compare the body language of Donald Trump with Justin Trudeau or Emmanuel Macron with Ueli Maurer (the president of Switzerland, for those few who even know his name). Observe how Daniel Ek, the Swedish founder of Spotify, speaks at the podium compared to, say, Travis Kalanick, the American former CEO of Uber. Think of how Roger Federer, the iconic Swiss tennis star, behaves when he wins, or even more importantly, when he loses.

At the Level of Society

What can modesty contribute at the level of society?

First, greater humility breeds fewer conflicts. Smaller countries have learned the advantages of avoiding geopolitical rivalry on the global stage, thus sparing themselves the hefty cost of military spending and the temptation to demonstrate its results. As Steven Pinker, himself a Canadian, points out, 'The cost of conflict as it relates to trust and long-term reciprocity almost always outweighs the benefit of what is being fought over.' TSTF countries have thus become adept at soft power, skilled at resolving conflicts and achieving their goals without aggression, through negotiation and tolerance – not coercion, payment or government fiat. They are also achieved through tolerance, as Simon Kuper, a witty journalist at the *Financial Times*, noted, 'Ever since the Dutch founded the Dutch East India Company in 1602, they have learnt to hold their noses and do business with anyone. A small country that trades globally learns to be cynical' (*Financial Times* 2018).

Second, modesty helps mitigate the debilitating effects of inequality. Studies show that social dysfunction arising from crime, depression, status insecurity, lack of trust and even social mobility, worsens when the prospect of being looked down upon increases. This is most pronounced in societies where the difference between the most and least fortunate are larger.

The Danish–Norwegian author, Aksel Sandemose, realized that greater equality makes societies stronger. He codified how typical Scandinavians downplay their differences in social status in his 1933 novel, *A Fugitive Crosses His Tracks*, which follows the life of a sailor from a typical Danish town called Jante. The 'Law of Jante' spells out ten principles – all variations of a common theme – which form the 'Jante's Shield' which protects Scandinavian culture. The overarching principle is to place the community ahead of the individual and not show-off or boast. The first law states, 'You're not to think you are anything special,' and then proceeds to counsel that we should not give the impression that we are 'smarter, better or more important' than others. These character traits are waning, especially in urban areas, but they nevertheless form a substrate of social norms which place the value of the community over the individual.

Modesty is under siege everywhere in this world of social media. This incessant advertising of self-importance arouses envy, resentment and anger between the 'haves' and the 'have-nots'. Studies show that threats to our social status cause the most stress and that our happiness, or lack thereof, is dependent on how we perceive our standard of living in relation to others. So Jante seems to be a kind of medieval Scandinavian elixir, which suppresses our temptation towards self-importance to the benefit of social cohesion. This 'we' versus 'me' orientation means that social norms are more effective at governing individual behaviour. They reduce the need to impose regulations, which bring the attendant costs and nuisance of policing and enforcement.

Community priority also encourages collaboration over competition. Paul Polman, the Dutch CEO of Unilever, told me, 'In Netherlands, because of our small size and intimate living conditions, the individual must be more considerate of the community.' Polman also echoes the sense of vulnerability which characterizes *TSTF* countries. Half of the Netherlands is below or barely above sea level and major floods have occurred every generation for hundreds of years. Large parts of the Netherlands consists of what are called polders – low-lying areas of land which have been reclaimed from the sea and are protected by dykes. These polders contain some of the country's biggest cities. Polman says, 'The threat of imminent flooding required community members to collaborate together to protect themselves, instilling a sense of community and common purpose which prevails over individual interests.'

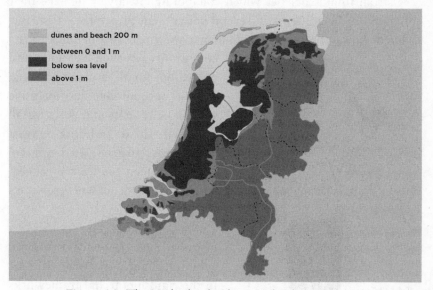

Figure 4.1: The Netherlands Above and Below Sea Level

Half of the Netherlands is below or barely above sea level, which makes the country liable to frequent flooding. This helps engender social cohesion.

Source: Simon, 2010

David Sloan Wilson and the late Elinor Ostrom, the only woman to receive the Nobel Prize for economics (in 2009), sought to determine what makes the collective strong from an anthropological perspective (Wilson 2019). Humans, after all, have spent the last two million years developing their roles as hunters and gatherers by working together in small groups and learning from one another. When individuals collaborate, they can compete against other groups more effectively – be it states, companies or football teams. From a Darwinian perspective, collaborative cultures survive longer and reproduce more if they possess virtues which improve trust and cohesion such as honesty, reliability, reciprocity and even heroism.

The challenge is finding solutions to 'tragedy of commons' and 'free riding' problems, which arise when 'me' overshadows 'we'. Commons facilities and pastures, without clear rules, are often overused and neglected. And trust breaks down if one member extracts what is perceived as an unfair advantage or if benefits are not reciprocated.

Ostrom found societies which collaborate effectively manage their communities by adhering to several core design principles – first, low levels of hierarchy with a clear demarcation of who belongs to the community, as well as rights and obligations for all those who belong; second, an equitable and inclusive sharing of benefits and costs for all involved; third, policing against violations; fourth, appropriate sanctions when rules are breached; and finally, quick and fair resolutions to conflicts.

Wilson felt these design principles can be difficult to achieve in large, transient cities or in the rigid hierarchal frameworks found in agriculture and heavy industry. He positioned Norway as a 'blueprint for the global village', but could have easily expanded this assessment to include similar *TSTF* nations.

Figure 4.2: Social Media Behaviour

'Right, let's post this up on mylifesbetterthanyours.com'

Source: Banx

This sense of modesty and community interest pervades all aspects of society, including business, in these countries. Ingmar Kamprad, the founder of IKEA and one of the wealthiest people in the world, flew economy class and drove a Volvo station wagon which had done more than 100,000 km. He felt that he was more effective bargaining with suppliers if they felt that benefits went to the customers rather than to him. Dutch and Danish monarchs traditionally attend public schools so they can share the same journey as their subjects. Hans Baer, a member of the Swiss banking dynasty, had two identical, modest, green Audis so people thought he only had one. When I asked Paul Bulke, the chairman of Nestlé, what the difference was between working at Nestlé or, say, Procter & Gamble, he told me, 'At Nestlé, we treat every worker with the same respect and dignity whether it is the person turning the lights on in the morning on the factory floor or running our most profitable division.'

It is this sense of respect which transcends society and may explain the greater degree of civility we find in public debate and dealings in smaller, successful countries. The level of acrimony and hostility directed towards personal attacks rather than deliberation about issues in the US and the UK has become so high that it is difficult for many citizens in more civil societies to imagine how the public is served by this.

When Lim Boon Heng was born in 1948, Singapore was in tatters. It had just emerged from being occupied by a defeated Japan and was still within the jurisdiction of a crippled British empire. Singapore would go on to become the most successful nation formation story of our, if not any, generation. Its per capita GDP has risen from a subsistence level at its birth ($428 per person) and now, at nearly $60,000 per person, eclipses that of Britain, Japan and the US (World Bank 2017). When I posted a photo of Lim Boon Heng, chairman of Temasek Singapore and responsible for one of the world's largest sovereign wealth funds, on Facebook, a classmate of mine responded, 'If he manages $275 billion, could he not afford a nicer suit?'

One of the decisive factors underpinning Singapore's success has been its commitment to meritocracy. The belief is that people are rewarded because they deserve it rather than because they are entitled to it. In this kind of a society, it is substance which counts rather than appearance.

Appearance also provides an indication of how elite or egalitarian a society is. Senior managers, heads of government and entrepreneurs in Denmark, Israel, Switzerland and Singapore are much harder to distinguish by their appearance. Ulrich Bremi, an icon of Swiss industry, might pass as a refrigerator delivery man; Ingvar Kamprad, the Swedish founder of IKEA with a net worth above $60 billion, could be a carpenter if he was judged solely by his appearance. These societies feel fashion is more closely tied to pretension than to achievement.

This attitude also transcends gender and youth. The objectification of women in popular culture is highly discouraged and cultural norms emphasize respectful interactions between the sexes. Is it a coincidence that women in these societies are better paid and are promoted to higher positions of responsibility than in other countries? Among youth, fashion trends in Scandinavia and Israel have become globally popular for their no frills, affordable, down-to-earth and breezy coolness. The Swedish clothing chain H&M, now worth over $200 billion, has built a successful business tapping this social characteristic.

In Denmark, there is no elite education and no advanced or gifted and talented programmes. Crown Prince Frederik's children attend the same public community school as a common citizen. Professor Ove Kaj Pedersen told me, 'All Danish children go to the same school for ten years and this ensures shared values, a common identity and equality of opportunity.' The kids work in groups and if your child is better than the others in a certain subject, he or she is expected to help the students who are not as gifted. Students do not receive grades until the eighth class and there's almost no standardized testing until the children are fifteen or sixteen. 'A child's job is to play,' says Pasi Sahlberg, a Finnish education expert. Children are inculcated with the notion that success need not be a zero-sum game; for you to win, it is not necessary that I should lose.

Compare this to the fierce competition in the US, the UK, China, Korea and Japan, where children fight to occupy the limited seats at the best schools. Add that to the stress on young students to achieve the highest scores in the 'all or nothing' entrance examinations. What kind of impact does this culture of competition have on those that are lucky enough to land at the top? A young Boris Johnson, writing in the *Eton Chronicle* aged 16, provides an adamant defence of private schools: 'I tell you this. Exercise your freedom of choice because, in this way, you will imbue your son with the most important thing, *a sense of his own importance*' (Mount 2019).

In a Danish school, the child's social life is considered most important. Do they have friends? Do they get along and are they able to work with the other children in the class? Do they like to go to school? The idea is that if a child enjoys school, then academic success will follow. It would be a mistake to think that the Scandinavian school systems are relaxed. Denmark has one of the highest educational levels in the world and children from Finland score among the highest PISA scores for both maths and reading. The systems also encourage a high degree of self-reliance. By age ten, it's common for Danish children to make the journey to school by themselves.

At the Level of the Individual

In addition to benefits at the collective level, modesty confers important advantages at the individual level. Life is easier when we take ourselves less seriously. It is costly to establish your own brand and constantly promote it through relentless publishing activity on Facebook, Instagram and Twitter. Life becomes a bit like a Pavlovian system, recording what we transmit to the world and eagerly awaiting how it reacts. This may lead some of us to succumb to the phenomenon that we spend most of our energies projecting ourselves rather than achieving the goals we hold dearest. It may also excite envy and recriminations from those who would like to spite us or degrade the world's perception of us. Charlie Munger, Warren Buffet's trusted partner, once said, 'envy is the only sin you can't have any fun at.' But it is nevertheless prevalent in proportion to what value the society places on social status.

Reducing the emphasis on self-branding also helps us to communicate and empathize with one another. It's difficult to do either if everyone is perpetually transmitting and not listening. When we turn down the transmitter and camera, it also allows us to focus on what is really important – whether that's work, family, friends or hobbies.

Modesty is also a good reality check. Knowing our limitations and weaknesses and acting according to that awareness is likely to lead to more desirable outcomes than overestimating ourselves. Those of us who do not try to project onto others or show that we are superior to them are likely to attract more collaborators and incite less envy, disdain or resentment. We're likely to be more attentive to reality, which in turn means we're apt to form better judgements and are thus more likely to succeed. We're also more likely to be considerate of others' interests, which means we're less likely to offend others and engage in avoidable conflicts.

Mark Zuckerberg declared a few years ago that his new year's resolution was to meet 'one new person outside of Facebook every day' (Carlson 2013). Most CEOs, chairmen and successful entrepreneurs in small countries encounter a multitude of people from all walks of life on a continuous basis. They take public transport, attend board meetings of the local school, shop at the community grocery store or eat in the local restaurants. When I met Lars Fruergaard Jørgensen, the CEO of Novo Nordisk, Denmark's leading pharmaceutical company, he didn't even have his own office and he walked me out to the lift.

Contrast this to the Belvedere hotel in Davos during the World Economic Forum when entourages of security, press and support staff form a parade which precedes and follows the CEO of a French, American, Chinese or Russian company, advertising their relative importance and superiority. Which person is closer in tune with the world we are living in?

Conclusion

To sum up – though difficult to measure, modesty offers a number of valuable attributes to a society and the individuals. The outperforming, small countries have a distinct advantage because differences in social status are not as large, so it is not quite the pot at the end of the rainbow everyone feels they need to chase.

It is important to note that there is no 'modesty' gene identified by scientists. Modesty is an attribute which has fortuitously manifested itself from adversity (war), necessity (community) and experience (success). As such, it is exogenously imposed rather than a natural characteristic. Again, Ove Kaj Pedersen told me, 'The trick in Denmark is to contribute something intelligent without appearing to stand out.'

Fortuitous because, as pointed out, lower costs of distance and greater connectivity means that the world should become more collaborative and less confrontational. So this subtle attribute should become more valuable. People prefer counterparts who they can like and trust – something which is hard to do if your prospective partner is arrogant or chauvinistic.

Humility may also act as a shield to ward off some of the invasive and corrosive aspects of the increasing supremacy of technology. Smartphones have enabled us to fill every moment of our lives with stimuli of one sort or another. They offer us a dizzying array of choices which have taken boredom out of our lives and replaced it with an incessant need for instant gratification and ceaseless flattering of our social status. Never mind if they are increasingly determined by algorithms designed to reinforce our known preferences, optimize advertising and exploit our addictions. The Pew Research Centre reported that nearly half of us could not live without our smartphones (Anderson 2015).

The same technology which has given us so many choices, has perversely relieved us of the need to take them. Meanwhile, we ask ourselves why our lives are filled with so many things we don't want and so few activities we really enjoy doing?

Nevertheless, the world feels as though it is coming around to the merits of modesty, and those who have it, stand to benefit disproportionately. Janan Ganesh, an insightful political commentator at the *Financial Times*, summed it up for me beautifully: 'I really think it is small nations' lack of entitlement which drives their success – they expect to have to adapt to outside forces, so they do.' In a rapidly changing world, with multiple vectors of exogenous forces, this feels like the winning strategy.

References and Further Reading

Anderson, M. '6 facts about Americans and their smartphones'. *Pew Research Centre*, 2015. http://www.pewresearch.org/fact-tank/2015/04/01/6-facts-about-americans-and-their-smartphones/.

Carlson, N. 'This year, Mark Zuckerberg is meeting a new person every day.' *Business Insider*, 2013. https://www.businessinsider.com/this-year-mark-zuckerberg-is-meeting-a-new-person-every-day-2013-4?r=US&IR=T.

Ganesh, J. 'The belle époque of the small nation is over'. *Financial Times*, 2018. https://www.ft.com/content/464edd30-c247-11e8-95b1-d36dfef1b89a.

'GDP per capita (current US$)'. *World Bank Group*. https://data.worldbank.org/indicator/NY.GDP.PCAP.CD?end=2017&locations=MY-SG-Z4&start=1960.

Kuper, S. 'When Trumpist rhetoric crashes into European reality'. *Financial Times*, 2018. https://www.ft.com/content/bbb3f7ba-0094-11e8-9650-9c0ad2d7c5b5.

Mount, H. 'What's Boris really like?' *The Oldie*, 2019. https://www.theoldie.co.uk/blog/boris-johnson-tory-leadership-poll.

Mueller, J.E. *The Remnants of War*. (Ithaca; London: Cornell University Press, 2004).

Sandemose, A. *A Fugitive Covers His Tracks*. Kindle Edition (Lulu.com, 2018).

Tilly, C. *Coercion, Capital and European States, A.D. 990–1992*. Revised edition (Malden, MA; Oxford: Wiley-Blackwell, 1992).

Simon. 'IPCC: sea level blunder angers Dutch environment minister. Australian Climate Madness, 2010. https://australianclimatemadness.com/2010/02/05/ipcc-sea-level-blunder-angers-dutch-environment-minister/.

Wernick, A. 'The Netherlands, always vulnerable to floods, has a new approach to water management'. *PRI*, 2017. https://www.pri.org/stories/2017-07-16/netherlands-always-vulnerable-floods-has-new-approach-water-management.

Wilson, D.S. *This View of Life: Completing the Darwinian Revolution* (New York: Pantheon, 2019).

Conversations and Interviews

Janan Ganesh, Lars Fruergaard Jørgensen, Simon Kuper, Ove Kaj Pedersen, Pasi Sahlberg, Paul Bulke, Paul Polman, Stephen Walt and Steven Pinker.

5

Education

The Holy Grail to Eradicate Inequality

Learning is Fun

Source: Wikimedia Commons

Education is an enigma. In the US or the UK, every few years a new secretary *or* minister of *education* is enthusiastically appointed to deliver on campaign promises to finally rescue the American or British derelict educational system. Euphoric sounding initiatives like 'Leave No Child Behind', 'Race to the Top' or 'Teach First' attempt to comfort, reassure and convince. The measures are often as bold as they are innovative. David Cameron even called for ending the 'state's monopoly' over Britain's state school system, endorsing instead the right of private companies, voluntary groups and charities to run schools (Curtis and Mulholland 2011).

Education is arguably the most valuable aspect of any social contract between a nation and its citizens. After all, children are the most precious resource of the future. In an increasingly knowledge-based economy, what factor could be more important in determining a nation's competitiveness than the education and skills of its workforce?

There is probably no area of politics which elicits as many heroic promises as education. It is a subject in which every parent sees themselves as an unmatched expert, based only upon the breathtakingly limited samples of their children. Unsurprisingly, hopes of reform often turn into disappointment, and the cycle continues and repeats itself.

Governments around the world spend over $2 trillion on education (Barber and Mourshed 2007). Despite massive increases in spending and ambitious attempts at reform, the performance of most school systems has barely improved in decades. The US has spent considerably more money per pupil than most other nations and its government officials have repeatedly attempted to introduce marketplace competition into public schools. Yet, for the past decade, the US has muddled along in the middle of the pack in terms of education scores. Similarly, Britain has reformed virtually every aspect of its school system without appreciable success, with each new education secretary proposing radical overhauls with short shelf lives, which are later abandoned with the arrival of a new government. As Richard Adams summed up, 'The results of the OECD survey, which put England close to the bottom in literacy and numeracy among sixteen to twenty-four-year-olds among developed nations, comes despite – or perhaps in part owing to – decades of permanent revolution aimed at improving the education system' (*Guardian* 2013).

The US and the UK are not alone in the desire to constantly change their education systems. Education reform is near the top of the agenda in almost every country in the world, and for obvious reasons. There is a consensus among experts that rising inequality is one of the more serious challenges which future generations will have to face, and education is probably the most effective means of combating this socially destructive trend.

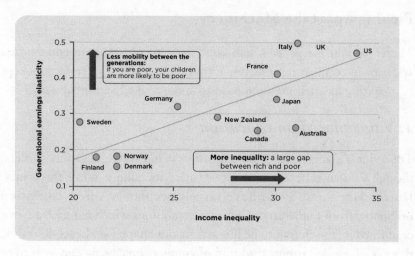

Figure 5.1: Intergenerational earnings elasticity vs income inequality

The Great Gatsby Curve shows a strong relationship between inequality and social immobility, indicating whether you are rich or poor depends to a great extent not on individual qualities or efforts, but on where you happen to be born and the education system offered.

Source: Corak (2013)

A handful of *TSTF* countries – Denmark, Finland, the Netherlands, Singapore and Switzerland – have managed to buck the trend, instituting reforms which have led to considerable improvements in their global rankings of their students in the knowledge of mathematics, reading and science. Their societies show higher upward mobility or so called 'intergenerational income elasticity', which means that the background of one's parents and wealth have less bearing on a child's ultimate success and citizens are able to switch their economic class with far greater ease. Most crucially, they show that outstanding education systems can contribute to a country's economic competitiveness and an absence of inequality can also help to eradicate youth unemployment and alleviate social tensions.

This chapter will analyse what makes an excellent education system and how it can lead to the outperforming of one's international peers. What have these countries done differently and can it be replicated elsewhere?

Picking Apart the Machinery

There are many aspects which contribute to outstanding educational systems. In conducting research across these countries, ten factors kept reappearing as attributes common to successful education systems:

1. Value placed on education

The value a society places on education is indispensable to its success, though value is different from price (mere spending). While the Danes, Dutch, Finns and Swiss have largely secular cultures, education originated from Lutheran or Calvinistic traditions which required anyone confirmed by the church to be literate. As our chapter on Israel describes, there is a long and robust tradition of young people being encouraged to read the Torah and argue, even to the point of anarchy, with the local Rabbis about possible interpretations. Traditional Confucian culture also values education highly, which explains not only Singapore's stellar results, but those in Korea, Japan, Taiwan and Shanghai. The Chinese proverb 'Give a man a fish and you feed him for a day. Teach a man to fish and you feed him for a lifetime' dates back thousands of years, and is still a source of inspiration for education.

Studies show that something as simple as parental expectation has an important impact on a child's education. Yossi Vardi, the father of Silicon Wadi, Israel's version of Silicon Valley, told me, 'Jewish mothers are our secret sauce. From birth till death, they tell us we must succeed.' He went on to say, 'Our main parameter of success is meeting the expectations of our mothers.' But it is not just in Israel that mothers contribute to the drive of their children. Amy Chua, a Professor at Yale, ignited a global parenting debate with her book about Asian 'tiger moms', reputed for the demands they place on their children to achieve academically.

It becomes very clear that the national attitude towards education contributes to the system itself. There are no Pew studies or PISA scores which measure *sisu* (a two syllable Finnish national anthem to describe their national character, roughly translating into 'stoic determination'), nor are there official measures for *chutzpah* (Hebrew for 'gall', or 'brazen nerve'), but who would doubt the value of this attribute?

2. *Equal opportunity for all: and for free*

The overriding philosophy among top performing nations is that education is a 'common good' and not a 'positional good'. A positional good, a description coined by the German economist, Thorstein Veblen, is one which individuals buy or invest in for the sake of, at least in part, demonstrating their status – a Bentley car, a Rolex watch, a Harvard degree or a Cy Twombly painting.

Treating education as a common good means that the same opportunities must be made available to all citizens irrespective of their ethnic origin, age, family wealth or stature, or where they live. Another distinguishing feature of successful education systems is that the schooling doesn't cost anything to the students. In most of these countries, education is free, or nearly free, at all levels from pre-primary to higher education. In Finland, this even includes meals, textbooks and healthcare insurance. By contrast, student debt taken on to fund university education in the US exceeds $1.5 trillion, surpassing the amount of debt incurred for credit card and automobile loans (Spicer 2019).

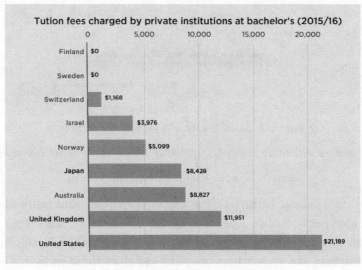

Figure 5.2: The Price of College

University tuition fees are substantially lower in TSTF nations than in the UK or the US.

Source: OECD, 2017

The more hard-nosed justification for a very good public-school education is that it will help the country become, and stay, competitive. A society where everybody is paddling the same boat at a decent pace will move quicker and more effortlessly than one with a few speedsters and many laggards.

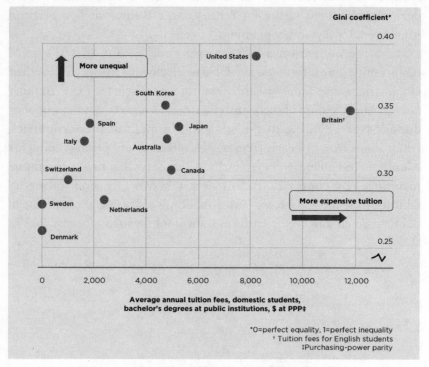

Figure 5.3: Gini coefficient vs tuition expenses

Countries with more expensive university tuition are also more unequal

Source: *The Economist* and Martin Vetterli

One surprising feature of successful systems is that more money does not simply lead to a better education. Finland spends 30 per cent less on primary education per child than some of their large-country counterparts and its teachers are paid less than those in most OECD countries. Singapore has among the most admired school systems in the world and spends less on primary education than twenty-seven out of the thirty countries in OECD (Barber and Mourshed 2007).

While the traditional response to improving school systems has followed the industrial or military logic of throwing more resources at the problem, Finland and Singapore have turned this orthodoxy on its head, demonstrating that more can indeed be achieved for less.

Figure 5.4: Education

Source: Banx

3. Public Schools are the preferred choice

Milton Friedman, the patron saint of free markets, argued vociferously that school vouchers should replace the American public-school system. He said, 'Parents could express their views about schools directly by withdrawing their children from one school.' The philosophy that unfettered free markets are superior to lumbering governments in the context of a nation's 'social contract' has been a determining characteristic of public policy formulation in the American and British traditions – whether it's in regard to education, healthcare or even prisons.

In *Exit, Voice and Loyalty*, Albert Hirschman provides an insight into how small, successful countries tackle their problems differently and more effectively. While the natural reflex of some countries is to throw more resources at a problem or to privatize, Hirschman felt these responses were flawed because they were imposed from the top rather than emerging from the bottom.

Hirschman was interested in contrasting the two strategies which people have for dealing with badly performing institutions. 'Exit' is voting with your feet and expressing your displeasure by taking your business elsewhere. 'Voice' is staying put, speaking up and choosing to fight for reform from within.

Societies which are confrontational in nature, like the US and the UK, tend to use 'exit' as a means for establishing policies, while more collaborative *TSTF* nations prefer to use their 'voice'. Hirschman points out that 'exit' may be more expedient, but it fails to send a useful message to underperformers. Hirschman felt that the worst thing which ever happened to incompetent public-school districts in the US was the growth of private schools. Private schools can afford to cherry-pick the best teachers and wealthiest students, leaving public-schools to deal with the rest. This cements social discrimination and inequality in the lives of children even before they have lost their first set of teeth. Hirschman argues that private schools also siphon off precisely the kind of demanding parents who would otherwise push for reform within the state sector. Freed from their critics, under-performing public schools are then no longer subject to the kind of robust and recurring criticism necessary to stay on top of their game. This turns into a vicious circle, where the quality of education deteriorates and the gulf between a nation's best and worst schools widens.

Hirschman went so far as to say that measures which result in 'exit' are silent protests, driven by cowardice and motivated by fear. 'Voice', while more laborious, requires courage and consensus and is thus a superior foundation for anything which serves as a 'common good'.

Most importantly, the fact is that the best PISA results are achieved by nations where there is an absence of competition between private and public schools and where the local public school is the predominant option for citizens, as in Finland, South Korea, the Netherlands, Japan, Singapore and Switzerland.

4. Common journey

If we compare Switzerland to the UK, we observe two incredibly different education systems. The UK system distinguishes between winners and losers, separating and dividing pupils into one of two categories. In Switzerland, the approach is instead to equip all students for life. Consequently, pupils are provided a more even platform to stand on, leading to a radically different mindset from what is found in a British school. Similar education systems exist in other smaller countries, where young people are permitted to thrive, partly due to the lack of engineered social segregation in the schools.

The lack of segregation means that young people in these nations share a common journey. They all participate in the same school system, often walking with classmates in their neighbourhood or riding their bikes to get there. Students come from diverse backgrounds, yet schools in these countries give their pupils very similar educational experiences. Education is usually economically integrated, so poor and rich students are in the same classrooms. By embracing students of all backgrounds and income levels, these countries have succeeded not only with stellar PISA scores, but with the elusive goal which so many advocates seek – equal opportunity for a nation's children. As a result, these societies become fairer, decreasing levels of inequality while increasing levels of social trust (a common feature of outperforming countries).

By contrast, the quality of schools in the US and the UK varies enormously. Schools are often effectively segregated by both race and income, with poor students having fewer resources and less experienced teachers in their schools. The McKinsey study cited earlier revealed that the annual expenditure per pupil in the US ranged from $5,700 to $12,700 (Barber and Mourshed 2007). It is not surprising that this is the case, as the US funds its schools through property taxes, which differ greatly based on neighbourhoods. Hence, massive disparity in funding is inevitable. These systems cause the most disadvantaged students to be warehoused together in the worst schools and thus, inequality is propagated in the US. While each of us wishes to 'give our child a better start', this becomes a means of unbalancing the playing field and reinforcing social divisions. Studies show that an eighth grade (fourteen-year-old) child from a lower income bracket who achieves maths results in the top quarter is less likely to graduate than a kid in the upper income bracket scored in the bottom quarter. As Edward Luce summarises, this is the reverse of how meritocracy should work.

5. Utilitarian care

We have all become aware as children that we have differing abilities and capacities. Who among us has not felt the humiliation of being the last person selected for a sports team? Talent is not distributed equally. Some are best suited to play the clarinet, while others might be best suited as the centre in a girls' basketball team.

What is damaging is when the variance of performance is a function of the school rather than the individual's talent. The variance in student performance among schools in Finland, for instance, is the narrowest in the world, with less than 5 per cent difference in results between the best and worst schools. Poorer students in the UK and the US are three times more likely to underperform than wealthier ones (Sahlberg 2011). Tony Little, the former headmaster at Eton, points out that a handful of private schools in Britain keep pace with the leading nations in education, but what about the students who are not accepted to the likes of Eton, Harrow and Westminster (Little 2015)?

In countries like Finland, the authorities ensure that, despite natural differences in abilities, there is help for those who are not as academically inclined. Professor Hannele Niemi of the University of Helsinki told me, 'Success depends on the way countries educate their bottom 50 per cent; the smartest 10 per cent tend to do well with any educational institution. It's especially those who are of below average ability that need special treatment and our help most.' Finland's utilitarian scheme has a 'whatever it takes' policy of detecting struggling children early and providing special help to keep them at the same paces as others. Smarter children are expected to help children who are having difficulty with their work and consequently, to quote Nieme, 'Nobody falls out of the boat.'

It is this 'whatever it takes' attitude of helping the neediest which helps explain why, in Finland, the discrepancies between the weakest and strongest students are amongst the smallest in the world.

6. Radical Reform

For those of us longing for educational reforms, the good news is that they can be done. The excellent school systems of Finland, Korea and

Singapore were founded upon radical reforms, where they achieved their goals in relatively short periods of time. Australia, Ireland, Portugal and Estonia have also undertaken important reforms and have steadily improved their scores across each subject, overtaking the US and Britain.

So there is proof that it can be done. Yet, how did they do it?

These education overhauls and reforms demonstrate that tinkering at the edges doesn't work. Rather than trying to graft new branches to the derelict existing systems, these nations opted to raze and burn the old legacy systems. In their place, they built new, solid foundations based on far-sighted principles. These principles and goals were ambitious and, as Tommy Koh, the spiritus rector of many of Lee Kuan Yew's reforms in Singapore, told me, they were 'broken into small steps'.

Finland rid itself of its inherited Soviet era education system and designed a system de novo (see chapter 9, 'God's Chosen Profession' for a more in-depth account of the Finnish education system), independent from the prevailing orthodoxy of the 1980s. Taiwan sought to break from the yoke of the Chinese communist school system.

Singapore also fought against its past. When under British rule, education in Singapore had been the preserve of the affluent and it was considered a privilege rather than a common good. Under the leadership of Lee Kuan Yew, the 'Singapore method' was born. It was created and moulded by a team of teachers – not sclerotic bureaucrats or theoretical university professors – who had the considerable latitude to create the foundations of a superior educational system.

The way children were taught in Singapore was radically altered. Aiming to move away from simple rote-learning, a new focus was placed upon teaching children about problem solving. Textbooks were influenced by the writings of educational psychologists such as Jerome Bruner, who posited that people learn in three stages: by using real objects, then pictures and then symbols (Vasagar 2016). This theory contributed to Singapore's radical move away from the prevailing German 'Lehrplan' (learning plan) system, which is based on traditional syllabus and orthodox teaching techniques. Instead, they placed a strong emphasis on, for example, modelling mathematical problems with visual aids, such as using coloured blocks to represent fractions or ratios. Finland recently moved to the so-called 'phenomenon-based learning' in which teaching is based on topics and context rather than classical subjects.

These educational systems establish a requirement for excellence at all levels. Ong Ye Kung, a former Minister for Education in Singapore, spelled out the four ingredients of the country's success – 'Every student, an engaged learner; every school, a good school; every teacher, a caring educator; every parent, a supportive partner.' Fixing one aspect of the system while neglecting others is not enough – and may help to explain why targeted reforms fail to achieve their desired impact.

All these reforms have been based on 'voice' rather than 'exit'. This means that ambitious overhauls were a matter of consensus and that they were designed for the long run, not quick-fix miracles which lasted until the ruling party lost the subsequent election. Lee Kuan Yew, for instance, linked educational reforms to the nation's goal of making manufacturing constitute 20 per cent of the economy from a virtual dead start.

Successful reform requires ambition and a tireless drive, as Professor Niemi explained to me that the 'reformation of Finish schools has been going on for forty years, and our experiments are continuing'.

7. A good place for mothers

Nations with successful education systems tend to be better places to live for mothers, as our later chapter about gender delves into. Studies show that much of a child's success is the result of a supportive home environment, and with women increasingly working full-time, measures to ease the burden of motherhood have become necessary. In the US, day care is expensive – the second-most costly expense after housing. While countries such as Finland provide three years of maternity leave and subsidized day care to parents, it is only, according to a UN report surveying 185 countries, Papua New Guinea and the US which do not guarantee paid maternity leave (Kim 2015). With more women in the work force, falling reproduction rates and ageing populations, societies which can offer families greater flexibility balancing the competing demands of career and parenthood stand to have a comparative advantage.

8. Vocation: no dead ends

Andreas Schleicher, the director for education and skills at OECD, asserts that 'nations have skill shortages, not degree shortages'. It is interesting that another important aspect among successful education systems in Finland, Denmark, the Netherlands and Switzerland is that when children share a common education journey, they are not channelled only towards university, but also towards vocational training. Some pupils are more academically inclined and others commercially. However, instead of commoditizing university educations for marginal students to the point that it becomes equivalent to a high school diploma, nations with excellent education systems channel commercially inclined students in their late teens to specialized crafts and trades.

Companies have begun to recognize that traditional education does not always lead to success in the real world. Google has found no correlation between GPAs (grade point averages), test scores and employees who do well and therefore has stopped looking at those academic qualifications altogether (Nisen 2013). In *TSTF* countries, there is no stigma surrounding craftsmanship; instead, it is embraced. In Finland, training in a specialized craft and trade also does not lead to a lack of future options. There is a belief that no educational pathway should result in a dead end where a student is unable to pursue a particular course because of a choice they made at sixteen. Students who choose vocational training can follow a track back to university later.

9. Conscription

When doing field work in *TSTF* countries, we notice a high degree of social trust. There is a greater emphasis on the community versus the individual; a greater sense of collaboration versus competition; a more pronounced collaboration between government and the private sector; and a sharpened sense of identity and a shared sense of belonging among the people. A good portion of this comes from the common journey described earlier. In small countries such as Finland, Israel, Norway, Singapore and Switzerland, participation in military training during the formative years of the youth is an important part of this common journey.

There are many other tangible benefits of conscription. Dr Fritz Gerber, the former chairman of Roche Holding AG and a colonel in the Swiss military, said that it is normal for a Swiss lawyer or PhD to report to a baker or plumber if the latter has a higher rank in the military, which encourages an egalitarian society founded upon mutual respect. Furthermore, a part of the feeling of belongingness is sacrificing self-interest to a greater purpose, and conscription is one of those rare opportunities to demonstrate this. Princeton's Daniel Rodger, author of the *Age of Fracture*, suggests that the US began to unravel socially after deciding to professionalize its military. He says, 'We lost our sense of what we were for and against' (Rodger 2012).

Gerber felt that conscription provides, in addition to social glue, valuable management training. Our chapter on Israel describes how the special UNIT 8200 members of the intelligence and cyberspace protection unit of the Israeli military almost single-handedly account for the country's vibrant business start-up scene, which is admired throughout the world. Military systems are also laboratories for identifying the nation's future talent and leadership. Only relatively recently has it become possible to be chairman or CEO of one of the Swiss powerhouse multinationals like Roche, Swiss Re or UBS without achieving at least the level of a captain in its military. Indeed, many leaders of major Finish, Israeli, Norwegian and Singaporean companies have also served as high ranking officers in the military.

Of course, the idea of conscription as a means of achieving social cohesion is not a new one. Jean-Jacques Rousseau argued vehemently against professional armies, feeling it was the right and privilege of every citizen to participate in the defence of the whole society and that it was a sign of moral decline to leave this responsibility to professionals. He based this view on the development of the Roman republic, which came to an end simultaneously with the Roman army's change from a conscript to professional force. Harvard's Stephen Walt traces the decline in the efficacy of the US military intervention to the same phenomenon. 'When children of voters put their lives at risk compared to professional soldiers, the inclination to engage in war is diminished,' he told me. Interestingly, Emmanuel Macron, France's youthful leader, recently brought back compulsory national service for all sixteen-year-olds, both boys and girls.

10. In teachers we trust

Workmen renovating a room in one of the medieval cloisters of Eton College in 2005 uncovered some faint images which read '*Virtus preceptoris est ingeniorum notare discriminia*', a Latin quotation from Quintilian, a Roman educator, which translates as 'The excellence of the teacher is to identify the differences in talents of their pupils.' More than 2,000 years old, the images are believed to be the earliest representation of a school scene in England.

Any successful school system requires a variety of systems, all working together in harmony to optimize the talent of its youth and future workforce. Any attempt to select the most important ingredient should be tempered with this caveat in mind. However, studies consistently show that teaching is the most significant explanation for the success (or failure) of any school system. McKinsey's landmark study of school systems around the world identified that 'getting the right people to become teachers and encouraging them to deliver the best possible instruction for every child' is the most important factor for any successful system (Barber and Mourshed 2007). Teaching is thought to account for more than 50 per cent of a student's performance. What these *TSTF* nations do better than other nations is have better teachers. As aptly summarized by Niemi, 'The quality of our education system cannot exceed the quality of our teachers.' In these nations, teaching is reserved for the brightest and most passionate students, who are well respected in the society.

Once these bright and passionate individuals become teachers, an environment of trust is built – another feature that distinguishes the teaching profession in top performing school systems. Unlike nations which have bureaucratic accountability systems which make teachers feel threatened, overcontrolled and undervalued, teachers in *TSTF* nations are trusted and respected. While the approach in Singapore is more industrious, teachers in Denmark, Finland, the Netherlands and Switzerland are often left to plan and carry out their lessons in whatever manner they see fit. They themselves decide upon the methods of teaching, the number of hours of instruction, what homework to assign, the types of testing as well as what textbooks and materials are necessary.

In Singapore, teachers are given time in the school day to evaluate their own work and to observe each other's lessons. A successful teacher is not pushed towards management, as is often the case elsewhere, but given opportunities to be a mentor or take a hand in designing the curriculum. Schleicher of OECD says, 'In other school systems we make the best teacher a poor administrator.' We can easily contrast this with the UK, where a lack of trust has led to a desire to control. Teachers are subjected to regular inspections and schools have data managers dictating which colour pens to use for marking tests, creating a culture of accountability through witch-hunts and sending a message of lack of regard for those who are teaching.

The irony of successful school systems is that their teachers spend less time teaching. This frees up more time to prepare lessons and work one-on-one with struggling students. In Finland, Korea and Japan, secondary school teachers spend 50 per cent less time teaching than secondary school teachers in the US and 25 per cent less than teachers in the UK (Sahlberg interview). In Singapore, the operating slogan is 'More learning and less teaching' – and it works.

Problems Remain

Successful school systems are not immune to the challenges facing teachers everywhere. In an interview with Sahlberg, he told me that the share of fifteen-year-olds in Finland reading more than thirty minutes per day has fallen from a half to a third since the iPhone was introduced. Sociologists are constantly warning of the danger of the my-life-is-better-than-your-life mindset which is instilled and characterized by social media. The *Economist* reported that 63 per cent of Instagram users are miserable, a malaise which transcends Finnish borders (*Economist* 2018). Furthermore, social media can prevent intellectual development, as it works to reinforce obstinacy rather than reason. Far from encouraging an understanding of different perspectives, platforms like Facebook, Instagram and Twitter confirm our own beliefs and inclinations rather than challenge them, often behaving as vacuumed echo chambers.

Technology has also come to threaten vocational training, with AI experts predicting that many of today's jobs will may not exist in fifteen years. An auto mechanic who trained a decade ago is being replaced by a software specialist. A travel agent is being replaced by websites such as Expedia and Booking.com, which lie at our autonomous fingertips.

Conclusion

There are compelling reasons for paying attention to these small, outperforming countries. They have been strikingly successful at the level of the individual, society and nation. Students at Beverly Hills High School are thought to be pretty good in maths and science, ranking in the top 12 per cent nationally in the US. They would be astonished to learn that, when compared to their Singaporean peers, they would rank in the bottom 34 per cent (MacLellan 2018). The *Economist* reported that Singaporean teens are roughly three years ahead of their US peers (*Economist* 2016). For a school system which lasts twelve years, this is significant. This example demonstrates the vast consequences which are at stake at the individual level.

At the collective level, the variance is even more staggering. The variance of performance among schools in Finland is about one tenth of the OECD average. The fact that there is so little educational inequality in Finland means that students get the same 'loaf of bread' when it comes to education; the difference or inequality which remains is mainly due to the natural variation of students' talents.

This means that these nations are running on more cylinders regarding their human capital, and their cylinders are firing faster. It is not surprising then that the competitiveness of these nations is rising while their larger counterparts are languishing.

The second reason to pay attention is that the small nations have managed to combine open economies and pro-business policies with public investment in human capital. They offer a more nuanced and responsive approach to the 'laissez faire' attitudes of the right and the 'tax and redistribute' mindset of the left, without meeting entirely in the middle.

The smaller nations also do a better job at drawing on the talents of their entire population. They have lower youth unemployment and exceptionally high rates of female labour force participation. They offer more equal opportunity of chance, not outcome. They enjoy the world's highest rates of social mobility and gender policies which encourage motherhood rather than punish it. Perhaps most remarkably of all, they have succeeded in doing all this by showing us that more money doesn't buy a better education.

Many US researchers and educators argue that it's misleading and unhelpful to compare the US or Britain to any small top performing country because of demographic and cultural differences. Is Niemi's assertion, 'The quality of our education system cannot exceed the quality of our teachers,' applicable across nations? Is this assertion any different in Helsinki from Manchester or Houston? Is it a coincidence that nations with better educated and skilled workforces are more competitive?

These are the sort of questions this chapter seeks to provoke. There are no easy answers. In closing, perhaps the final and most important reason to pay attention to these countries is that they have fixed something which was broken in the not-too-distant past. To do so, they had to do some soul-searching regarding issues of fundamental concern to all of us. What are schools for? How should teachers be educated? How should good schools work? They have been victorious by coming up with highly innovative solutions that rejected the tired orthodoxies of the left and right and worked irrespective of which political party was in power. Improving education became a national imperative.

References and Further Reading

Adams, R. 'OECD literacy leagues: poverty and inequality blamed for England's poor results'. *The Guardian*, 2013. https://www.theguardian.com/education/2013/oct/08/oecd-adult-literacy-numeracy-uk-poverty-inequality.

Barber, M. and M. Mourshed. 'How the world's best-performing school systems came out on top'. *McKinsey & Company*, 2007. https://www.mckinsey.com/industries/social-sector/our-insights/how-the-worlds-best-performing-school-systems-come-out-on-top.

Curtis, P. and H. Mulholland. 'David Cameron promises to "end state's monopoly" over public services'. *The Guardian*, 2011. https://www.theguardian.com/society/2011/jul/11/david-cameron-promises-end-state-monopoly-public-services.

'Education at a glance 2017: OECD Indicators'. OECD Publishing, 2017. https://www.oecd-ilibrary.org/education/education-at-a-glance-2017_eag-2017-en.

Friedman, M. *Capitalism and Freedom: Fortieth Anniversary Edition* (Chicago; London: University of Chicago Press, 2002).

Hirschman, A.O. *Exit, Voice and Loyalty: Responses to Decline in Firms, Organizations, and States.* (Cambridge, Mass.: Harvard University Press, 1970).

'How heavy use of social media is linked to mental illness'. *The Economist*, 2018. https://www.economist.com/graphic-detail/2018/05/18/how-heavy-use-of-social-media-is-linked-to-mental-illness?fsrc=scn/tw/te/bl/ed/?fsrc=scn/tw/te/bl/ed/howheavyuseofsocialmediaislinkedtomentalillnessdailychart.

'How to be top'. *The Economist*, 2007. https://www.economist.com/international/2007/10/18/how-to-be-top.

Kim, S. 'US is only industrialized nation without paid maternity leave'. *ABC News*, 2015. https://abcnews.go.com/Business/us-industrialized-nation-paid-maternity-leave/story?id=30852419.

Krueger, A.B. 'The Rise and Consequences of Inequality in the United States', 2012. https://cdn.americanprogress.org/wp-content/uploads/events/2012/01/pdf/krueger.pdf.

Little, T. *An Intelligent Person's Guide to Education.* UK edition (London; New York: Bloomsbury Continuum, 2015).

Luce, E. 'Amy Chua and the big little lies of US meritocracy'. *Financial Times*, 2019. https://www.ft.com/content/7b00c3a2-8daa-11e9-a1c1-51bf8f989972.

MacLellan, L. 'The best US high schools aren't as good as they think they are'. *Quartz*, 2018. https://qz.com/work/1266735/us-only-rankings-for-schools-like-beverly-hills-high-mislead-students/.

Nisen, M. 'Google HR boss explains why GPA and most interviews are useless'. *Business Insider*, 2013. https://www.businessinsider.com/how-google-hires-people-2013-6?r=US&IR=T.

'Relationship between Economic Inequality and Mobility across Countries'. *Equitable Growth*, no date. https://equitablegrowth.org/another-attack-on-the-great-gatsby-curve/roadtoserfdom1/.

Rodgers, D.T. *Age of Fracture* (Harvard: Belknap Press, 2012).

Sahlberg, P. 'Paradoxes of educational improvement: The Finnish experience' in *Scottish Educational Review*, vol. 43, no. 1, 2011. pp. 3–23 (p. 17). Available at: https://pasisahlberg.com/wp-content/uploads/2013/01/Paradoxes-of-improvement-SER-2011.pdf.

Spicer, J. 'Red flags emerge as Americans' debt load hits another record'. *Reuters*, 2019. https://www.reuters.com/article/us-usa-economy-debt/red-flags-emerge-as-americans-debt-load-hits-another-record-idUSKCN1Q11YV.

'The Great Gatsby Curve: Declining Mobility'. *Bloomberg*, 2013. https://www.bloomberg.com/graphics/infographics/the-great-gatsby-curve-explained.html.

Vasagar, J. 'Why Singapore's kids are so good at maths'. *Financial Times*, 2016. https://www.ft.com/content/2e4c61f2-4ec8-11e6-8172-e39ecd3b86fc.

'What the world can learn from the latest PISA test results'. *The Economist*, 2016. https://www.economist.com/international/2016/12/10/what-the-world-can-learn-from-the-latest-pisa-test-results.

Conversations and Interviews

Fritz Gerber, Hannele Niemi, Pasi Sahlberg, Stephen Walt, Tommy Koh and Yossi Vardi.

6

Who Are 'We the People'?

Rembrandt's *The Night Watch*

Source: Rijksmuseum

Rembrandt's *The Night Watch*, one of the world's most admired paintings, sits on the wall of the Rijksmuseum in Amsterdam, where it attracts over two million people a year. The painting depicts the civic guardsmen of Amsterdam, who volunteered to put out the odd fire or quell the occasional brawl, adopting the roles of policemen and firemen. Traditionally, group portraits were stoic replications of rows of monotonous figures. By contrast, each member in Rembrandt's painting performs a specific action which defines his role in the group. Art historians rave about Rembrandt's use of light and shadow to accentuate the figures. The intricate detail of each individual is what brings the painting to life.

The Night Watch is symbolic of the Dutch Golden Age, a period of unparalleled Dutch success in art, science and trade. In 1642, when Rembrandt completed his masterpiece, the Netherlands was freeing itself from the yoke of the Spanish empire and the Roman Catholic Church, an institution which had effectively controlled the minds and hearts of people throughout Europe for more than a thousand years. Lidewij de Koekkoek, Director of the Rembrandt House Museum, says that the period was characterized by 'creativity, entrepreneurship and an international outlook' – words which continue to define the Dutch mindset till today.

The seventeenth century also saw the rise of mercantilism. Dutch ships sailed around the world to places hitherto unreachable such as Indonesia and Japan, searching for exotic goods. Ships laden with precious cloth, porcelain and spices from Africa to Asia captivated curious European consumers and resulted in a spectacular surge of wealth to this newly independent nation. Large numbers of sailors, map makers, engineers and shipbuilders relocated to its port cities to meet the increasing demands for their skills. Canals, ports and infrastructure were put into place to handle the growing trade. In 1602, a few years before Rembrandt's birth, the world's first multinational company, The Dutch East India Company, was formed to finance the risky voyages to foreign lands. This led to the world's first stock exchange in Amsterdam and the world's first central bank. The *Gazette de Leyde* (Gazette of Leiden), published in French, was considered the world's most authoritative newspaper.

I chose to open this chapter with *The Night Watch* not for Rembrandt's artistic brilliance but for how the painting reflects the society in transition at that time. No longer was it vertically integrated between subordinate and superior; a serf ploughing land for his master or sitting obediently in a rear pew during a Sunday church service. Participation could no longer be accommodated by existing political institutions, and people had to organize themselves without the guidance of a king or a bishop. In other words, they became citizens.

The Night Watch oozes with civic pride and duty. Eighteen members of the civic guard company, Kloveniersdoelen, commissioned the painting to distinguish themselves and broadcast their allegiance to the community they served. *The Night Watch* thus captures the transcendence of 'we' over 'me'. It depicts a call to collective action, that pivotal moment when an individual is asked to devote himself to the service of a common good. A young boy in the left foreground carrying a powder horn dashes off to collect more gun powder. Another member loads his firearm. A drummer taps out a cadence and members spring dutifully to action.

How do prosperity, power and wealth arise? What helps preserve them? Why do some nations have more and others less? Organizations such as the World Economic Forum and the World Bank routinely analyse and rank well-known performance indicators, including innovation, education and ease of doing business. This chapter argues that they may have overlooked one of the most important factors of all – social cohesion, a force which Rembrandt captures vividly in *The Night Watch*.

We start by asking what cohesion is, and why it is so important. We then observe that smaller, outperforming nations are better at getting and maintaining it, and explain why. We conclude that this comparative advantage is likely to take on more importance in the future, as larger, diverse societies struggle with the increasing cost of social cohesion and trust.

Recent political upheavals, such as Brexit, the election of Trump and the surging right-wing movements in France, the Netherlands and Germany, are telling us, among other things, that societies are not as cohesive as they once were. *TSTF* countries offer an alternate picture – one which more closely resembles the social cohesion depicted in *The Night Watch*.

* * *

Why Social Cohesion Is Important

A quick glance at synonyms for 'cohesion' yield familiar and comforting words – togetherness, solidarity, bonding, continuity, connection. The word is used in chemistry to describe which natural elements have an affinity for each other and the propensity for molecules to cling together. Software geeks use 'cohesion' to measure how lines of source code work effortlessly together. Who among us hasn't rooted for the underdog sports team which prevailed against a superior team because of more cohesive teamwork?

Human beings are a unique species. We live constantly with dual claims for our allegiance. There is self-interest against consideration for others; collaboration against competition; confrontation against compromise; the supremacy of the individual against that of the community. And we can transition from one to the other depending on circumstances. Our chapter on openness highlights our tendency to seek out opportunities and convert possibilities into realities. It suggests that this requires some form of collaboration – and suppression of selfishness. Working with others is thus essential.

Jonathan Haidt, a professor at New York University, agrees that collaboration is central to social cohesion. He describes cohesion in the form of moral capital as 'the degree to which a community possesses interlocking sets of values, virtues, norms, practices, identities, institutions and technologies that mesh well with evolved psychological mechanisms and thereby enable the community to suppress or regulate selfishness and make cooperation possible' (Haidt 2013).

The proclivity to collaborate voluntarily and spontaneously is one of the most important and underrated attributes of successful societies. Alexis De Tocqueville once said, 'It is the *art* of *association that becomes* the *mother* of *action*' (Tocqueville 1835). He argued that this is what distinguished America's exceptional emergence as the world's most powerful economy. 'Americans of all ages, all conditions, and all dispositions, constantly form associations,' he said (Tocqueville 1835).

Tocqueville felt that there was a continuum of collaboration with kinship or family on one side and the state or the monarchy on the other. A vital factor for a cohesive society is a wider circle of trust and collaboration which does not rely on either of these two limiting frameworks. Excessive reliance on family results in nepotism and stunts society's development. Over reliance on the state deprives the society of initiative and competition. Instead, a society should be fostering an abundance of spontaneous and voluntary collaborations which emerge to suit a particular purpose – whether it's a new Rotary club, building a hospital or a division of boy scouts.[5]

---

5. Tocqueville recognized that collaboration was integral to democratic nations. He said, 'In aristocratic (or plutocratic) societies men do not need to combine in order to act, because they are strongly held together. Every wealthy and powerful citizen constitutes the head of a permanent and compulsory association, composed of all those who are dependent upon him, or whom he makes subservient to the execution of his designs. Amongst

The essential ingredient of voluntary collaborations is trust – the expectation that members exhibit predictable, honest and collaborative behaviour based on shared values. Whenever we depend on the contribution of another, we place a wager on them not to disappoint us. Anthropology suggests that we are wired to trust people who perform as advertised and distrust those who don't. The biological term 'reciprocal altruism' can be applied to many of life's transactions – 'I help you if you help me.' If a person does a service for another person, the recipient will feel grateful and be inclined to reciprocate in some manner they feel is commensurate to the value of maintaining the relationship.

Reciprocity is a norm shared by all cultures. Sometimes it can carry an explicit expectation – as when a customer buys bread from the local baker, who expects to be paid in return. Every buyer and seller expects to be better off as a result of a transaction. Why else would they undertake it? At other times, reciprocity is deferred for a favour we expect (or hope for) in return – as when we invite someone to a dinner party or give someone a gift. Even the efficacy of bribes depends on reciprocity.[6]

Reciprocity is also the basis of many social norms. Swiss people place an enormous value on being punctual because they view it as a contract where both sides agree to meet at a certain time and place. If one party doesn't show up or feels they are superior and can keep the other party waiting, it is considered a breach of trust. Trust is derived from doing what one says, repeatedly. This is why brands are valued so highly. They give promises which we expect will be fulfilled. We are also genetically wired to punish freeloaders and betrayers, which explains why 'prisoners' dilemma' outcomes are so complex.[7]

---

democratic nations, on the contrary, all the citizens are independent and feeble; they can do hardly anything by themselves, if they do not learn to collaborate voluntarily to help each other.'

6. Gary S. Becker and Richard A. Posner of the University of Chicago posited that any organization produces suboptimal outcome because individuals' preferences and goals may differ from those of the group, so there are friction costs, another form of agency cost. Once again, more like-minded or cohesive nations produce more like-minded results.

7. The prisoners' dilemma is a hypothetical scenario that shows why two individuals may choose self-interest over cooperation to their own detriment. The concept was formed by Merrill Flood and Melvin Dresher.

All of this is important because studies show persuasively that capitalism flourishes best in societies with high degrees of cohesiveness and trust. Steve Knack, an economist at the World Bank and a student of social cohesion and trust, went so far as to say, 'It would explain most of the difference between the per capita income of the United States and Somalia' (Keefer 1997). In other words, without trust – and its vital complement, social cohesion – the prospect of economic development is bleak.

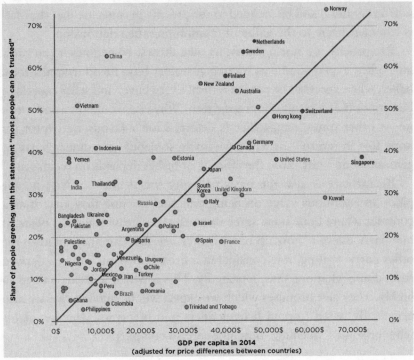

Figure 6.1: Trust and Prosperity

This graph shows the relationship between GDP per capita and institutional trust. TSTF nations perform highly.

Source: Boda and Medve-Bálint, 2012

When examining the correlation between the level of cohesiveness in a society and its economic success, *TSTF* nations rank the highest. This occurs at two levels – external and internal. Denmark, Finland, the Netherlands, Singapore, Sweden and Switzerland routinely rank among the world's most trusted nations by their peers. They also exhibit the highest degrees of mutual trust among their own citizens. Trust brings a host of advantages. For example, people who trust one another are more likely to collaborate for mutual gain. They are also more likely to share the profits with one another, and with those who are less fortunate.

The advantages are not only economic. The Nobel Prize-winning economist Kenneth Arrow has shown that smaller, more cohesive societies are easier to govern (Arrow 1974). Consensus formation is difficult when electorates become substantially more diverse and polarized. Pew research reports state that nations exhibiting high levels of trust have lower levels of crime and corruption (Holzwart and Wike 2008). It is not surprising that these nations are staunchly meritocratic, with systems which reward talent, hard work and encourage upward mobility. Contrast this with places such as the US, Britain, France, Korea and Japan, where social mobility may occur only once in a lifetime when a teenager succeeds in a gruelling entrance exam or when universities like Oxford, ENA, University of Tokyo or Yale decide who will ostensibly be set for life.

Nations vary according to their emphasis on the community and their degree of social cohesion. Stanford's Francis Fukuyama distinguishes between 'high trust' and 'low trust' societies. Whilst citizens in a high trust society exhibit predictable behaviour towards one another, citizens in a low trust society are challenged by divergent or opaque behavioural norms. As behaviour is less predictable, citizens are more likely to experience high levels of corruption, rent-seeking behaviour and inequality.

People who trust one another are less dependent on formal rules and regulations. They cooperate without a system which must be negotiated, agreed to, litigated and enforced often by coercive means. This regulatory apparatus serves as a costly substitute for trust, entailing what economists call 'transaction costs'. Widespread distrust in a society imposes a kind of tax on all forms of economic activity, which high-trust societies do not have to pay. Just think of the nuisance of airport security procedures as one small example where regulations seek to compensate for lost trust. Simple activities become arduous in societies which lack cohesion and trust. How can you be sure someone will pay their bill? Or that you won't be robbed on the way to the neighbourhood grocery store? It can't be a good sign if armed guards are needed at elementary schools, movie theatres and nightclubs. The US pays significantly more than other industrialized nations for police protection and imprisonment because of a lack of trust and social cohesion.

The costs arising from a lack of social cohesion are substantial and growing almost all over the world. Researchers at Stanford University's financial fraud research centre estimate that 'consumer fraud' alone costs Americans more than $50 billion annually (*Economist* 2018). In *Phishing for Phools*, Nobel Prize-winning economists George Akerlof and Robert Shiller argue that markets are inherently deceitful as profit-seeking companies manipulate and exploit their consumers. While no nation is immune to fraud, studies show that *TSTF* nations consistently rank among the least corrupt nations and have substantially less incidences of fraud per capita compared with larger G7 nations (*NationMaster* 2002).

"WE MAY BE SMALL BUT WE'RE HIGHLY SOCIALLY COHESIVE."

Figure 6.2: Social Cohesion

Source: Banx

What Creates Cohesion?

That high trust levels promote prosperity seems uncontentious, but understanding what contributes to greater social cohesion is more difficult to establish. Several aspects coalesce to determine the degree of cohesiveness of any society. To begin with, smallness helps. With fewer degrees of separation, there is a greater frequency of dealings and a higher likelihood of getting called out for free riding, deception or cheating. Since reciprocity happens more often, it is more easily enforced.

The signal-to-noise ratio is also superior in smaller societies, so spreading 'fake news' or deceiving people is more difficult. Large, remote and diverse nations are ideal for the propagation of misinformation via social media channels, as transmission tends to compound errors and the time required to validate the truth undermines the validation. Such twitter tactics involve dissemination of falsehoods and moving on to the next tweet before the factual discovery process can occur. This leaves the audience in a perpetual state of misinformation. The strategy of touting shamelessness as a comparative advantage, or the prospect of 'fake it till you make it' as a viable tactic for advancement, would never work in a small, cohesive society.

With smallness comes vulnerability, which encourages communities to come together to find solutions. We have earlier discussed polders in the Netherlands and how they build cohesiveness in their society. We have also mentioned how Swiss alpine communities collaborate to reduce damage from avalanches. The same is true of other *TSTF* countries. Citizens of Israel are among the most cohesive in the world, in good part because it only takes a few minutes for a devastating warhead to reach them from their hostile neighbours. Humility and cohesion exhibit a high degree of affinity.

Another possible explanation for why *TSTF* countries enjoy top-tier social cohesion is that many still retain learnings from conscription time. For a few years, during their formative years of adolescence, citizens are taught that the nation is worth fighting for and belonging to. Like Rembrandt's *The Night Watch*, they suspend the self-interest and tendencies of 'me' in favour of the common good of 'we'. It is in those years and in close experiences that 'we the people' is reinforced.

A society's architecture also has a substantial impact on its degree of cohesion. We can see this in three crucial areas. First, it helps having a dominant belief to shape a common sense of values, identity and belonging. Scandinavian nations, though non-religious, have a strong sense of Lutheran values which still determine their social norms. Similarly, Ireland has the religious values of Catholicism and Israel has those of Judaism. Despite their more heterogenous mix, 70 per cent of Singaporeans are ethnically Chinese with Confucian values and 70 per cent of Swiss are Swiss–German or of Protestant origin. The important point here is not about race, ethnicity or religion but about the impact of differing preferences and norms on a society's social cohesion. Multiculturalism, like Malaysia's 'three cultures, one nation' policy, is a laudable goal, but in practice it can be costly and problematic to maintain. Having a dominant belief and a values doctrine also enables immigrants to assimilate more readily.

Second, an urban–rural divide is becoming the axis of politics in many large nations. America is divided between the liberal-dominated west and north east coasts, and a vast expanse of a conservative-dominated interior. In *The Road to Somewhere*, David Goodhart finds that Britain is similarly divided. He argues that Brexit stemmed from the emergence in the past generation of two big value clusters – the educated, mobile people who see the world from 'anywhere' as against the more rooted, less educated people who see the world from 'somewhere' and prioritize group attachments and security. The 'anywheres' are more upwardly mobile, leaving the 'somewheres' far behind. To some, this explains why London has become a nation within a nation, and why more than 60 per cent of British people still live within twenty miles of where they grew up. Rural populations account for an increasingly smaller share of the national experience, but they tend to have a stronger grip on the national conscience and are perceived as its seat of virtue. Electoral systems such as the Electoral College and the US Senate give 'somewheres' power that is disproportionate to their number.

Earlier, nations needed domestic automobile production, which required steel and therefore iron ore and coal. So cities like Cleveland, Detroit, Pittsburgh and New York were inextricably linked in the value chain. The same went for Essen, Dresden, Munich, Stuttgart, Coventry, Birmingham and London. But these capital and labour-intensive industries are today a fraction of their former selves, leaving hollowed out communities with dwindling living standards. In the extreme, as with Great Britain, it can feel like two nations within one.

Take the recent rise of the gilets jaunes – the yellow vest movement in France. According to geographer Hervé Le Bras, the highest concentration of gilets jaunes as a share of the population falls along a diagonale du vide (empty diagonal), which is a long band of French territory stretching from the department of the Meuse to Landes, with a low density of population caused largely by rural exodus and urbanization. This is 'in-between France', according to Raymond

Depardon, a photographer whose stills depict derelict high streets and empty roundabouts – the very places now occupied by gilets jaunes. Similarly, *Hillbilly Elegy*, a book which became Trump's battle cry, is a story of a family from a small town in Ohio, which is characterized as 'in-between America'.

By contrast, *TSTF* nations do not have vast hinterlands. Their industrial heritage formed as ateliers rather than hierarchically managed industrial complexes. This may help explain part of their advantage with respect to social cohesion. Most people in *TSTF* nations are both 'anywhere' and 'somewhere'. They have access to similar-level high education possibilities, they speak multiple languages and are encouraged to travel and live abroad during their youth. But they can maintain their roots in their communities, not the least because the maximum distance from the most remote farming village in Denmark, the Netherlands or Switzerland and their largest cities, for example, is often only a few hours' drive.

Third, *TSTF* nations are better at empowering their people. Abraham Lincoln's famous dictum at Gettysburg – 'Government of the people, by the people, for the people' is a more apt description of democracies in Denmark, the Netherlands, Switzerland and Sweden. Societies in these nations are organized as networks rather than hierarchies, so power is more broadly dispersed. People in *TSTF* nations have much greater confidence in their governments in large part because they feel they are heard. Each member of Congress in the US represents around 600,000 citizens; in the UK, it is 100,000 citizens per legislator. This compares to less than 40,000 for most *TSTF* nations, the approximate number of constituents envisaged by the authors of the Federalist Papers. It is not hard to see why citizens in *TSTF* nations feel better represented.

TSTF nations are characterized by proportional representation, or 'consensus democracy' as described by the Dutch academic Arend Lijphart in *Patterns of Democracy*. Lijphart contrasted majoritarian, 'winner take all' democracies in the US, the UK, New Zealand, etc. with electoral systems which foster coalition building, as in Denmark, Germany, the Netherlands, Switzerland and Sweden. He found that *TSTF* nations select political leaders whose views correspond more closely with those they are representing. He also found that there is less corruption, greater inclusivity with respect to gender, LGBT and minority interests, more civil and less adversarial interactions and a greater emphasis on longer term, important issues which require stable policies. Studies show that citizens of nations with proportional representation compared to 'winner take all' systems exhibit greater engagement and voter participation. Greater inclusiveness is likely a major reason why policies requiring long term commitment – such as education, pensions and the environment – have garnered enduring support in these nations.[8] Britain, by contrast, increasingly feels like two nations within one. Its new prime minister was chosen by 0.3 per cent of the electorate to form a government by a party speaking for 20 per cent of the people, who will then try to deliver what the majority of the country is set against.

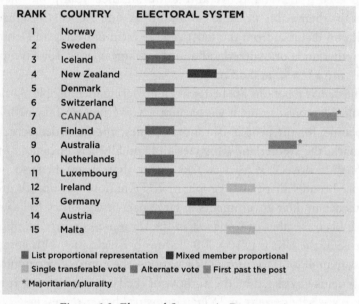

Figure 6.3: Electoral Systems in Democracies

TSTF nations tend to use some form of proportional representation rather than 'winner takes all' systems so a greater portion of citizens feel their voices are heard.

Source: Moscrop, 2016

---

8. Denmark, for example, has seventeen districts which elect on an average eight representatives. Minority parties with as little as 8 per cent of the vote are represented and thus have a voice.

By contrast, 'winner take all' electoral systems incentivize politicians to over promise and under deliver. It is no surprise that citizens in these countries have little trust in their governments. According to Pew Research Centre, fewer than three in ten Americans trust their federal government (Holzwart and Wike 2008). This is only slightly higher than the level of trust in a used car salesperson, and is down precipitously from nearly eight in ten a generation ago. The UK has experienced a more moderate yet similar decline. Part of this is no doubt explained by the 'Yoyo' effect, when a newly elected party enacts reforms, which are reversed or squelched when they are ousted from power.

Laborious yet Self-Reinforcing

Social cohesion requires considerable effort. It takes a preponderance of like-minded participants and there needs to be a common yardstick to measure morality. This encourages consensual rather than confrontational behaviour and is important for establishing reliable social norms. If someone simply walks away and feels they may never see the person they have dealt with again, the incentive to remedy dissatisfaction or honour reciprocity is virtually eliminated. Then, life is based around transactions rather than relationships.

The good news is that social cohesion is self-reinforcing. Ultimately, high-trust societies are positive equilibriums in which most people behave as they should because the gains from behaving are higher than the gains from defecting. Economic out-performance not only requires trust, but encourages it. Why bother to cheat when you are already comfortable? By contrast, in a leaky society, where there are low likelihoods of getting caught, the incentives to cheat are high.

Building, maintaining and shoring up social cohesion is programmed to become more expensive for large and small nations alike. We live in an era which puts increasing emphasis on the self at the cost of the community, so the forces are at work against social cohesion. With more emphasis on personal identity, people are moving away from traditional structures such as the family and religion. It remains to be seen whether the new affiliations that take their place will be as cohesive.

Just as high levels of social cohesion produce a virtuous spiral, low levels produce a vicious one. Low trust societies experience greater economic inequality, which exacerbates the costs of social cohesion. Citizens may polarize themselves between 'those who do' and 'those who mooch off those who do', undermining the acceptance of redistribution policies aimed at reducing inequality. When an 'every man for himself' mentality sets in, the strongest will feel authorized to indulge in value extraction or rent seeking. Academic studies by Berkeley psychologists Paul Piff and Dacher Keltner show that rising wealth reduces our empathy and encourages unethical behaviour towards others, thus eroding social cohesion (Piff et al. 2012).

So much attention is given to governments and markets, but very little is paid to what the renowned German philosopher Jürgen Habermas describes as the 'public sphere'—the central nervous system that operates between and penetrates every pore of society (Habermas 1991).

Habermas argues that successful societies work best when they consist of networks rather than hierarchies, which means people are free to communicate horizontally instead of vertically. Social cohesion is easier, and friction is reduced, when people speak the same language, understand the same idioms, and share similar backgrounds, values and beliefs.

What is important is that political impetus is rational rather than emotive. And for this to happen, citizens need to be well-informed, critically minded and able to express, in an unrestricted fashion, their honest opinions. Thus, the contest of deliberation ensues, and the best arguments win the day. Sovereignty rests with the people, and their elected leaders march to the tune of the public consensus constructed bottom up.

On the opposite side of this utopia are political systems struggling to intermediate a consensus due to a perplexing variety of competing interests fixated among identity groups. To gain power, politicians appeal to the emotive (not the rational), and take positions to please its most passionate members. This is how political discourse becomes polarized. Edward Luce, a political commentator with the *Financial Times*, sums up this disturbing development in the US: 'The more [Trump] demonises minorities, the more liberal America shifts leftward, which in turn boosts Mr Trump's politically incorrect allure' (*Financial Times* 2019).

In instances like these, there is no public chorus or 'sphere': no common voice, but a cacophony of disjointed discussions among isolated audiences. Due to echo chambers fostered by social media algorithms and the proliferation of 'fake news', the citizen's ability to discover, digest and adjudicate information is severely weakened. Since participation and rigorous critical debate are essential for an effective democracy, any system of 'res publica' is rendered less workable.

TSTF nations are by no means utopias, but they do score higher across the range of metrics Habermas had in mind for a well-functioning society.

Conclusion

Social cohesion and trust are fragile. They can be dissipated easily with costly consequences to society. When trust breaks down, relations have to be spelled out in detail, unwritten rules codified and third parties appointed to arbitrate disputes. Spontaneous and cooperative collaboration ceases. For the legal profession, this is a gold mine; for society, a plague.

The cult of the individual has been on the rise everywhere and 'whoever dies with the most toys wins' seems to be the prevalent mantra. Simon Kuper, who grew up in the Netherlands, describes how life in high-trust societies feels different: 'Get home from work in time for dinner with the kids; no stress about paying for their education or healthcare; safe streets in a safe region; an affordable home near your extended family; frequent holidays and a long life. You won't get rich, but you won't need to either' (Kuper 2018).

Maybe the potential for progress in large nations has less to do with growth or the next wonder innovation. Instead, these nations should be focusing on how to eke out ways to create more trust and to improve on what binds people.

Times have changed. The cost of distance may have declined dramatically due to technology but the cost of cohesion has increased significantly, precisely when it is needed the most. As with *The Night Watch*, this will likely call for a new social order.

The most distinctive feature of Rembrandt's *The Night Watch* is a mysterious, angelic girl emerging from the darkness behind the brave, stately members of the garrison. Hanging upside down from her waistband are the claws of a chicken. Each militia had an emblem and this was theirs. Members wore it as symbol of belonging. A testament of their willingness to suspend 'me' for 'we' when the moment called for it. Herein may lie the secret.

References and Further Reading

Alberto, A., E. Spolaore and R. Wacziarg. 'Economic Integration and Political Disintegration'. American Economic Review, vol. 90, no. 5 (2000): pp. 1276–96. doi:10.1257/aer.90.5.1276.

Alberto, A., R. Baqir and C. Hoxby. 'Political Jurisdictions in Heterogeneous Communities'. Journal of Political Economy, vol. 112, no. 2 (2004): pp. 348–96. doi:10.1086/381474.

Alberto, A., R. Baqir, and W. Easterly. 'Public Goods and Ethnic Divisions'. *The Quarterly Journal of Political Economy*, vol. 114, no. 4 (1999): pp. 1243–84. doi:10.1162/003355399556269.

Arrow, K.J. *The Limits of Organization* (New York: Norton, 1974).

Blais, A. and M.A. Bodet. 'Does proportional representation foster closer congruence between citizens and policy makers?' *Comparative Political Studies*, vol. 39, no. 10 (2006): pp. 1243-1262. doi:10.1177/0010414005284374.

Boda, Z. and G. Medve-Bálint. 'Figure 3: Association between Institutional trust and per capita GDP (2010)'. *Blogs.lse.ac.uk* (2012). https://blogs.lse.ac.uk/europpblog/2012/08/21/institutional-trust-zsolt-boda/.

Butler, J.V., P. Giuliano and L. Guiso. 'The Right Amount of Trust'. *Journal of the European Economic Association*, vol. 14, no. 5 (2016): pp. 1155-80. https://doi.org/10.1111/jeea.12178.

——'Trust, Values, and False Consensus'. *International Economic Review*, vol. 56, no. 3 (2015): pp. 889–915. https://doi.org/10.1111/iere.12125.

Campbell, J.L., J.A. Hall and O.K. Pedersen. *National Identity and the Varieties of Capitalism: The Danish Experience* (Canada: McGill-Queen's University Press, 2006).

'Edelman Trust Barometer'. *Edelman*, 2019 https://www.edelman.com/trust-barometer.

'Frauds: Countries Compared'. *NationMaster*, 2002. https://www.nationmaster.com/country-info/stats/Crime/Frauds.

Fukuyama, F. *Trust: The Social Virtues and the Creation of Prosperity* (London: Penguin, 1996).

Goodhart, D. *The Road to Somewhere: the Populist Revolt and the Future of Politics*. (London: Hurst & Company, 2017).

Goodhart, D. 'Why I left my liberal London tribe'. *Financial Times*, 2017. https://www.ft.com/content/39a0867a-0974-11e7-ac5a-903b21361b43.

'Governments need better ways to manage migration'. *The Economist*, 2018. https://www.economist.com/briefing/2018/08/25/governments-need-better-ways-to-manage-migration.

Grewal, D. 'How Wealth Reduces Compassion'. *Scientific American* (2012). https://www.scientificamerican.com/article/how-wealth-reduces-compassion/.

Guiso, L., H. Herrera M. Morelli. 'Cultural Differences and Institutional Integration'. *Journal of International Economics*, vol. 99 (2016). doi:http://dx.doi.org/10.1016/j.jinteco.2015.11.005.

Guiso, L., P. Sapienza and L. Zingales. 'Civic Capital as the Missing Link'. *Handbook of Social Economics*, vol. 1 (2011): pp. 417–80. http://dx.doi.org/10.1016/B978-0-444-53187-2.00010-3.

——'Long-Term Persistence'. *Journal of the European Economic Association*, vol. 14, no. 6 (2016): pp. 1401–36. http://dx.doi.org/10.1111/jeea.12177.

Habermas, J. *The Structural Transformation of the Public Sphere: An Inquiry into a Category of Bourgeois Society* (Cambridge, MA: MIT Press, 1991).

Haidt, J. *The Righteous Mind: Why Good People are Divided by Politics and Religion* (London: Penguin Books, 2013).

Hirschman, A.O. *Exit, Voice and Loyalty: Responses to Decline in Firms, Organizations, and States* (Cambridge, Mass.: Harvard University Press, 1970).

Holzwart, K. and R. Wike. 'Where Trust is High, Crime and Corruption are Low'. *Pew Research Centre*, 2008. http://www.pewglobal.org/2008/04/15/where-trust-is-high-crime-and-corruption-are-low/.

Horst, H.V.D. *The Low Sky: Understanding the Dutch* (Schiedam: XPat Scriptum Publishers, 2016).

Hume, D. *A Treatise of Human Nature*. (London, Clarendon Press, 1896).

Israel, Jonathan. *The Dutch Republic: Its Rise, Greatness, and Fall 1477-1806* (Oxford: Clarendon Press, 1998)

Keefer, P. and S. Knack. 'Does Social Capital Have an Economic Payoff? A Cross-Country Investigation'. *The Quarterly Journal of Economics*, vol. 112, no. 4 (1997): pp. 1251–88. doi:10.1162/003355300555475.

Koot, T. *Rembrandt's Night Watch: A Fascinating Story* (Amsterdam: Meulenhoff International, 1969).

Kuper, S. 'The new American dream? Northern Europe'. *Financial Times*, 2018. https://www.ft.com/content/4ccd99be-f2a1-11e8-ae55-df4bf40f9d0d.

Lijphart, A. *Patterns of Democracy: Government Forms and Performance in Thirty-six Countries*. 2nd ed. (New Haven; London: Yale University Press, 2012).

Luce, E. 'US liberal over-reach on gender identity risks benefiting Trump'. *Financial Times*, 2009. https://www.ft.com/content/065210f0-87f2-11e9-a028-86cea8523dc2.

Moscrop, D. 'An Electoral System for All'. Broadbent Institute, 2016. https://www.broadbentinstitute.ca/an_electoral_system_for_all.

Mueller, J. *The Remnants of War* (Ithaca; London: Cornell University Press, 2007).

Norris, P. 'Choosing electoral systems: proportional, majoritarian, and mixed systems'. *International Political Science Review*, vol. 18, no. 3 (1997): pp. 297-312. https://sites.hks.harvard.edu/fs/pnorris/Acrobat/Choosing%20Electoral%20Systems.pdf.

Piff, P.K., et al. 'Higher social class predicts increased unethical behavior'. *PNAS*, 2012. https://www.pnas.org/content/109/11/4086.

Porta, R.L. et al. 'Trust in Large Organizations'. *The American Economic Review*, vol. 87, no. 2 (1997): pp. 333–38. http://www.jstor.org/stable/2950941.

Putnam, R.D. *Bowling Alone: The Collapse and Revival of American Community* (New York; London: Simon & Schuster, 2000).

'Renewal of Swiss residence permits now depends on good behavior and integration'. *Le News*, 2019. https://lenews.ch/2019/01/04/renewal-of-swiss-residence-permits-now-depends-on-good-behaviour-and-integration/.

Schama, Simon. *The Embarrassment of Riches: An Interpretation of Dutch Culture in the Golden Age* (London: Collins, 1988).

Smith, A. *The Theory of Moral Sentiments* (CreateSpace Independent Publishing Platform, 2016).

Tocqueville, A. de. 'Chapter V: Of the Use Which the Americans Make of Public Associations in Civil Life'. *Democracy in America* (New York, Harper Perennial Modern Classics, 2006).

'Why do so many people fall for financial scams?'. *The Economist*, 2018. https://www.economist.com/finance-and-economics/2018/12/08/why-do-so-many-people-fall-for-financial-scams.

Conversations and Interviews

Paul Polman and Ove Kaj Pedersen.

7

Critical but Not Urgent

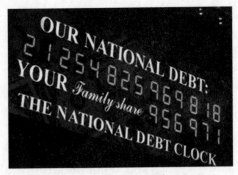

US National Debt as on July 2018

Source: Wikimedia Commons

You don't believe the sky is falling until a chunk of it falls on you.
—Margaret Atwood, *The Testaments*

Fear is natural. It often manifests itself in the most ordinary of actions and activities. There is the fear of not being liked, not completing a degree, not securing a job, not finding the right partner or not having enough savings to fund our retirement. Fear in moderation can be healthy because it is an important source of motivation. It prods us to make an extra effort, think of alternate solutions, take a chance, fine-tune our priorities and, ever so often, surprise ourselves.

I recall Harvard's Daniel Gilbert, author of *Stumbling on Happiness*, describing the threat of a rapidly approaching spear, the sort of incident which was not uncommon in the savannahs of Africa where our human evolution took shape. 'We duck,' he said, explaining how thousands of years of evolution has programmed us to avoid immediate danger. The problem, Gilbert explained, is that 'when it takes fifty years for this spear to reach us, our brains are not wired to react'.

People are very good at dealing with what is urgent and has their self-interest. Free markets thrive on these human traits as people are quick to act when they need to replace a burned-out light bulb, buy a birthday present or pull into the next Burger King to cure hunger pangs.

Individuals and societies, it turns out, are much worse at dealing with problems on the opposite side of the continuum – the issues which are important, but not necessarily urgent. Democracies are particularly handicapped in this regard, as they are based on the assent of the people. To some extent, markets which tend to have a strong place in democratic societies can be effective long-term actors, but not reliably so.

The problems in democratic societies come in a number of forms. One category could be called 'consume now and pay later'. Elected officials' prime motivation is to get re-elected. Reducing taxes and increasing spending is a tried-and-tested method of gaining popular support. A second category of problems are the so-called 'tragedy of the commons' issues, which have adverse consequences to us all, but are not reflected in the price set by free markets. Pollution, traffic and noise are the common examples. The third category of problems deal with blind spots which arise because, as consumers, we are not fully aware of the long-term consequences of our behaviour. This would include not saving or investing properly during our youth. Obesity, known as a 'silent killer', is a blind spot for many of us; it can lead to a cascade of diseases like renal failure and heart disease.

The libertarians among us will tout the superiority of individual will and freedom of choice and rightly point out that many of our challenges are within human reach to understand and resolve. They will argue, as Churchill once said, 'Society should be a ladder, not a crutch.' Most of us celebrate free markets and consider consumer sovereignty to be supreme. If people are buying iPhones, a pair of new shoes or making risky investments, then that's their business; they know their own values and tastes. Markets rely on consumers fending for themselves, invoking caveat emptor as capitalism's manifesto for consumers' self-reliance.

But our lives are more nuanced. There are signs of consumer frailty everywhere which are routinely exploited. Fitness clubs are profitable because they can expect people to take membership, normally during the new year, only to stop coming a few months later. Yes, we should save more when we are young, pay off that costly credit card debt early or lose those extra pounds. We would all like to keep our new year's resolutions, but how many of us actually do?[9] Knowing and desiring is one thing but doing is quite another. We prefer not to think that Facebook and Google are profit-seeking advertising companies, and are surprised to learn that their vast system of algorithms is actually designed to optimize their revenue and exploit our human frailty rather than fortify our well-being. These occur not necessarily because companies are malicious or venal, but because the profit-seeking markets incentivize them to do so. Akerlof and Shiller's book about how companies exploit human weaknesses raised considerable controversy, but each of them has won the Nobel Prize and rank among the most important economists of the last half-century. They are also intellectual rebels.

When we survey the world, the types of problems which are the greatest source of social tension and are becoming the most intractable to solve seem to have a common typology. They often occur at the intersection of Gilbert's defunct genetics and Akerlof and Shiller's vulnerability to being deceived. Whether it's climate change, underfunded pension schemes, bloated national debt, obesity on an epidemic scale or eroding infrastructure, most of us would agree that these are significant and growing problems which affect us all. So what can be done to compensate for our obsolete genetic wiring and proneness to deceit and manipulation?

This chapter describes how *TSTF* societies have been better than other countries at solving tomorrow's problems today. We survey three areas where the extent to which societies are willing to look at the long term can be fairly compared – government debt, retirement schemes and global warming.

This approach is more nuanced than merely choosing between ladders or crutches. It turns out that there is much to be afraid about.

* * *

9. Only 8 per cent of people keep their new year's resolutions according to a study by Joseph Luciani, an American clinical psychologist.

Taming the Leviathan

There has been no shortage of warnings about the use of debt throughout history. Emerson felt debt threatened our freedom. He said, 'A man in debt is so far a slave.' Thomas Jefferson warned, 'Public debt is the greatest danger to be feared.' There have also been a number of real-life experiences to remind us of its dangers. Think of the Roman empire, France in 1789, the Confederacy during the US Civil War or the Weimar Republic. There have been nearly three hundred incidents of government default since 1800 and little suggests that governments have learned their lessons. Consider Turkey or Venezuela now.

Memories seem short and temptations to spend today on the basis of the promises of tomorrow loom large around the world. Government debt in rich countries has exploded between 2007 and the present, nearly doubling from an average of 53 per cent of GDP to almost 100 per cent.

Larger countries have, on balance, been more profligate than smaller ones. Japan's debt-to-GDP has surged to 248 per cent from 50 per cent in the mid-1980s, and this coincided with tepid economic growth. The US is among the countries doing the least to curtail its debt. By the IMF's calculation, the US's debts as a proportion of GDP currently stand at 105 per cent, up five times since the 1980s. Similarly, the UK has debt amounting to 89 per cent of its GDP, up substantially over the same period (IMF 2018).

By comparison, *TSTF* countries live much more within their means. Scandinavian countries and the Netherlands have the costliest social security systems in the world. Nevertheless, they manage debt levels of between 40 to 60 per cent. Israel has 64 per cent, Denmark has 35 per cent and Norway has 39 cent (IMF 2018).[10]

Historically, government debt has been cyclical in nature. Debt was taken to finance wars and then paid during peacetime. Later, governments adopted the Keynesian theory of stimulating the economy during cyclical downturns and then reducing debt levels once the economy recovered. What is remarkable about the latest debt build-up is that it has occurred in the absence of wars and continues to

---

10. Ireland, at 79 per cent, is high owing to the public bailout resulting from the collapse of its banking system in 2008.

expand despite economic recovery. Many suggest that it is politically motivated since politicians have an incentive to lower taxes and increase expenditure to get elected, regardless of fiscal and economic conditions; the burden of repayment can be painlessly passed on to a successor government or even future generations.

Excessive government debt levels have become a gauge for fiscal laxity and political opportunism. *TSTF* countries demonstrate that their societies are more capable of providing checks on such short-sighted abuses. Swiss citizens, for example, took matters into their own hands in 2001, when 85 per cent of voters-imposed limits on the amount of government debt and spending. The reform, considered by many as a role model for others, was called a 'debt brake' (*Schuldbremse*). It sent a clear signal to elected officials that there is no such thing as 'government funded'; it is all 'taxpayer funded'. Since its enactment, government spending growth has declined from 4.3 per cent per annum to only 2.6 per cent (Mitchell 2012). Switzerland now ranks among the most debt-free countries in the world with a debt to GDP ratio of just 33 per cent (IMF 2018).

Sweden also imposed a fiscal straitjacket on its politicians with its pledge to produce a budget surplus over the economic cycle. Since then, its public debt has fallen from 80 per cent of GDP in 1995 to 41 per cent in 2017. Its annual government budget also moved from an 11 per cent deficit to a 0.9 per cent surplus over the same period (Wooldridge 2013). Ireland probably embraced austerity more enthusiastically than most countries following the collapse of its banking system in the wake of the financial crisis and has, since, fully recovered (with the exception that it used government credit to bail out its banks and still nurses a high debt to GDP ratio). Singapore, a bastion of fiscal prudence, enjoys a significant surplus.

Through a different lens, capital markets arguably provide the most independent scorecard on how nations manage their fiscal affairs. Denmark, the Netherlands, Singapore, Sweden and Switzerland all enjoy AAA credit ratings from S&P, a financial ratings agency. The UK is rated AAA, but has a negative outlook, meaning that its fiscal situation is deteriorating. The US and Japan have been downgraded to AA+ and AA- respectively, and both have a negative outlook, meaning that their ability to fund future obligations is deteriorating.

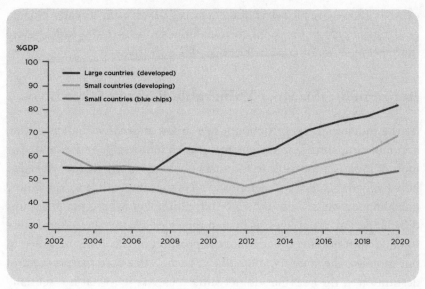

Figure: 7.1: Large Nations have Taken on Greater Debt

Source: World Bank, Credit Suisse

With a robust economy and low interest rates, why fret? Because these conditions are unlikely to remain favourable indefinitely. Debt levels would be less dangerous if societies were growing with young, vibrant populations and expanding productivity. But populations are stagnating, which results in fewer workers relative to retirees. This, in turn, increases the liabilities for pensions and health care. These two most important determinants of government debt are highly geared to ageing societies.

The point is that a lot of things can happen when a country has too much debt, and none of them are good. Carmen Reinhart, in her work with Kenneth Rogoff, found that periods of high debt were paired with long periods of weak economic growth. Countries with high debt levels are less able to respond to the next economic downturn. In contrast, countries with lower debt burdens have more fiscal space when recessions materialize to take counter-cyclical measures rather than being forced to take dreaded austerity measures which make bad times worse. A world of low growth and high debt is a risky combination.

Part of the belief of *Too Small to Fail* is that these countries have a greater sensitivity to fear and vulnerability to fail. Dependency on exports, viable social contracts and confidence of citizens in their elected officials are all a part of their success. Increasing already-bloated government debt, mortgaging their children's futures and spending more than income are not compatible with this narrative.

Retirement: the Most Vulnerable Period of Our Lives

At the individual level, there are few areas of greater challenge than accumulating sufficient savings to fund a comfortable retirement. For most of us, it is impossible to forecast how long we will live or when and how badly our health will deteriorate. It is thus impossible to know how much money we will need. As a result, retirement is becoming the most difficult period of our lives, as by that time we have exhausted our ability to build up more savings and face the prospect of becoming a burden to our families, the state or, most likely, both. Some face the prospect of destitution, if their savings do not suffice. Inevitably, what is essentially an individual problem has become accepted in most advanced countries as a social problem. How are various countries coping with this challenge?

The financial outlook for all governments is dire due to rapidly ageing societies. Pensions are a heavier burden when the retired population expands relative to those working, which means that fewer young people have to support more retirees. According to the *Economist*, in 1950, 13.9 people in the OECD countries were over 65 for every 100 people of working age (20–64). As of 2015, the proportion of elderly people had doubled to 27.9. By 2050, it will have nearly doubled again to 53.2. In part, this is due to lower fertility rates. Many countries are now below the 2.1 children per couple needed to keep the population growing. Improved longevity is another contributing factor. Since 1970, the life expectancy of the average OECD retiree aged 65 has risen 4–5 years (*Economist* 2018). It is a small wonder that retirement systems throughout the world are in a funk.

In the US, more than half of private sector workers do not have a private pension plan at all. The median pension savings for those aged 55–64 is just $80,000 (Buttonwood 2018). The usual benchmark for a viable middle-class retirement plan – which provides 70 per cent of employment earnings – is now clearly unattainable for a large number of Americans.

| 1. Netherlands |
| 2. Denmark |
| 3. Finland |
| 4. Australia |
| 5. Sweden |
| 6. Norway |
| 7. Singapore |
| 8. Chile |
| 9. New Zealand |
| 10. Canada |

Figure 7.2: The World's Best Pension Systems

Small countries dominated the 2018 Mercer rankings of the best pension systems in the world.

Source: Solanki, 2018

Mercer, a pension advisory firm, together with the Australian Centre for Financial Studies, annually analyses and ranks the quality and efficiency of pensions systems globally. Their study looks at more than forty indicators to determine the relative 'fitness' of a nation's pension system. The ranking is dominated by small, outperforming countries. In 2019, the Netherlands topped the ranking and the top nine pension systems in the world are from nations with populations with less than twenty-five million people.

According to the OECD, retirees in the Netherlands can expect 101 per cent of the level of earnings they enjoyed as workers. This compares to 29 per cent for the UK and 63 per cent for the average OECD country. Individuals in Singapore and Switzerland have separate social security savings accounts in their own names, which are funded with real contributions. These systems are ranked higher because they do not rely on promises from the government, which could decide at any time to reduce benefits (OECD 2017).

By contrast, the outlook for pension funds in large countries looks grim. According to a recent report from Citi, the total value of unfunded government pension liabilities for twenty OECD countries is $78 trillion (2016), or almost double the outstanding government debt.

Projections show that living to one hundred is well within technological reach, and even likely. Assuming one starts working at twenty-five and finishes at sixty-five, this means that forty years of work must finance thirty-five years of retirement. Moreover, trends now show a growing portion of work in the future will be conducted on a freelance basis. This development shifts the burden to fund retirement from employers to the individual or the state. *Scientific American* reported that in the US, the ratio of active workers to retirees is currently 4:6, down from 16:5 in 1950. It is projected to decline to 1:9 by 2100, which means there will be less than half the number of workers to support a retiree as there are now. Germany's ratio will drop from 2:9 to 1:4. Rapidly growing nations will see even greater collapses – China from 7:8 to 1:8; Brazil from 8:6 to 1:5; and India from 10:9 to 2:3 (Fischetti 2014).

A part of the shortfall in pension funding has been due to suboptimal returns and gouging on the part of the financial services sector. Retirement savings are vulnerable to abuse and manipulation by professional fund managers because of the relative financial illiteracy of many savers and slack regulation. Banks across the world have paid about $321 billion in fines since the 2008 financial crisis for various illegal or careless practices, according to a note by the Boston Consulting Group (Finch 2017). Pensioners have been among the most significant victims. It is noteworthy that these infractions occurred in large countries. None of the countries featured in our survey have been materially implicated (except the US and the UK activities of the large Swiss banks).

Some of the devastation of retirement savings is perfectly legal, even if not defendable morally. Studies show that clients of mutual funds receive only a minor portion of the actual returns because of high fees. Additionally, the tendency of both fund managers and investors to panic when markets drop and invest at the top of markets when the mood is most euphoric also contributes to low returns to consumers.

Ageing societies, underfunded pension schemes, consumer illiteracy and abusive practices, as well as a low-return outlook, combine to paint a fairly bleak picture. This is a tall order for any society to cope with so there is plenty to fear. Well designed and effective pension funds will take on greater importance. It is again the small, nimble nations grappling with the daunting challenges inherent to retirement savings who are showing us the way.

Global Warming

The alerts are by now all too familiar – warnings that beachfront homes will soon be submerged, reports of farmers' crops devastated by intense droughts and photos of polar bears teetering on rapidly diminishing islands of ice.

It would be difficult to overestimate the scope of damage to the world arising from substantially higher temperatures. Threats to our environment are the quintessential example of the collective losing out to self-interest; the immediate prevailing over of the long term. These threats also remind us how free markets are ill-equipped to come to the rescue. Which profit-seeking company has any inclination to forego shareholder profits to invest in protecting our environment unless it is compelled to do so? To borrow Gilbert's visual metaphor, global warming is for many experts the sharpest and most dangerous spear coming imperceptibly towards our heads.

Luc Hoffmann, the late co-founder of the World Wildlife Fund, once said, 'They have to know in order to care.' Temperatures have indisputably risen substantially compared to historical averages, and most of the increases have happened in the last thirty-five years (*Economist* 2016). Studies show that 97 per cent of peer-reviewed articles published by scientific experts on climate agree that 'climate-warming trends over the past century are extremely likely due to human activities'. But, as we have seen with government debt and retirement savings, knowing, while necessary, does not seem to be sufficient to catalyse the doing.

The climate change debate has been polarized for political reasons into a simple dichotomy. Either global warming is 'real, human-made and dangerous', as scientists contend, or it is a 'hoax', as President Trump and others argue, unified by their reluctance to divert profits from industry towards protecting the environment. A third camp begs to hedge, arguing that nothing can be certain in predicting the far reaching and inextricable consequences of higher emissions. 'Why take the risk?' they ask.

Against this cacophony of debate, many parts of the world are awash with plans, promises and policies to tackle climate change. But little has actually happened at the collective level due to a lack of consensus. Matt Ridley, an acclaimed sociologist and climate change sceptic, points out, 'Ten years ago the world derived 87 per cent of its primary energy from fossil fuels; today, according the widely-respected BP statistical review of world energy, the figure is still 87 per cent' (Ridley 2015).

The good news is that the seemingly relentless rising trajectory of carbon-dioxide emissions from burning fossil fuels appears to be stabilizing. Now they need to fall.

While much of the world has been collectively twiddling its thumbs or making bold but empty speeches at conferences, *TSTF* nations have been taking concrete measures and walking the walk. The industrial nations with the lowest CO_2 emissions per capita are dominated by *TSTF* countries. Moreover, they also count as the countries making the most inroads towards carbon neutral growth.

Sweden and Switzerland have per capita emissions of less than thirty per cent compared to the US, despite having a larger share of their economies dedicated to manufacturing. They have reduced emission levels by one third since 1990. While California and a few other US states have made progress, the modest reduction of per capita CO_2 emissions in the US over this period can be attributed to outsourcing its pollution-intensive manufacturing to China. The US still contributes a remarkable 2–3 times more towards global warming on a relative basis than most industrial countries.

Looking at a more comprehensive metric, the Environmental Performance Index (EPI), calculated through a collaboration of Columbia, Yale and the World Economic Forum, is a wide-ranging assessment of how well countries perform on environmental issues. It looks at twenty leading indicators such as air pollution, pesticides, sanitation, fish stocks and ecosystems. Once again, *TSTF* nations dominate the rankings. The countries contributing the most amount of CO_2 emissions in the world include Japan (#20), US (#27) and China (#120), which performed substantially worse (Emerson et al. 2018).

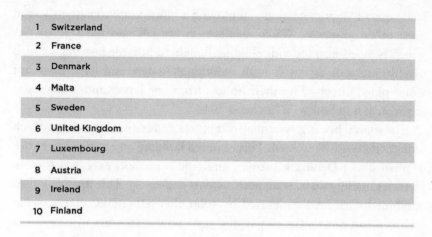

1	Switzerland
2	France
3	Denmark
4	Malta
5	Sweden
6	United Kingdom
7	Luxembourg
8	Austria
9	Ireland
10	Finland

Figure 7.3: The Most Environmentally Responsible Nations

Small countries dominate the rankings of those most likely to meet the environmental targets set forth in the United Nations Millennium Development Goals.

Source: Environmental Performance Index 2018

A more environmentally friendly nation is a result of more effective policies and not just chance. The Dutch, for instance, charge car buyers a fee that funds the recycling of end-of-life vehicles. Denmark, meanwhile, turned its efforts to reduce pollution into an economic advantage. When the oil crisis of 1973 hit and the price per barrel quadrupled, it should have been a disaster for Denmark. The country depended on imported oil for nearly 90 per cent of its energy (Whitehead 2014). Denmark used this adversity as a catalyst to invest heavily in renewables and other forms of energy efficient systems. Denmark has become the global leader in wind energy with an ecosystem of companies servicing the world's growing need for renewable sources of energy. Around 42 per cent of all electricity consumption in Denmark is generated from wind, and it's expected to grow to 50 per cent by 2020. Wind energy (knowledge or know-how as well as products) has also become one of its most important exports. A third of the world's wind turbines originate from Denmark (Nielsen 2017).

The Danes have an expression that 'the cheapest and cleanest form of energy is saving energy which is wasted'. The Danes also refined the technique of 'district heating', employing it much more consistently than most other countries. While residents in the UK and the US buy gas which is piped into individual home boilers to provide heating, Danish neighbourhoods do away with individual boilers and have their hot water piped directly into their houses from one larger and much more efficient shared boiler (Whitehead 2014).

The shared heating system also captures and redistributes heat which would otherwise be wasted. This required building an extensive network of pipes under Denmark's towns and cities to collect excess heat from factories, incinerators, transport systems and so on. This heat was then combined with heat generated by solar thermal energy plants, wind turbines and conventional gas and coal power stations to produce a low-cost and highly efficient heat supply system.

Once dependent on the whims of OPEC, Denmark has become a net exporter of energy and is now a market leader in housing cloud storage for the likes of LinkedIn, Google and Facebook, owing to its cool climate, cheap and clean energy, and political security.

Figure 7.4: Complacency

Source: Banx

The success of a nation will increasingly be measured by its ability to deal with precisely those areas where free markets fail. These problems will not go away. Instead, they will become a substantial burden for society to deal with, if not now, then in the future, usually at a far greater cost to future generations.

This chapter shows us that innovative, effective policy changes have been enacted by small, outperforming countries. We are also reminded that their achievements, while laudable, are not sufficient. The vectors driving retirement, including prolonged ageing and meagre returns, mean that the goal posts will continue to retreat. Problems like climate change are of a global scale and thus the response must be a collaboration at an international level.

Commenting on his recent book, *Skin in the Game*, Nassim Nicholas Taleb said, 'We've survived 200,000 years as humans. Don't you think there's a reason why we survived? We're good at risk management. And what's our risk management? Paranoia. Optimism is not a good thing' (2018).

It's hard to be optimistic about debt levels, retirement savings and global warming. Maybe a healthy dose of paranoia would do some good, as we have seen in *TSTF* nations.

References and Further Reading

Akerlof, G.A. and R.J. Shiller, *Phishing for Phools: The Economics of Manipulation and Deception* (Princeton, NJ: Princeton University Press, 2015).

Breiding, J. 'Heaven's eyes: Luc Hoffmann, unsung hero of nature conservation'. *The Ecologist*, 2016. https://theecologist.org/2016/nov/23/heavens-eyes-luc-hoffmann-unsung-hero-nature-conservation.

Buttonwood. 'Fixing America's pensions: A plan that needs more money'. *The Economist*, 2018. https://www.economist.com/buttonwoods-notebook/2018/04/09/a-plan-that-needs-more-money.

Churchill, W.S. *A History of the English Speaking Peoples* (London; New York: Bloomsbury Academic, 2015).

Cohen, S.S. and B. DeLong. *The End of Influence: What Happens When Other Countries Have the Mone* (New York: Basic Books, 2010).

'Countries with the best pension systems in the world'. *Consultancy.uk*, 2015. https://www.consultancy.uk/news/2932/countries-with-the-best-pension-systems-in-the-world.

DeLong, J. B. 'When is Government Debt Risky ?' *Project Syndicate*, 2013. https://www.project-syndicate.org/commentary/the-impact-of-public-debt-on-economic-growth-by-j--bradford-delong?barrier=accesspaylog.

Emerson, J.W. et al. '2018 EPI Results'. *Environmental Performance Index*, 2018. https://epi.envirocenter.yale.edu/epi-topline.

Finch, G. 'World's biggest banks fined $321 billion since financial crash'. *Bloomberg*, 2017. https://www.bloomberg.com/news/articles/2017-03-02/world-s-biggest-banks-fined-321-billion-since-financial-crisis.

Fischetti, M. 'Ratio of Workers to Retirees Will Plummet Worldwide'. *Scientific American*, 2014. https://blogs.scientificamerican.com/observations/ratio-of-workers-to-retirees-will-plummet-worldwide1/.

Gilbert, D. *Stumbling on Happiness* (London: Harper Perennial, 2007).

Greshko, M., et al. '*A running list of how President Trump is changing environmental policy*'. https://www.nationalgeographic.com/news/2017/03/how-trump-is-changing-science-environment/

'Hope I save before I get old'. *The Economist*, 2018. https://www.economist.com/buttonwoods-notebook/2018/04/27/hope-i-save-before-i-get-old.

'IMF DataMapper: Debt % of GDP'. *International Monetary Fund*, 2018. https://www.imf.org/external/datamapper/DEBT1@DEBT/OEMDC/ADVEC/WEOWORLD.

'Life Expectancy for Social Security'. *Social Security*, no date. https://www.ssa.gov/history/lifeexpect.html.

Mitchell, D.J. 'How the Swiss "Debt Brake" Tamed Government'. *CATO Institute*, 2012. https://www.cato.org/publications/commentary/how-swiss-debt-brake-tamed-government.

Nielsen, V.V. 'The Danish Wind Cluster: The Microeconomics of Competitiveness', 2017. https://www.isc.hbs.edu/resources/courses/moc-course-at-harvard/Documents/pdf/student-projects/Denmark_Wind_2017.pdf.

'Net pension replacement rates'. *OECD Data*, 2019. https://data.oecd.org/pension/net-pension-replacement-rates.htm.

'Pensions at a Glance'. *OECD*, 2017.

https://www.oecd-ilibrary.org/social-issues-migration-health/pensions-at-a-glance-2017/old-age-dependency-ratio_pension_glance-2017-22-en;jsessionid=P-NV_gvA9kEO5u8mKkKFLIkL.ip-10-240-5-110.

Reinhart, C.M., V.R. Reinhart and K.S. Rogoff. 'Public Debt Overhangs: Advanced-Economy Episodes since 1880'. *Journal of Economic Perspectives*, vol. 26, no. 3 (2012). https://www.aeaweb.org/articles?id=10.1257/jep.26.3.69.

Ridley, M. 'Fossil Fuels Will Save the World (Really)'. *The Wall Street Journal*, 2015. https://www.wsj.com/articles/fossil-fuels-will-save-the-world-really-1426282420.

Rust, S. 'Melbourne Mercer: Netherlands beats Denmark as world's top system'. *IPE*, 2018. https://www.ipe.com/news/pensions/melbourne-mercer-netherlands-beats-denmark-as-worlds-top-system/www.ipe.com/news/pensions/melbourne-mercer-netherlands-beats-denmark-as-worlds-top-system/10027394.fullarticle.

Solanki, M. 'The Netherlands has the best pension system in the world'. I Am Expat, 2018. https://www.iamexpat.nl/expat-info/dutch-expat-news/netherlands-has-best-pension-system-world.

Taleb, N.N. *Skin in the Game: Hidden Asymmetries in Daily Life* (New York: Random House, 2018).

'The Coming Pensions Crisis'. *City GPS*, 2016. http://www.agefi.fr/sites/agefi.fr/files/fichiers/2016/03/citi_retraite_hors_bilan_21_mars_1.pdf.

'Too darn hot'. *The Economist*, 2016. https://cdn.static-economist.com/sites/default/files/images/2016/11/blogs/graphic-detail/20161119_woc234_0.png.

Whitehead, F. 'Lessons from Denmark: how district heating could improve energy security'. *The Guardian*, 2014. https://www.theguardian.com/big-energy-debate/2014/aug/20/denmark-district-heating-uk-energy-security.

Wooldridge, A. 'Northern Lights'. *The Economist*, 2013. https://www.economist.com/special-report/2013/02/02/northern-lights.

'You'll fail your New Year's resolutions by this date'. *Newscorp Australia*.

https://www.news.com.au/lifestyle/real-life/the-date-most-people-give-up-on-their-new-years-resolution/news-story/91f50b7c5eef040100fcdd04963efd15

Zumbrun, J. 'Since 1880, Global Government Debts Have Rarely Been So High'. *The Wall Street Journal*, 2018. https://blogs.wsj.com/economics/2018/04/18/since-1880-global-government-debts-have-rarely-been-so-high/.

Conversations and Interviews

Dani Rodrik and Daniel Gilbert.

8

Responsible Ownership

A National Treasure

Siemens Annual Shareholders' Meeting 2015

Source: Wikimedia Commons

> Where stock is held by a great number, what is anybody's business
> is nobody's business.
>
> *—Andrew Carnegie*

There's a colour for every mood, I discovered, while touring the Geneva
manufacturing unit of Caran d'Ache, the iconic Swiss maker of pens,
pencils and crayons. Over the past century, scores of these colouring
pencils have been used by schoolchildren to express their artistic
fantasies – a simple pleasure. But for Carole Huebscher, the chairperson
and fourth-generation owner, there is an art to the manufacturing of

writing instruments. It is no wonder that Caran d'Ache was Pablo Picasso's brand of choice.

Switzerland's first pencil factory originated in Geneva in 1915, conveniently close to the mountains where the graphite, raw material for pencils, was abundantly available. During the factory tour, it occurred to me that there is nothing particularly proprietary about their technology or methods. Instead, Caran d'Ache has relied on a strong culture of ownership to navigate the many crossroads of the past hundred years. Huebscher reflects this commitment to strong ownership. Throughout our talk, I could see the pride in her eyes at leading what is now the go-to brand for pencils. This commitment gets transferred to every person touched by the business. On my way out, I met a cheerful receptionist and former Swissair flight attendant, who told me that Caran d'Ache is among the most attractive employers in Geneva.

Caran d'Ache is one of the several businesses in Switzerland which are a shining example of business legacy and old-world ownership systems. They have always paid taxes and are committed to retaining manufacturing processes within the country. The owners believe in staying relevant and recognize the value of investing in research and development. Consequently, Caran d'Ache has a history of creating innovative and iconic products – they introduced the first push-button pencil, Fixpencil, in 1929; wax oil pencils (crayons) in 1952; the Ecridor range of ballpoint pens in 1953; and the 849 metal-finish pens in 1969 (Caran d'Ache 2015). Now, they are creating an elegant pen made from recycled Nespresso capsules in collaboration with Nestlé.

Caran d'Ache is a success story in responsible ownership. There are many others like it around the world. Yet, in large economies like the US and the UK, a different model is surfacing – one which has led to excessive executive pay, the embedding of professional parasites and the abandoning of community responsibility. In this chapter, we will suggest that some of the seediest corporate trends of our age have been driven by subtle but dramatic changes in ownership. Then, we will discuss why this plague is less rampant in *TSTF* nations. The Caran d'Ache story is a part of a wider narrative, which suggests that *TSTF* countries have a superior attitude and approach towards ownership.

* * *

Problems with Too Many Owners

Ownership is critical to entrepreneurship and development of the business. It helps to advance capitalism by providing incentives for which innovations to pursue, technology to research, enterprises to initiate and companies to turn around or rescue. The lure of ownership can make an ambitious employee sacrifice the safety net of a stable job and embrace the uncertainty of setting out on his or her own. Bernard Arnault, the Chairman of LVMH, and richest man in Europe, sums it up, 'the wealth of a country is made by the success of its companies'.

Historically, multiple ownership has been a great asset because risks could be shared. For example, the invention of limited liability companies meant projects could be funded by a multitude of investors who were only liable for the amount of capital they had invested. With the potential for loss limited to this initial investment, investors began to fund more innovative, risky projects. Take the East India Company, one of the first companies to offer limited liability to its shareholders. Investors funded risky sea voyages knowing that if the ships sank, their loss would be limited. The possibility that the ships would return safe, full of valuable goods and provide profits at multiples of what they invested, justified their investment.

Limited liability companies are still immensely popular and it's not hard to see why. They give investors a sense of having 'skin in the game'. They also instil a degree of prudence, creating a healthy balance between greed and fear. Above all, they encourage innovative, out-of-this-world projects. Elon Musk has raised some $2 billion in speculative capital for SpaceX (Knapp 2018). The novel transportation company seeks to send spacecraft into the earth's orbit.

As both the East India Company and SpaceX prove, limited liability companies when managed efficiently have their advantages. The problems begin with the democratization and fungibility of ownership. While limited liability was designed to shield shareholders from the responsibility of all of the company's liabilities in the case of failure, no one thought there was an uglier side to the same coin – the tendency of boards and managements of widely-owned companies to abdicate responsibility of the business.

Ownership Revisited

A classic account of the problems and ambiguities of the concept of ownership was given more than fifty years ago by the British legal scholar, Anthony Maurice Honoré. He felt ownership has many attributes and real ownership depends on having enough of them. Can I use it or not use it, sell it, rent it, give it to others, throw it away or appeal to the police if a thief steals it? Is it mine to the exclusion of others? Do I have responsibility for its misuse if, say, I lend my car to someone who then gets into an accident? And so on. Some would argue that the real litmus test for ownership is risk – who suffers most if an asset is destroyed? Isn't this the 'real' owner, whatever the law may say?

When examining the ownership of widely-held major multinational companies, it can be tempting to look towards the shareholders. But, as the economist John Kay suggests, the shareholders have no more right to the products or services of the business they 'own' than the average customer. If shareholders go to the company premises, they will more likely than not be turned away. The company's actions are not their responsibility and corporate assets cannot be used to pay off their debts. Nor do shareholders have the right to manage the company in which they hold an interest and even their right to appoint the people who do so is more theoretical than real. They are entitled only to such part of the income as the directors declare as dividends. They don't have any say over most decisions – that is the domain of the board of directors and management. Indeed, of the eleven tests of ownership Honoré put forward in a scholarly manner, Kay points out that shareholders in many large listed companies can satisfy only two – and these are rather minor, three are satisfied in part and six are not met at all.

In practice, there is a strong case for asserting that most big companies are controlled by their directors and management. Adolf Berle and Gardiner Means famously observed in 1932 that shareholders in widely-owned public corporations are subservient to directors who can exploit widely dispersed and disinterested share ownership to become self-perpetuating bodies. Andrew Carnegie put it more pragmatically: 'Where stock is held by a great number, what is anybody's business is nobody's business.'

Little changed in more than three-quarters of a century after Berle and Means. For decades, it was customary to see boards of big companies, such as AT&T or General Electric, stuffed with worthy, aged friends of the chief executive, making it perfectly clear that the CEO ran things. But as long as they did so responsibly, CEOs encountered little opposition.

Executive pay challenged the idea of responsible ownership and shattered the illusion that CEOs had their company's best interests at heart. Since 1990, executive pay has increased five-fold while workers' wages have stagnated (Frydman and Jenter 2016). At the same time, there is little evidence that higher remuneration has resulted in increasing shareholder value or greater competitiveness. Studies show that this is at best random, and at worst negatively correlated (more pay = worse performance). All of this suggests that remuneration of executives in large, widely-held companies has become a means of extracting existing value rather than a catalyst to create new value.

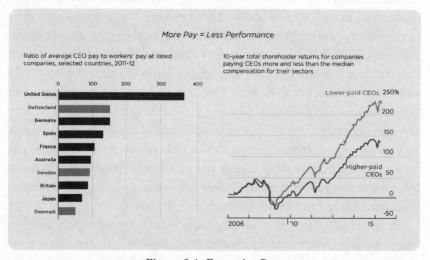

Figure 8.1: Executive Pay

The figure on the left shows that CEOs in the US are paid, on average, much more than the rest of the world. The figure on the right shows that higher-paid CEOs translate (perversely) to lower returns for shareholders.

Source: The Wall Street Journal

Things get worse. Typically, senior executives also have share options, aimed at aligning their interests with those of the company. The worth of these options is totally dependent on a rising share price. These incentives incite a model of common behaviour. As the average tenure of CEOs has declined to a handful of years, the optimal strategy for a new CEO is to concentrate on boosting the share price quickly. They can achieve this by selling an underperforming division instead of fixing it, cutting overheads and/or repurchasing the company's own stock instead of investing shareholder funds in viable projects. Why risk making long-term investments to strengthen the company when the fruition of such undertakings will likely be long after their tenure as bosses?

The fallout from this extraordinarily short-sighted focus spreads far and wide. Management attracting short-term-oriented investors are then beholden to their short-term perspective, engendering short sighted decisions. CEOs are likely to struggle with succession plans, given that nobody within their company has proved themselves worthy by coming up with an innovative new product or conquering a new market. The CEO turns to an executive search firm (head-hunter) and pays handsomely to recruit someone, often from a different industry and without any institutional memory or relationship to the business. What they do have is a compelling narrative, especially for the short-term minded investment community. The newly appointed CEO, realizing that his or her tenure will probably be less than five years, repeats the script. The cycle continues with the result being that the company contracts and becomes less competitive over time. A cover of the *Economist* some time ago featured global multinational companies 'In Retreat' and explained their deteriorating returns and profitability (*Economist* 2017).

John Gapper recently suggested that CEOs earn so much money because the board of directors, aware of their information deficits, fearful of reproaches and lacking any real personal commitment, are content to accommodate.

Whatever the reason, we have underappreciated the value of companies as the store of a nation's treasure and become complacent with a widespread culture of irresponsible ownership. Executive pay suggests that we reward those who partake in it.

Figure 8.2: All Mine!

Source: Banx

Towards Unintended Ownership

Adam Smith wrote in *The Wealth of Nations* that corporate executives are 'managers of other people's money', so they cannot be expected to look after that money with the same care which partners or sole proprietors would. Justin Fox and Jay W. Lorsch suggest that such an idea helps explain the current problems of ownership. They trace the modern understanding of this difficulty back to an article by Michael Jensen and William Meckling, 'who framed the issue as a conflict between what they called "principals" (shareholders) and "agents" (managers). If an agent owned the business, Jensen and Meckling argued, there was no conflict. But as the ownership percentage went down, agents inevitably faced the temptation to do things that benefited themselves rather than the principals' (Fox and Lorsch 2012).

The welfare of agents over owners in widely-held companies has been facilitated by the unstoppable trend of share ownership passing from individuals to collective investment vehicles managed by fiduciaries, such as mutual funds, pension funds, hedge funds and exchange traded funds (ETFs). These funds are known pejoratively in the trade as OPMs or 'other peoples' money', and they are not especially interested in the long-term prospects of the companies whose shares they hold. The simple proof of this is in the length of time shares of big companies are now held. The average holding period of an investor in large multinationals is less than one year (Bogle 2010), which means that the 'owners' are likely to be replaced in a sort of 'musical chairs exercise' before the company's next annual meeting.

Unintentional Ownership (ETFs)

The abdication of ownership responsibility by collective funds has taken a new, and almost comical, twist. Index ETFs (exchange traded index funds) have become the most popular type of OPM. These are funds which buy shares of companies based only on the fact that those shares happen to be in the index which the Index ETF is tracking. Thus, ownership has become unintentional. This trend towards transient and complacent ownership is already decisive and programmed to increase. Blackrock, the world's largest manager and custodian of Index ETFs, is now the most important owner of multinational companies. Bizarrely, our capital market system, based on wide ownership of joint stock companies, has evolved to confer ownership on a group of fund managers with no intention, incentive or mandate to act in a responsible manner.

This was demonstrated blatantly in the case of Unilever, the Anglo-Dutch foods group, wanting to abandon its UK domicile for a single home in the Netherlands. The move was motivated by the directors' desire to build stronger defences against activist investor challenge. However, ETF and other passive fund managers blocked the move without considering whether it was a good or bad idea for the long-term prospects of the company. Their opposition was based on the fact that if Unilever dropped its UK share listing, those shares would drop out of the FTSE 100 share index, which many of the OPM funds were tracking. That would mean that the funds would immediately have to sell their Unilever shares, whether they wanted to or not. And, in those circumstances, the volume of shares put up for sale would almost certainly be so great as to depress the price the funds could get for them.

Typically, with ownership by OPM institutions, one name is recorded in a share register and someone else decides to buy or sell the shares.

Yet another may decide how the shares are to be voted, if at all, and another, the real investor, benefits from the returns from the company's activities. ETFs, mutual funds and big pension funds are not known for confronting boards, except on self-serving issues like the Unilever case mentioned. Their modus operandi is to 'vote with your feet' or 'exit rather than voice' (Hirschman 1970). If they do get involved in governance issues, they usually do it through specialized agents (more rent-seekers).

This is very disturbing, coming at a time when the largest multinational companies have become so valuable that the only owners with the weight to have their say are in reality the least likely to do so. It is precisely at the intersection of lumbering size and complacent ownership that some of the most outrageous abuses have occurred – think of mishaps like Enron, Hewlett Packard and Royal Bank of Scotland.

TSTF Countries: How They Differ

Cornell's Peter Katzenstein points out in *Small States in World Markets* that successful, small nations are often dependent on their export industries and thus need to promote and support responsible ownership to protect the viability (and national allegiance) of their most successful companies. There is safety in numbers in economies like the US and the UK, where the ecosystems are large and diverse enough to adopt a permissive attitude about company formation and destruction. Small countries tend to rely on a relatively small number of industrial firms, which means that losing one could have a major impact on their entire value chain.

Smaller countries tend to provide their citizens with more protective social contracts than large countries, partly as buffers to the effects of dependency on volatile global trade. This means that the cost to society can be very high when an important firm ceases to exist. The issue with small countries is that while their companies' successes are almost always achieved abroad, failure must be borne at home. In this respect, they are too small to fail and so they tend to focus on fixing ailing companies rather than discarding them. Nokia dominated the global mobile phone sector before Apple invented the iPhone. It was Finland's most important company before becoming a public disgrace. It has since reinvented itself and prospects are upbeat.

Take Switzerland as an example, which has the highest density of leading multinational export companies in the world (Breiding 2012). The country's success can be largely attributed to the longevity and adaptability of these companies. The average age of a Swiss multinational company is 125 years compared with an average company age of 15 years in the S&P 500 index (Breiding 2012; Sheetz 2017). But it has not always been easy. Companies such as Nestlé and Roche have been on the brink of bankruptcy. The Swiss watch industry did go bankrupt. And UBS, the largest wealth manager in the world, only survived the financial crisis with the support of the government.

Duration of ownership is not only a Swiss phenomenon, but one shared by other *TSTF* nations. Danish companies such as Carlsberg (1847), Novo Nordisk (1923) and William Demnant (1904), Swedish companies such as Ericson (1876), Enskilda (1871) and Philips (1891) and Finland's Kone (1910) have thrived well past their third generation. And, as in the Swiss case, there has been substantial pain along the way. Unilever and Royal Dutch Shell have successfully merged Dutch with British businesses, which resulted in more competitive companies. Volvo, at the time listless, had to be resurrected, but is now a leading producer of trucks following its merger with Geely Holdings, the Chinese auto concern.

As a result of this continuity, these smaller outperforming countries have managed to grow larger and become robust, industrial oak trees. Switzerland has four times the number of firms in *Fortune* magazine's Global 500 ranking of the most valuable multinationals as Germany, the US or Japan. The Netherlands, Sweden and Denmark also rank highly in their per capita density of large multinationals. Unilever's Paul Polman reminded me, 'Unilever started in 1872, and Nestlé in 1857. These companies have been around for so long because they are in tune with the needs of society. Sure, they've had plenty of challenges to deal with, and their fair share of criticism, but they succeed because they adapt responsively and responsibly.'

Another good reason for their success is that these countries have historically treated ownership with greater care than most others. They are more dependent on their industrial legacy and more vulnerable to losing it. While the notion of 'disruption' or 'creative destruction' are fashionable in London and Silicon Valley, 'reinvention', 'reconstruction' and 'survival' are the key words among *TSTF* countries.

More Sustainable Ownership

Carnegie would probably have approved of the form of ownership practised by most *TSTF* countries. Here ownership tends to be characterized by the existence of larger individual shareholders, with long-term horizons and a more responsible attitude concerning their roles as owners. The result is that they pay close attention to the operations and ensure that transitions are smooth to ensure continuation.

All the countries featured in *Too Small to Fail* advocate free markets and are decidedly pro-business. In any free market system, companies prosper, perish and are ultimately replaced by more viable competitors. There are mergers, there are bankruptcies, which are often painful. The essential point is that actions result in creating a more competitive business. But in *TSTF* countries, the idea of selling to the highest bidder to add a trophy to the acquirers' showcase is disdained – even if it were to result in generous returns to those selling out.

Each of these countries have their own idiosyncratic methods of preserving their industrial treasures. In Sweden, Investor AB and Industrivarden have influential and long-term ownership stakes in the country's most important companies. Most major companies in Denmark, including Carlsberg, Lego, A.P. Møller-Mærsk and Novo Nordisk, are controlled by foundations which have an inter-generational view of the company's activities. In Singapore, Temasek has an active role in shaping and controlling the country's industrial base.

Paul Polman, CEO of Unilever, denies that the company's aborted attempt to move its headquarters to the Hague was intended to protect the group following the unwelcome takeover approach by Kraft and 3G. But studies show that the Dutch system of shares with preferred rights and the use of Dutch foundations and fiduciaries to hold voting rights, while leaving investors only with financial entitlements, has been an effective method of retaining the Netherlands' industrial base and preventing unwanted takeovers (Kabir, Cantrijn and Jeunink 1997).

The source of their success can be traced to differences with respect to ownership. Two Danish professors, Steen Thomsen and Torben Pedersen, examined the impact of ownership structure on the economic performance of 435 of the largest European companies (Pedersen and Thomsen 2000). Accounting for industry, capital structure and nation effects, they found that ownership concentration correlates significantly with shareholder value (market-to-book-value of equity) and profitability (asset returns), though the benefits taper off after the majority control is reached. Studies in the US and elsewhere have reached similar conclusions.

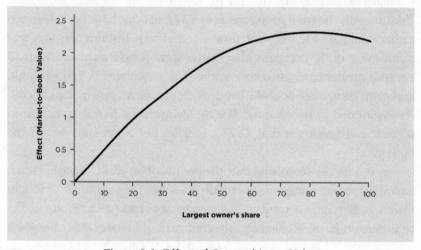

Figure 8.3: Effect of Ownership on Value

This figure demonstrates that companies are more competitive and profitable when they have large, long term owners.

Source: Pedersen and Thomsen, 2000

A by-product of concentrated and engaged ownership, which is a characteristic of companies in *TSTF* nations, is that they invest more in new product development and are more likely to retain, rather than outsource, manufacturing capability. *TSTF* countries have retained or built up stronger manufacturing bases and spend more on Research & Development (R&D), so they tend to be more innovative and export-oriented, as discussed in previous chapters.

In *Hidden Champions*, Hermann Simon points out how niche manufacturing companies in Germany, Denmark, Switzerland and Sweden spend three times the expenses on R&D, generating five times the number of patents per employee and experience one fifth of the level of employee turnover compared to average companies in the US. These companies are also more likely to invest in their own product development and less likely to repurchase their own shares, which is a gimmick used by large, widely-owned companies to shore up their share prices.

With a more engaged ownership, the appointment of board members is more likely to be based on their allegiance to owners (instead of management) and ability to serve the long-term interest of the company. Traditionally, board appointments in *TSTF* nations have been deserved rather than paid for, and with power comes responsibility. History and significance of the company also matter since people are more likely to exercise greater care when they know that a company is 120 years old and contributes meaningfully towards employment, research and taxes. As mentioned in the chapter 'We the People', the narrative taught in schools and families is that *TSTF* countries put community before the individual.

So, it is hardly surprising that the boards of Swedish, Danish, Dutch and Singaporean companies normally look like the equivalent of knight orders rather than a result of appointments stacked in favour of the chairperson. Jacob Wallenberg, the chairman of Investor AB, summed it up at a speech I attended at the Swedish Swiss Chamber of Commerce. He said, 'We really only have one job – to make sure we put the right people in the right place.'

Management in these companies is often recruited and promoted from within because stable, engaged and familiar shareholders prefer stable, engaged and familiar managers. Thomas Oetterli, who was appointed CEO of Schindler in 2016, had been working for the company for twenty-three years; the company has never appointed an external CEO. Similarly, Søren Skou joined A.P. Møller-Mærsk aged nineteen and worked his way up through various functions. CNBC reported that CEOs in Scandinavia earn less than 75 per cent of the European average and about 50 per cent of the American average. Even then, Novo Nordisk's share price has vastly outperformed those of its global peers over the past two decades.

Thus, we see that significant owners tend to exercise power responsibly while insignificant ones don't – and sometimes can't. Once there is a loss of owner oversight, the balance, instead of value creation, is usually tipped radically in favour of value extraction.

**"Yes, the planet got destroyed.
But for a beautiful moment in time we created
a lot of value for shareholders."**

Figure 8.4: Invaluable Lesson

Source: Wikimedia Commons

Conclusion

Too little attention is paid to the nature and importance of ownership. It is arguably the DNA of capitalism. Bernard Arnault is right; a nation's companies are its national treasure, and how it treats ownership has a substantial impact on its ability to maintain national prosperity, offer high-paying jobs and retain the competence and scope for innovation.

Despite this, few seem to care about ownership. In its landmark annual study, 'Doing Business', the World Bank investigates factors which promote or constrain business across 190 countries. It considers parameters such as construction permits, credit, international trade, contract enforcement and insolvency, but ownership is not included. Similarly, the World Economic Forum's annual 'Global Competitiveness Report' examines hundreds of factors but ownership doesn't feature prominently. Harvard's Michael Porter does not have a single entry under 'ownership' in the bibliography of his 831-page epic, *The Competitive Advantage of Nations*.

This chapter presents a different perspective and suggests that small, outperforming countries are prosperous because they have a more responsible attitude towards ownership. Above all, *TSTF* countries recognize the value of continuity; companies with stable ownership are more likely to consider long-term performance, which is conducive to greater investment, research and innovations. Their companies are more efficient at countering the wealth extraction tendencies inherent among those who follow less responsible ownership practices. They foster fairness by rewarding value creation and discouraging value expropriation. In terms of CEO and board appointments, they are inclined to respect the more sustainable relationship between achievement and reward, and duty over self-interest.

TSTF countries also recognize the need for industry to co-exist with society. Business leaders tend to be of the 'lower profile, lower pay' disposition. Individually, they may be weaker, but collectively they are more effective than their multinational peers. Their voices are heard in the national dialogue, in part, because they are perceived as being less self-interested. Charles Erwin Wilson, the longstanding CEO of General Motors, is purported to have said, 'What's good for General Motors is good for the country, and vice versa.' Who in Britain or the US can say this with sincerity today? For *TSTF* nations, there are several candidates from each country, such as Alfred Schindler, Paul Polman or Jacob Wallenberg, who could cite this with ease and authenticity.

After more than a hundred years, Caran d'Ache is still making colouring pencils. It strikes me that, in other countries, the company may have fallen victim to a chairperson's bout of hubris or been bought out by a private equity firm which cut costs and racked up debt. There are many roads to Rome, and in the rough-and-tumble world of capitalism, there are few holds barred. Yet, as Caran d'Ache illustrates, when companies operate in better sync with society, they can transcend generations and become a store of national wealth. If these *TSTF* nations can continue to hold their agency costs and abuses in check, they have a comparative advantage, and may continue to see the longevity of their industrial bases eclipse those of larger countries. This means they will reap the benefits of greater and more inclusive returns for their investors, workers and taxpayers.

References and Further Reading

Berle, A.A. and G.C. Means. *The Modern Corporation and Private Property*, 2nd edition (New York: Transaction Publishers, 1991).

Bogle, J.C. 'Restoring Faith in Financial Markets'. *Wall Street Journal*, 2010. https://www.wsj.com/articles/SB10001424052748703436504574640523013840290.

Breiding, R.J. Introduction. *Swiss Made: The Untold Story behind Switzerland's Success* (London: Profile Books, 2013).

'Doing Business 2019', *The World Bank*, 2018. http://www.doingbusiness.org/en/reports/global-reports/doing-business-2019.

'Executive pay: Neither rigged nor fair'. *The Economist*, 2016. https://www.economist.com/briefing/2016/06/25/neither-rigged-nor-fair.

'Fortune Global 500'. *Fortune*, 2018. http://fortune.com/global500/.

Fox, J. and J. W. Lorsch. 'What Good Are Shareholders?'. *Harvard Business Review*, 2012. https://hbr.org/2012/07/what-good-are-shareholders.

Gapper, J. 'It is a mystery why bankers earn so much'. *Financial Times*, 2018. https://www.ft.com/content/760fb4c2-7eb3-11e8-bc55-50daf11b720d.

Hirschman, A.O. *Exit, Voice and Loyalty: Responses to Decline in Firms, Organizations, and States* (Cambridge, Mass.: Harvard University Press, 1970).

'In retreat: the multination company is in trouble'. *The Economist*, 2017. https://www.economist.com/leaders/2017/01/28/the-multinational-company-is-in-trouble.

Jensen, M.C. and W.H. Meckling. 'Theory of the Firm: Managerial Behaviour, Agency Costs and Ownership Structure'. *Journal of Financial Economics*, vol. 3, no. 4 (1976): pp. 305–360. https://papers.ssrn.com/sol3/papers.cfm?abstract_id=94043.

Kabir, R., D. Cantrijn and A. Jeunink, A. 'Takeover defences, ownership structure and stock returns in the Netherlands: an empirical analysis'. *Strategic Management Journal*, vol. 18, no. 2 (1997): pp. 97–109. https://ris.utwente.nl/ws/files/6899459/Kabir_SMJ_1997.pdf.

Katzenstein, P.J. *Small States in World Markets: Industrial Policy in Europe* (Ithaca; London: Cornell University Press, 1985).

Kay, J. 'Shareholders think they own the company – they are wrong'. *Financial Times*, 2015. https://www.ft.com/content/7bd1b20a-879b-11e5-90de-f44762bf9896.

Knapp, A. 'SpaceX is raising a $500 million funding round at a $25 billion valuation'. *Forbes*, 2018. https://www.forbes.com/sites/alexknapp/2018/04/12/spacex-is-raising-a-500-million-funding-round-at-a-25-billion-valuation/#2bd44c02055c.

'Lower CEO pay and better results in Europe?'. *CNBC*, 2013. https://www.cnbc.com/id/100540655.

'Manufacturing, value added (% of GDP)'. *World Bank Group*, 2017. https://data.worldbank.org/indicator/NV.IND.MANF.ZS.

'100 years of history'. *Caran d'Ache*, 2015. https://www.carandache.com/100/history.php?lang=en.

Pedersen, T. and S. Thomsen. 'Ownership structure and economic performance in the largest European companies'. *Strategic Management Journal*, vol. 21, no. 6 (2000): pp. 689–705. https://doi.org/10.1002/(SICI)1097-0266(200006)21:6<689::AID-SMJ115>3.0.CO;2-Y.

Porter, M.E. *The Competitive Advantage of Nations* (Basingstoke, UK: Palgrave Macmillan, 1998).

Schwab, K. and X. Sala-i-Martin. 'The Global Competitiveness Report 2016-2017'. *World Economic Forum*, 2016. http://www3.weforum.org/docs/GCR2016-2017/05FullReport/TheGlobalCompetitivenessReport2016-2017_FINAL.pdf.

Sheetz, M. 'Technology killing off corporate America: Average life span of companies under 20 years'. *CNBC*, 2017. https://www.cnbc.com/2017/08/24/technology-killing-off-corporations-average-lifespan-of-company-under-20-years.html.

Simon, H. *Hidden Champions of the Twenty-first Century: The Success Strategies of Unknown World Market Leaders* (New York; London: Springer, 2009).

Smith, A. *The Wealth of Nations* (New York, Random House, 2016).

Zaretsky, S.. 'The big law firms with the highest partner billing rates'. *Above the Law*, 2014. https://abovethelaw.com/2014/01/the-biglaw-firms-with-the-highest-partner-billing-rates/.

Conversations and Interviews

Carole Huebscher, Jacob Wallenberg and Paul Polman.

Part B

Leading by Example

9

Finland: Education

God's Chosen Profession

Learning

Source: Wikimedia Commons

Seasons in Finland tend to be all or nothing, with endless summer days followed by long winter nights. Moods were already dampened on a dreary afternoon in December 2000, just a few days before the winter solstice, when the OECD revealed the long-awaited results of their initial Programme for International Student Assessment (PISA) tests. The triannual test, which has since become the most influential and revealing research of its kind, compares fifteen-year-olds' abilities in reading, mathematics and science across more than fifty countries.

139

Finns swallowed hard and teachers trembled as they anticipated embarrassment and disrepute for their nation's schools. The worries were real. Finland had just completed a massive restructuring which had turned its primary education system upside down. In 1963, the Finnish Parliament made the bold decision to choose public education as the key propellant of the country's economic recovery. 'I call this the big dream of Finnish education,' said Pasi Sahlberg, a former director general in the ministry of education and culture, who has written multiple books on the Finnish education system, including *Finnish Lessons*. 'It was simply the idea that every child would have a very good public school [education]. If we want to be competitive, we need to educate everybody. It all came out of a need to survive,' echoing the theme of *Too Small to Fail*, and an inspiration for our title (Hancock 2011).

Over the years, the Finnish journey has been a rocky one. The country was wedged between the Swedish monarchy and the Russian Czar for seven hundred years before the twentieth century brought crippling civil and world wars. But the Finns emerged as staunchly independent people. 'Neither Scandinavian nor Baltic, Finns were proud of their Nordic roots and a unique language only they could pronounce,' wrote LynNell Hancock in her insightful piece, 'Why Are Finland's Schools Successful?' (Hancock 2011). It is this Nordic DNA that provides the foundation to its society including its rule of law, institutes of democracy, sense of egalitarianism and the university system. Culturally, Finns resemble the more shy, resourceful Japanese than nations with Anglo-Saxon, Germanic or Latin heritage.

Until the late 1960s, Finns were still emerging from the yoke of Soviet influence. Finland's schools at the time were substandard. Most children left public school after six years. Only one in ten adult Finns had completed more than nine years of basic education (Hancock 2011). Receiving a university degree was uncommon and reserved for the privileged few. According to Sahlberg, 'Finland's education level was comparable to that of Malaysia or Peru and lagged substantially behind our Scandinavian neighbours Denmark, Norway and Sweden. Dropout rates were high, and universities complained of increasingly apathetic candidates seeking admission. Industry lamented the progressive decline of skills.'

Coming back to Finland's bold restructuring of its education system, the educators were sceptical in 2000 whether it was working. The public discourse and media were critical, touting that Finland had fallen hopelessly behind others in mathematics and sciences in an increasingly knowledge-based economy which created Nokia, a leading mobile phones company, and several other successful high-tech enterprises.

Thus, when the 2000 PISA results were announced, the Finns were as astonished as most other nations. Finnish fifteen-year-olds outperformed most students from other OECD members (forty-three countries took part in the first test and ranked the best young readers in the world). The results of the tests in science and mathematics were also promising, chalking up third and fourth places respectively. Three years later, they led in maths. By 2006, Finland was first out of fifty-seven countries in science and maths, and had achieved second place in reading (Ministry of Education and Culture 2016). The nation had not experienced such a swell of national pride in its young people since 1952, when seventeen-year-old Armi Kuusela became the first Finn to win the Miss Universe pageant. Arjariita Heikkinen, principal of a Helsinki comprehensive school, was dumfounded. 'I didn't realize we were that good,' he said (Hancock 2011). Martti Ahtisaari, the president of Finland at that time (and later Nobel laureate), commented with characteristic Finnish modesty and dry humour, 'How bad did the others do?' (Niemi interview).

Anyone who cared about education must have been curious to learn how the Finns so drastically turned around their education system. The reactions of critical peers from other nations ranged from envious to confounded. Surely, they must pay their teachers more money, or invest in state-of-the-art infrastructure and razzle dazzle technologies. Most theories on education draw on classic industrial or military logic – if progress is sought, more or better resources must have been thrown at it. So observers were surprised to learn that Finland achieves more with less. As previously mentioned in our chapter on education, Finland spends 30 per cent less on primary education per child than many large countries, and its teachers are paid less than teachers in most OECD countries (OECD Data 2019). Similarly, Singapore, one of the world's top PISA performers, spends less per capita on primary education than twenty-seven of the thirty countries in the OECD (Barber and Mourshed 2007).

These countries differ in *how* they spend. Finland prefers to spend money on learning than administration. As Sahlberg told me, its ratio of administrators to students, for instance, is one-tenth that of the city of Los Angeles, providing another example of what we saw in the chapter 'Fallacy of Scale'. As for fashionable theories on education, Finnish classrooms have the technological feel of the 1950s. There are no fancy digital whiteboards costing $4,000 each, and classrooms have an austere, unpretentious feel to them.

An established management dictum is 'what is measured is what gets done.' So do the Finns achieve superior results by testing their students and teachers more often and using rankings as a means of incentivizing performance? In fact, students are rarely teste and teachers are not evaluated at all. Do the Finns pack more intensive learning into kindergarten, giving kids a head start over other nations, or do they receive more lessons per week and grind out more homework? No. The Finns start school at age seven, a year or two later than most developed countries, and children are encouraged to enjoy their childhood. A typical middle school teacher in Finland teaches just under 600 hours annually. In the US, a teacher at the same level typically devotes 1,080 hours (Sahlberg 2011). Homework assigned is minimal. Some surmised that the Finns must 'divide and conquer,' segregating students according to their ability and streaming them with teachers and a syllabus suited to the pace of their ability to learn. *No!* The Finnish system adheres to a 'we are all in the same boat' concept. Four children with mixed abilities normally sit at a table and the brightest students are expected to help the laggards. More on this later, as this is fundamental to minimizing the variation in levels of education and hence equalizing the opportunities available to children.

In short, the Finns seemed to have cracked the Gordian knot of education by turning conventional thought on its head. The Harvard education expert Howard Gardner summed it up: 'Learn from Finland, which has the most effective schools and which does just about the opposite of what we are doing in the United States' (Doyle 2016).

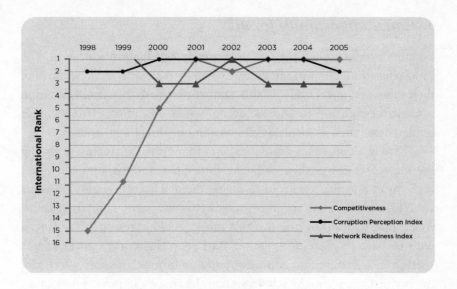

Figure 9.1: Finland's Ascent

Finland increased its global competitiveness ranking substantially following improvements to its education system.

Source: World Economic Forum

We start by looking at the key tenets of the Finnish education model and then focusing on the importance of teachers. We'll close by looking at some of the limitations of the system, the challenges confronting it and then postulate whether major aspects of the system offer any useful instructions for nations struggling to improve their own education systems.

* * *

Key Tenets

Many factors contribute to the extraordinary success of Finnish primary schools. Here are the seven which strike me as the most profound.

1. Equal opportunity for all

Equality in education is the foremost principle of Finnish education. The same educational opportunities are available to all citizens irrespective of their ethnicity, age, family wealth, stature or where they live. Education is also free right up to and including higher education. This includes hidden costs such as meals, textbooks and healthcare insurance.

There is a consensus among experts that rising inequality is among the most pressing challenges facing future generations, and education is the most effective means of resolving them. This is arguably the most valuable aspect of any social contract between a nation and its citizens. After all, children are the future's most precious resource. Yet, even with massive increases in spending (last year, the world's governments spent over $2 trillion on education) and ambitious attempts at reform, the performance of many school systems has barely improved in decades (Barber and Mourshed 2007). The US, for instance, has muddled along in the middle of the pack for decades despite repeated efforts by government officials to introduce marketplace competition in public schools. Britain has reformed virtually every aspect of its school system without appreciable success, including admission, funding, curriculum standards, the relationship of communities with schools and governance.

Far more impressive than their superior absolute scores was the fact that Finland somehow achieved the 'greatest good for the greatest number.' The variance of student performance between schools in Finland was the narrowest in the world, with less than a 5 per cent difference in results between the best and worst schools. Germany has a variance of over 60 per cent. This means that a student in the worst German school can conceivably achieve less than half the level of education as a student attending its best school (Sahlberg 2011).

Figure 9.2: Unequal Opportunity

Source: Banx

2. Common journey

Finland's youth share a common journey. They all attend the same school system. The society's social norms – which govern the vast portion of our behaviour – are instilled at a young age in a similar environment, fostering a sense of belonging and social cohesion. Everyone of course wishes to be different, but community and social cohesion are about similarities. Finnish education is about learning, not social status. There are no admission restrictions, so parents don't need to game the system to get their children into the best schools, as happens in New York or London. There are no elite private schools limited to those with means and privilege. The absence of a sizable private school system avoids the inevitable competition with public schools in which private schools cream off the best teachers and the wealthiest students. This competition has a way of cementing social distinction and inequality before children lose their first baby tooth. Children from the wealthiest 1 per cent take more Ivy League places than the bottom 60 per cent combined (Luce 2019). For what is 'giving my child a better start' but a means of unbalancing the playing field and increasing social divisions?

It is not an accident that the best PISA results are achieved by nations where there is an absence of competition between private and public schools and where the public school alternative is the predominant route as in Finland, Korea, Japan, Singapore and Switzerland. Indeed, in these countries, attending private schools tends to be designed for those unable to make it in the superior public school system. Since private schools are negatively perceived, even stigmatized, a child's opportunities there are seen as restricted rather than privileged.

3. Fun not fear

There is a well-known Finnish saying that 'a child's job is to play'. Finns discovered that fun is a superior motivator for learning than fear and that the joy of learning is enhanced if children and teachers learn how to think critically and solve real-life problems. Finnish education is built on the notion that intrinsic motivation, not external pressure, is what matters most to encourage learning. This means turning away from test-centric learning. Tests also create a demarcation between the elite and the rest. Hannele Niemi, a highly regarded educator from the University of Helsinki, told me, 'No clear evidence has been found showing a positive impact of high-stakes testing policies on student learning, while the unintended consequences associated with these policies can be considerable, such as increased student drop-out rates, cheating in exams, burnout and other stress related ailments.'

Most education systems across the world are based on competition and are authoritative in nature. It is the ability to score well on a few standardized tests which matters most, so the systems are geared to focus on these specific events. In the educational field, this is termed 'teaching to the test.' 'All of this comparing and ranking has its drawbacks,' says Amanda Ripley in her revealing book, *The Smartest Kids in the World: And How They Got That Way*. Ripley believes that systems based on high stakes standardized tests promote a 'culture of educational masochism.' She points out that in Korea, pupils must study relentlessly in the hope of securing a precious spot in one of the country's three prestigious universities. Misery is coupled with a lower sense of self-esteem for youth in nations with poor education systems where intense competition can destroy a child's motivation. When they aren't feeling miserable or despondent, they feel stressed. A recent survey conducted by Marc Brackett at Yale using a nationally representative sample of 22,000 US high school students indicated that students felt stressed 80 per cent of the time (Brackett 2015).

Finnish youth score well on PISA scores, in part because its methodology is designed to do what PISA measures – 'the ability to complete tasks relating to real-life situations, depending on a broad understanding of key concepts, rather than assessing the possession of specific knowledge' (OECD 2001, p. 19). Sahlberg told me, 'Rather than testing children with multiple choice questions that usually test memory retention and recall, pupils are usually required to compose their own written answers in long narrative form, demonstrating they have internalized the lesson and really understand what it's about.'

Companies have begun to recognize that performing well in traditional education does not always lead to success in the business world. Google has said that it has found no correlation between GPAs, test scores and employees who thrive, and therefore has stopped looking at those academic qualifications altogether (Lamb-Sinclair 2016).

Boredom is an enemy of learning anywhere and anytime, especially among high school students. Forever experimental, Finland adopted 'phenomenon-based learning', in which teaching is based on topics and context rather than classical subjects for some aspects of its curriculum. The Finnish system is based on collaboration, not competition; on support, not rivalry; on a sense of comfort, not fear; and on trust, not authority. The absence of fear also means that pupils say whatever comes to their minds rather than repressing their views, because they feel safe and don't feel defensive about their views. Pupils work in small groups to solve problems, which improves their communication skills. They call their teachers by their first names. This collaborative, uninhibited, learning-by-doing approach is a far cry from the traditional lecture-style format, in which pupils are often too afraid to ask questions.

At a Helsinki primary school, I observed an orientation exercise being conducted in the woods. Children had to navigate from one milestone to another, picking up information about different kinds of plants, insects and rocks. Then they gathered in the classroom, where they felt excited and compared their experiences and exchanged knowledge. It's not unusual to hear the noise of children giggling, shouting and singing during their breaks, or to observe children playing chess in a corridor. 'It's a chorus of happiness,' a teacher told me proudly.

Kati Levoranta, the effusive CEO of Rovio, the makers of the video game *Angry Birds*, explained, 'The attitude is that high school should be like kindergarten.' With four billion downloads ('yours truly' not among them), *Angry Birds* is the most popular video game in history. Finland is the only country with a dense cluster of top talent around computer coding for games. She feels it may be due to the long, lonely winters and a childlike approach to education. 'Children are encouraged to experiment and take chances. And this is what tends to make a great game coder,' she says.

4. Whatever it takes

Students often have the same teacher for their initial six years of school, so teachers know every student intimately. Teachers are trained to notice when a child is falling behind as early as possible. 'Early detection and intervention is very important. We start to correct certain problems already in the first grade,' explained Niemi. She adds, 'We have teachers specialized in the correction of the problems in reading, writing and speech. They go around to the schools and ask the teachers, "Do you have students who have problems like that?" And if they have students like that, each is trained with special methods to correct that kind of problem.' Nearly 30 per cent of Finland's children receive some kind of special help during primary school (Hancock 2011). And, again, the school system pays for this.

It is this whatever-it-takes attitude of helping the neediest which helps explain why the differences between weakest and strongest students in Finland are amongst the smallest in the world.

5. *Maximize the pupil's potential (not SAT or A-level scores)*

'The Finnish model is pupil-centric and improvement-led. Our objective is to maximize the potential of each pupil,' continued Niemi. There are no formal standardized tests, apart from one exam at the end of the student's senior year in high school. Results and rankings of students and schools are not published, so the typical comparisons and competition between students, schools or regions is avoided. Pedagogical emphasis is on helping children fulfil their potential based on their particular strengths and weaknesses. Continuous assessment is provided to guide and help pupils according to their needs. Each student receives a customized report at least once every school year. Tests are frequent, but they are designed to inspire confidence rather than instil fear.

Finnish teachers expect a lot from their students, and studies show that this is an important factor in determining the success of a school system. Once children share a common journey, they are channelled towards university or vocational training. There is no stigma associated with specialized crafts and trades – skilled craftsmen are needed and required in society. As Finland's wealthiest person Antti Herlin, the chairman of Kone (the world's largest producer of elevators for high-rise buildings), told me, 'Maintaining an elevator is a large, complex responsibility, so it deserves a high salary. The job demands specialized and practical skills, not an abstract university education.'

The underlying idea is that no educational path should result in a dead-end situation where the students' prior choices would block their eligibility for higher education. So, students who choose vocational training can follow a track back to university. The universities themselves are also excellent, with free tuition ensuring that there are no debilitating student loans which may compromise a student's future career choices and constrain their financial means.

6. Integrated

There are many parts of Finland's social contract which act as supports to reinforce its education system. Some of these are idiosyncratic to the Finnish culture and difficult to replicate, while others are more easily replicated.

The value a society places on education is important, as we have seen in top performing nations such as Korea, Israel and Singapore. In Finland, education seems to be ingrained into the country's DNA. While Finns have a largely secular culture, it originated from a staunch Lutheran tradition which held reading as a prerequisite for getting married. *The Seven Brothers* (1871) by Aleksis Kivi is widely regarded as Finland's national novel and is a story of the importance of education for seven rural peasants. Today, by way of example, the average Finn checks out sixteen books a year from their public libraries, which is among the highest in the world (Ministry of Education and Culture 2019). These reforms would not have achieved their full effect unless people placed value on the importance of education.

The foundation of Finland's education system, indeed the entire social contract, is trust. Finland lives and breathes trust. Like any honour system (think of the voluntary petty cash system at the Rotary Club), everyone must 'play ball' for it to work. It is thus not a coincidence that the nation ranks third on Transparency International's list of the least corrupt nations (2018). It helps that Finland has been characterized as a consensus society where major political decisions have been agreed by all key players in the society, as compared to all the political jockeying which happens with special interest groups trying to gain advantages for themselves in more contentious societies. Finland never had an aristocracy, and social divisions never took root. It's dependence on peasant farming and fishing in harsh climate has shaped a stoic national character of hard work and good behaviour, as well as an appetite for self-improvement. Any teacher can tell you how desirable these traits are in their students.

Finland is also a great place to live for mothers. Female participation in the workforce and their level of education is among the highest in the world. Finland provides three years of maternity leave and subsidized day care to parents. At universal pre-school for all five-year-olds, the emphasis is again on play and socializing (Hancock 2011). Finnish women receive 70 per cent of their pay for nine months, starting five weeks before their due date. The benefits decline after twelve months but last for three years.

I visited a playful day care centre conveniently located next to the large office complex of *Angry Birds*, so commuting for the mother or father working there are streamlined. A working mother with three children who I met told me, 'They take better care of my children than I do,' acknowledging her complete confidence in the teachers and system. Contrast this with America, where day care is a giant expense, often second only to housing costs. A recent study found that in twenty-eight US states the annual cost of putting an infant in a full-time day care was higher than a year's tuition and fees at a four-year public college (Zillman 2018). A 2015 UN report surveying 185 countries revealed that the US is the only industrialized country to not guarantee paid maternity leave (Kim 2015).

As mentioned in other chapters, *TSTF* countries tend to have stable political structures which enable impactful reforms and steadfast execution. Educational reforms require at least one generation to have an impact. Finland, Singapore and Korea demonstrate that school systems can go from low to high performance within a few decades, but there are no quick fixes. So it is important to persevere to stay the course. Initiating and then abandoning over-arching programmes, as has been the case with the Affordable Care Act in US, is costly and counterproductive. Sometimes even small measures can result in a big impact. Sahlberg pointed to Finland's decision in 1957, which required foreign television shows to include subtitles, as a key ingredient to the success story; it meant children were required to read while watching interesting films.

Finland, with long hunting traditions, has nearly as many guns per capita as the US, but the sort of atrocities which occur in the US never happen in Finland due to tight regulations. President Trump's suggestion that teachers should be armed to prevent future attacks would strike any Finn as absurd. The sheer possibility that a teacher could be murdered while teaching children is unimaginable. This is a nation where I saw eight-year-old girls taking the underground train system in Helsinki unaccompanied by adults.

7. In teachers, we trust

All these aspects are important, but I have saved the most significant explanation for Finland's extraordinary success for the last. While working on my previous book, I learned that Johann Heinrich Pestalozzi, an influential Swiss educational reformer, described teaching as 'God's chosen profession.' When I conducted my work on Finland's education system, this expression kept coming back to me, like a familiar song which plays over and over in our head. What Finland does perhaps better than anywhere else is make better teachers.

Teachers enjoy an extraordinarily high level of esteem in Finland. The profession is consistently ranked among the most desired careers by Finnish high school students. Men rate a teacher as the most desirable mate in marriage. Women rank it second after a medical doctor. Social status is ironically more important than wages. Teachers earn very close to the national average salary level for all occupations, typically equivalent to what mid-career middle school teachers earn annually in the OECD nations – about $41,000 (Sahlberg 2011). According to Sahlberg, 'Teachers routinely meet with students before and after school to shape their development, examine student work to improve lesson plans, reach out to students' families in the evenings and on the weekends and strive to increase their own knowledge and skills; so, it's important that they feel appreciated, even revered.'

Since becoming a primary school teacher in Finland is a very sought-after profession, the selection of teachers is a highly competitive process. Applicants must hold a master's degree from one of the top universities. Annually, only about one in ten applicants will be accepted to study to become a primary school teacher (Sahlberg 2015). Only

Finland's best are accepted on the course and this means having a whole host of skills alongside the necessary academic requirements. Successful candidates must have not only good scores and excellent interpersonal skills, but also a deep personal commitment to teach and work in schools (Sahlberg 2011). The candidates go through observed clinical activity replicating school situations, where social interactions and communication skills come into play. Finally, the candidates are interviewed by experienced instructors and asked, among other things, to explain why they have decided to become teachers. A teacher's passion to teach is as important as ability.

Autonomy is another feature which distinguishes the Finnish approach to teaching. There are no regulations governing class size, which means schools are free to determine how to group pupils and students. The curriculum is designed for the whole nation and every school has the same goals and draws from the same pool of university-trained educators. Funding does not vary by the wealth of the community. In this manner, each Finnish child has a good chance of getting the same quality education irrespective of their parent's financial position and no matter whether he or she lives in a rural village or a university town.

By contrast, in the US, money spent per pupil differs by more than 200 per cent (Barber and Mourshed 2007). The US funds its schools through property taxes which differ vastly in value based on neighbourhoods. This leads to a massive disparity in funding for primary schools – schools in expensive neighbourhoods have larger budgets. This causes the most disadvantaged students from poorer neighbourhoods to be warehoused together in the worst schools. Thus, inequality is created in the US from a young age.

A key characteristic of the work environment in Finnish schools is that teachers have a lot of freedom. They are left to decide on everything from lesson plans to the frequency of homework, which means they can tailor their teaching style to suit the needs of the class. In short, they are trusted and respected professionals. Contrast this with the UK, where schools have data managers, teachers are told which colour pens to use for marking and books are periodically checked to ensure that learning intentions are neatly stuck in place.

Furthermore, when new teachers are employed in a school in Finland, they usually stay for life. An official estimate suggests that only 10 to 15 per cent of teachers leave the profession during their entire career (Sahlberg 2011). This is about the annual attrition rate in the UK and the US.

The feedback from Finnish teachers is that they enjoy the freedom to truly exercise the knowledge and skills they have learned. 'We can shape the development of a child during the formative stage of their life,' comments Niemi. Others find the emphasis on personalized learning and creativity as rewarding. And they have six years to do this. 'Compare this to the attitude of a teacher who inherits a troubled child, but knows that it is only a matter of months before they will wash their hands off them,' laments Sahlberg. There is also less routine and repetition since teaching is personalized and holistic. Teaching for only the tests is not especially rewarding and can be as demotivating for teachers as they are for pupils. 'For the right type of person, our approach can be invigorating,' says Sahlberg. 'I enjoy discovering who they are and what they are best at doing,' commented a primary school teacher I spoke to about her students. Another preferred the collaborative Finnish approach against the US system, which places a high value on competition. 'This competition creates a radically different feeling in the classroom and requires a completely different culture of teaching which wouldn't suit me,' she said.

Outcome

The results speak for themselves. Finland upgraded its human capital by transforming its education system from mediocre to one of the best international performers in a relatively short period. The absolute PISA scores of students in Finland are among the highest in the world across the range of subjects tested. Only in Japan, Singapore, South Korea and the richer parts of China do students score higher than their Finnish counterparts. But unlike these places, Finland achieves its results without working its pupils into the ground.

Most importantly, the amount of variance between schools in Finland is about one-tenth of the OECD average. This means that whatever inequality remains is mostly due to the natural variation of students' talent. We can't all play centre for the Los Angeles Lakers or striker for Real Madrid. Here, we are actually bothered by something which is often confused with inequality – unfairness. Who among us feels it is fair to start 20 metres behind in a 100-metre race? The Finnish education reforms have achieved fairness at the individual level. And they have done much more at the collective level. Since that dark, skeptical December afternoon in 2000, Finland has been ranked as the world's most competitive economy by the World Economic Forum four times.

Challenges

While this is a love story about the Finnish education system, the system has its own challenges. Teachers bemoan the ubiquitous smartphones and the fact that students are reading less as a result. Far from encouraging an understanding of different perspectives, Facebook, Instagram and Twitter confirm our own beliefs and inclinations rather than challenge them. Increased use of social media can also have an adverse effect on mental health, though this is not specific to Finnish young people.

Finland's gap between rich and poor pupils is smaller than in most OECD countries, but it has widened since 2000 (*Economist* 2016). Part of the reason is immigration. Pia Pakarinen, the vice mayor of Helsinki, believes that integration of immigrants is vital to social cohesion. The emergence of ghettos in parts of Copenhagen and Stockholm cause her great consternation. Finland has thus far resisted this trend, but it is natural for ethnic groups to stick together (Singapore's public housing scheme requires people of Chinese, Indian and Malay origin to co-mingle). 'In Finland, we don't have any suburbs where I wouldn't live in,' Pakarinen told me.

Moreover, vocational training has been a route to middle class jobs in egalitarian countries like Finland, Denmark and Switzerland, but most of today's jobs are unlikely to exist in fifteen years – if you believe the predictions of AI experts. Jobs with repetitive tasks are the most vulnerable to automation, such as cashiers, cooks, paralegal or those filing tax returns. Maintaining such a high level of performance is never easy, especially in rapidly changing times. Sahlberg warns that Finland should avoid Nokia's error – failing to innovate at the top.

Conclusion

As a resource-scarce nation, Finland has always depended on creative people who have used their skills effectively and productively. This has not changed and if anything will become more pronounced in a vastly competitive world where ideas, research, funding, means of production and clients are agnostic to borders. Finland's remarkable reform of its education system has led to it becoming the envy of the world. It seems trivial to say, but nevertheless worth emphasizing, that in a knowledge-driven economy, knowledge improves competitiveness. Finland has harnessed this principle not by doing the same thing better, but by throwing out orthodox methods and replacing them with a novel and effective approach.

Sahlberg likes the old Finnish proverb, 'Only dead fish follow the stream.' There is a word in Finnish, 'sisu' – a term the Finns use to describe their national character. It roughly translates into 'stoic determination', tenacity of purpose and grit. Changing people's minds about anything is difficult. But isn't this what learning is all about after all? Who would have believed spending less time in class, assigning less homework, dismantling school inspectorates, rarely testing pupils and refusing to publish exam results helps you find education's holy grail?

The Finnish miracle is, to some extent, culture specific. But it seems to offer a rich treasure of common sense lessons for those open enough to consider them. Is it not possible to make teaching a more attractive profession and to elevate its social stature? Is it necessary or constructive that private schools compete with the public school system? Does it make sense to fund public schools via property taxes? Countless other questions arise from the Finland experience. One irony is that the country has become more competitive by being more collaborative. It has succeeded by doing more with less and proved that money doesn't actually buy a better education.

Another bumble bee that is not meant to fly.

References and Further Reading:

Abrams, S.E. 'The children must play'. *The New Republic*, 2011. https://newrepublic.com/article/82329/education-reform-finland-us.

Alexander, H. 'OECD education report: case study Finland'. *The Telegraph*, 2013. https://www.telegraph.co.uk/education/10489225/OECD-education-report-case-study-Finland.html.

Anderson, J. 'From Finland, an Intriguing School-Reform Model'. *The New York Times*, 2011. https://www.nytimes.com/2011/12/13/education/from-finland-an-intriguing-school-reform-model.html.

Barber, M. and M. Mourshed. 'How the world's best-performing school systems came out on top'. *McKinsey & Company*, 2007. https://www.mckinsey.com/industries/social-sector/our-insights/how-the-worlds-best-performing-school-systems-come-out-on-top.

Brackett, M. 'Emotion Revolution–Student'. *Yale Center for Emotional Intelligence*, 2015. http://ei.yale.edu/what-we-do/emotion-revolution-student/.

'Corruption Perceptions Index 2018'. *Transparency International*, 2018. https://www.transparency.org/cpi2018.

Doyle, W. 'How Finland broke every rule – and created a top school system'. *The Hechinger Report*, 2016. https://hechingerreport.org/how-finland-broke-every-rule-and-created-a-top-school-system/.

'Education spending'. *OECD Data*, 2019. https://data.oecd.org/eduresource/education-spending.htm.

'Finland and PISA'. *Ministry of Education and Culture*, 2016. https://minedu.fi/en/pisa-en.

Gross-loh, C. 'Finnish education chief: "we created a school system based on equality" '. *The Atlantic*, 2014. http://www.theatlantic.com/education/archive/2014/03/finnish-education-chief-we-created-a-school-system-based-on-equality/284427/.

Hancock, L. 'Why are Finland's schools successful?'. *Smithsonian*, 2011. https://www.smithsonianmag.com/innovation/why-are-finlands-schools-successful-49859555/.

Hart, J. 'The big lesson from the world's best school system? Trust your teachers'. *The Guardian*, 2017. https://www.theguardian.com/teacher-network/2017/aug/09/worlds-best-school-system-trust-teachers-education-finland.

'Helsinking: Europe's top-performing school system rethinks its approach'. *The Economist*, 2016. https://www.economist.com/europe/2016/05/12/helsinking.

'How heavy use of social media is linked to mental illness'. *The Economist*, 2018. https://www.economist.com/graphic-detail/2018/05/18/how-heavy-use-of-social-media-is-linked-to-mental-illness?fsrc=scn/tw/te/bl/ed/?fsrc=scn/tw/te/bl/ed/howheavyuseofsocialmediaislinkedtomentalillnessdailychart.

'How to be top'. *The Economist*, 2007. https://www.economist.com/international/2007/10/18/how-to-be-top.

Kim, S. 'US is only industrialized nation without paid maternity leave'. *ABC News*, 2015. https://abcnews.go.com/Business/us-industrialized-nation-paid-maternity-leave/story?id=30852419.

'Knowledge and Skills for Life First Results from the OECD Programme for International Students Assessment (PISA) 2000'. *OECD Publishing*, 2001. http://www.oecd.org/education/school/programmeforinternationalstudentassessmentpisa/33691596.pdf.

Lamb-Sinclair, A. 'What If High School Were More Like Kindergarten?' *The Atlantic*, 2016. https://www.theatlantic.com/education/archive/2016/08/learning-versus-education/494660/.

'Library Network'. *Ministry of Education and Culture*. 2019. https://minedu.fi/en/library-network.

Luce, E. 'Amy Chua and the big little lies of US meritocracy'. *Financial Times*, 2019. https://www.ft.com/content/7b00c3a2-8daa-11e9-a1c1-51bf8f989972?shareType=nongift.

Nelson, L. '9 reasons Finland's schools are so much better than Americas'. *Vox*, 2015. https://www.vox.com/2015/2/18/8063785/finland-schools-education.

Nisen, M. 'Google HR boss explains why GPA and most interviews are useless'. *Business Insider*, 2013. https://www.businessinsider.com/how-google-hires-people-2013-6?r=US&IR=T.

Partanen, A. 'What Americans keep ignoring about Finland's school success'. *The Atlantic*, 2011. http://www.theatlantic.com/national/archive/2011/12/what-americans-keep-ignoring-about-finlands-school-success/250564/.

Ravitch, D. 'Schools we can envy'. *The New York Review of Books*, 2012. https://www.nybooks.com/articles/2012/03/08/schools-we-can-envy/#fn-1»».

Resmovits, J. 'Finland schools' success story: lessons shared at California forum'. *The Huffington Post*, 2012. https://www.huffingtonpost.co.uk/entry/finland-schools-success-equality-collaboration_n_1219780.

Ripley, A. *The Smartest Kids in the World, and How They Got That Way* (New York: Simon & Schuster, 2013).

Sahlberg, P. 'A Model Lesson: Finland Shows Us What Equal Opportunity Looks Like'. *American Educator*, 2012. https://www.aft.org/sites/default/files/periodicals/Sahlberg_0.pdf.

——'Education policies for raising student learning: the Finnish approach'. *Journal of Education Policy*, vol. 22, no. (2007): pp. 147–171. https://doi.org/10.1080/02680930601158919.

——'Finland's success is no miracle'. *Education Week*, 2012. https://www.edweek.org/ew/articles/2012/01/12/16sahlberg.h31.html?tkn=OWPFl oO0pT21GWKAWwclMsNRce9j%2BOQp%2BqLg&cmp=ENL-EU-VIEWS1&intc=EW-QC12-ENL.

——*Finnish Lessons: What Can the World Learn from Educational Change in Finland?* (New York: Teachers College Press, 2011).

——'Lessons from Finland'. *American Educator*, 2011. https://pasisahlberg.com/wp-content/uploads/2013/01/Lessons-from-Finland-AE-2011.pdf.

——'Paradoxes of educational improvement: the Finnish experience'. *Scottish Educational Review*, vol. 43, no. 1 (2011): pp. 3–23. https://pasisahlberg.com/wp-content/uploads/2013/01/Paradoxes-of-improvement-SER-2011.pdf.

——'Q: What makes Finnish teachers so special? A: It's not brains'. *The Guardian*, 2015. https://www.theguardian.com/education/2015/mar/31/finnish-teachers-special-train-teach.

Strauss, V. 'Why Finland's schools are top-notch'. *CNN*, 2014. http://edition.cnn.com/2014/10/06/opinion/sahlberg-finland-education/index.html.

——'No, Finland isn't ditching traditional school subjects. Here's what's really happening'. *The Washington Post*, 2015. https://www.washingtonpost.com/news/answer-sheet/wp/2015/03/26/no-finlands-schools-arent-giving-up-traditional-subjects-heres-what-the-reforms-will-really-do/.

——'The brainy questions on Finland's only high-stakes standardized test'. *The Washington Post*, 2014. https://www.washingtonpost.com/news/answer-sheet/wp/2014/03/24/the-brainy-questions-on-finlands-only-high-stakes-standardized-test/.

——'What if Finland's great teachers taught in U.S. schools?'. *The Washington Post*, 2013. https://www.washingtonpost.com/news/answer-sheet/

wp/2013/05/15/what-if-finlands-great-teachers-taught-in-u-s-schools-not-what-you-think/.

The Hechinger Report. 'Standardized Testing a Foreign Concept in Finland with World's Top Students'. *The Huffington Post*, 2012. https://www.huffingtonpost.co.uk/entry/standardized-testing-a-fo_n_2145623?guccounter=1.

Wilby, P. 'Finland's education ambassador spreads the word'. *The Guardian*, 2013. https://www.theguardian.com/education/2013/jul/01/education-michael-gove-finland-gcse?CMP=twt_gu.

Zillman, C. 'Childcare Costs More Than College Tuition in 28 U.S. States'. *Fortune*, 2018. http://fortune.com/2018/10/22/childcare-costs-per-year-us/.

Conversations and Interviews

Antti Herlin, Hannele Niemi, Kati Levoranta, Pasi Sahlberg and Pia Pakarinen.

10

Singapore: Health Care

Power to Patients

Sing Health

Source: Hian; cited in Koh, 2015

Kishore Mahbubani shakes my hand and pats me on the back as though he is my uncle. As former dean of the Lee Kuan Yew School of Public Policy, and a jet-setting attendee of Davos forums, he is probably Singapore's most prominent global personality following the death of Lee Kuan Yew, the first prime minister of Singapore. He has been a ceaseless ambassador, reminding us whenever a podium presents itself that Singapore started not long ago as a small, poor fishing village with paltry wealth and resources. At just fifty-four years, Singapore feels as if it is in the prime of its life.

Singapore has arguably been the most impressive national success story of modern history. Few gave tiny Singapore much chance of survival on its formation, and none would have predicted it would emerge from a third- to a first-world country in less than two generations. GDP per capita was less than $500 when it declared its independence in 1965 and now exceeds $53,000, whizzing past economic titans like Britain, Japan and even the US (*Economist* 2015).

Whether we are measuring innovation, connectivity, education, urban planning, healthcare, foreign investment or citizen's trust in its government, this tiny country is at the front of the pack. At the same time, it has conceived, invested in and maintained one of the most enviable social contracts in the world. The facts speak for themselves – children educated in Singaporean schools achieve among the highest PISA scores in the world (Coughlan 2016); 90 per cent of Singaporean households own their homes thanks to government incentives and assistance (Capestany et al. 2018); people have peace of mind due to negligible crime rates; and retirement schemes for the elderly are among the most reliable and best-funded in the world.

When I ask Kishore why Singapore has been so successful, he talks about the country's 'm.p.h.' – but he is not referring to the speed of a new Tesla model S. 'Singapore's secret sauce is our combination of meritocracy, pragmatism and honesty,' he says, with the confidence expected of someone who was president of the United Nations Security Council. Since the purpose of our visit is to understand Singapore's healthcare system, I thought we could do so using Kishore's acronym as a guide. Surely it must take more to tame the healthcare beast which has forced patients and insurance companies to their knees and challenged policy makers wherever one goes in the world.

Healthcare systems everywhere are struggling to make ends meet and the reasons are now well known – underfunded insurance schemes, relentless rises in costs, accelerating innovation in treatments and devices and, above all, increases in longevity, which means providers must spend more and more on treating costly illnesses such as arthritis, Alzheimer's, cancer, diabetes and obesity. In most countries, these challenges are combined with misaligned incentives to create what may be one of the greatest threats to our physical and social well-being.

Rather than arguing while the boat is sinking, now might be a good time to try to understand what makes Singapore's healthcare system uniquely effective and see whether it holds any lessons for the rest of the world.

* * *

Health care is in a quagmire. Around the world, cost increases are rampant and governments are struggling to fund their healthcare systems. With populations ageing and wages languishing, this vicious cycle will only get worse.

Positions on opposite sides of the political continuum are entrenched and in radical disagreement. The right argues that single payer systems like those used in Britain and Canada are monopolies which stifle innovation, discourage efficiency and promote mediocrity. The left argues that healthcare in countries like the US represents the worst market failure of modern history, providing endless incentives for abuse.

Singapore has learned that both sides are right. Conceived as a single payer monopoly, their healthcare system initially failed. Revamped to embrace free markets, Singapore encountered the same malfunctions and traps experienced in the US and elsewhere. Drawing lessons from its experience of grappling with the shortcomings of each, the city state gradually crafted an amalgam of the best of both systems.

Today, it is clear that the critical innovation in the Singapore system was to bring the patient to the forefront. This meant dethroning the priestly status of the physician and weakening the power of the insurers. As a result, a more self-reliant consumer has emerged – one compelled to put skin in the game and salt away savings while young to provide for the inevitable health expenditure which comes with age.

The Economist Intelligence Unit recently ranked Singapore number two in the world for healthcare outcomes across a sweeping 166-country comparison (Nicholls and Pannelay 2014). Bloomberg went so far as to declare Singapore the healthiest country in the world, a conclusion reached by several independent observers around the world (Sims 2015). Whether it is life expectancy, infant mortality or recovery from cancer, Singapore tops the charts of measurements of key metrics in delivering world class healthcare.

Most surprisingly, these outstanding results are achieved at only a quarter of the cost of the US system and half that of the UK National Health Service (Haseltine 2013). And everyone seems to enjoy the benefits. Every Singaporean citizen is assured basic health care of an above average standard, receiving treatment in well-equipped public hospitals which offer technically sophisticated services. By contrast, one in ten Americans still lack health insurance of any kind. And in 2017, one in four Americans reported foregoing medical care because they couldn't afford it (Chin 2017).

So how did Singapore get there?

M.P.H.: Not the Kind of Horsepower You Think

Reversing the sequence of Kishore's catchy formula, 'm.p.h.', we begin with the 'h' which stands for honesty. Singapore, from the outset, felt that a nation with zero tolerance for corruption would have a comparative advantage in a part of the world often characterized by the colonial hangover of deceit, bribery and payoffs. Corruption often occurs when public officials wield power and influence significantly greater than their annual salary, so the incentive for others to offer bribes and the temptation to accept them are considerable. US congressmen meet these criteria fairly well, so it is hardly a coincidence that four of the largest six spenders for lobbying in Washington are healthcare businesses (Wilson 2017). While lobbying may be legal, it can feel like legalized bribery. These companies would not divert scarce funds from research, new hires or advertising to lobbying unless they felt the benefits outweighed the costs compared to these alternatives.

The primary strength of the Singaporean system is its ability to prevent healthcare providers from enticing politicians to maximize their interests. Singaporeans view lobbying by healthcare providers as an additional cost which brings no tangible benefit to society and which, at the end of the day, has to be borne by patients and taxpayers. So the practice is generally frowned upon.

The middle pedestal of Kishore's three-pronged success formula is meritocracy. There are plenty of good concepts and ideas discussed and even agreed upon among policy makers, but it is quite another matter to execute them effectively (think of Obamacare). Tommy Koh, Ambassador-at-Large at Singapore's MFA and a Spiritus Rector of Lee Kuan Yew, emphasized that good people were just as important as good policies: 'The success of Singapore is due, in part, to the high competence, integrity and dedication of its civil servants.'

Singapore's civil service drew on the tradition of British civil servants and Chinese Mandarins – and then raised the bar a few notches higher. The principle was that political parties may come and go, but a solid substrate of civil servants provides ballast and continuity to the system. In *A Mandarin and the Making of Public Policy*, Ngiam Tong Dow, a longstanding civil servant during Singapore's formative years, described how 'in those early days there was a sense of mission. Pay wasn't on our mind. It was getting the job done.'

Singapore has, like other *TSTF* countries, a steady pro-business, political leadership through either dominant parties or enduring coalitions. Its founding PAP party, while declining in significance, is still the dominant party with 70 per cent of voters casting their votes in its favour (Holmes 2015). Stable and cooperative leadership means they have been able to enact far-reaching and long-lasting policies. Singapore's healthcare reforms have been a continuous work in progress since the 1950s.

The final component of Kishore's acronym is pragmatism, and I can tell it's his favourite by the way his eyes light up. He points out self-effacingly that Singapore had a few things going for it. 'It helped that we were new and young,' he begins. 'Lee Kuan Yew modernized Singapore by learning from the experiences of other, more established countries and then adapting their best practices. We studied and learned from those who had already built up their health-care systems like the Australians, Americans and Japanese.'

Singapore had a young population, so it built up its healthcare system while the population was still active and healthy, with a low geriatric burden. The nation also had rapid economic growth and therefore could improve infrastructure and public health standards and, at the same time, educate its population on the merits of taking better care of themselves.

An advantage of having come from nothing is that you have little to lose, since you are free from the burden of maintaining legacy systems or tolerating legacy lobbies. So Singapore was in a better position to experiment. It started with a single payer system in the 1950s based on the British, Canadian and Australian models. The advantage of these systems was that everyone was covered and purchase was centralized. But Singapore found that some patients made frivolous visits to the doctor, knowing that their insurance would pay for it. The system was an invitation to excess. Once consumers know they are insured and that the costs are sunk, the system attracts more waste of healthcare services, which insurers then reflexively pass on in the form of higher premiums. Society has to bear a heavier, collective burden. There was also public criticism about waiting lists, limited choice and unresponsive bureaucracies.

Singapore then experimented with the free market models prevalent in the US and elsewhere, but the results were even worse. It became clear that a fee-for-service model provides highly perverse incentives for doctors and hospitals – and a moral hazard where insiders game the system by over-treating patients to secure lucrative profits. Since more care translates into more costs, the system becomes 'a tapeworm eating at our economic body,' as Warren Buffett, the astute investor, once vividly described it (Stempel 2010). Similarly, Nobel Prize winner Sir Angus Deaton of Princeton noted, 'Inequality is not killing capitalism in the United States, but rent-seekers like the healthcare sector.' He summarized, 'All that talent is devoted to stealing things, instead of making things' (Robb 2017). Like Buffet and Deaton, Lee Kuan Yew had earlier recognized that once vested interests are entrenched, whether it's doctors, insurance companies or lawyers, it becomes impossible to remove the excesses because they are programmed into the system and defended fiercely by those benefitting from them.

Pragmatism means dealing with things realistically in a way which is based on practical and rational rather than on theoretical and emotional considerations. But few subjects are more emotive than healthcare and thus more prone to sensationalism. There is no perfect system and trade-offs are inevitable, whichever way you go. The spirit of the Singaporean healthcare system, and the secret to its success, has been to reframe the focus of healthcare around efficiency – doing more with less.

Lee and his team were perplexed about how exactly to do this. A devout advocate of free markets, Lee understood that it is competition which drives innovation and creates value for consumers. This philosophy has characterized the nation's progress to become the second-most competitive country in the world, as ranked by the World Economic Forum (Schwab 2018).

But Lee noticed that healthcare seemed to defy the cardinal rules of innovation and competitiveness prevalent in other markets.

These rules explain that the number of hours we need to work compared to our grandparents to purchase a pair of shoes, a dozen oranges or a car has declined by several orders of magnitude over our lifetime (Cox and Alm 2008). But our outlays for healthcare seem to have risen inexorably higher and relentlessly outpace wages, suggesting that value extraction may be at work rather than value creation (Our World in Data 2017). This is a sign of market failure rather than market victory.

Market Victories Vs Market Failures

The late Nobel laureate Ken Arrow pointed out that healthcare simply doesn't work like normal markets (Arrow 1963). To start with, most of us don't understand what we're buying, what it costs and whether it even works. Second, because medical knowledge is so complex and specialized, the physician always has an information advantage vastly superior to the patient. Third, our needs for healthcare are unpredictable, unlike food or clothing, and we can often be in a desperate state just when we need it most. Who is in a position to shop or bargain for a better price or doctor just after suffering a heart attack? If disappointed by the services provided, recourse is impossible, or very costly. Moreover, the personal bill we receive is often only vaguely related to the services provided and the expense is often determined by how many procedures were done, not whether the problem was fixed (Brooks 2017). Finally, a patent behind a prescription drug is effectively a twenty-year monopoly so drug companies have considerable pricing latitude compared to markets offering greater consumer choice. Any one of these attributes put the healthcare system at odds with free markets. Collectively, they produce distortions and abuses of an unparalleled magnitude and breadth.

Thus, Lee came to realize that something was amiss. 'This is not the way I would buy a bicycle or pair of shoes,' he felt. He also recognized that the cadence of our healthcare needs do not follow a normal bell shape curve distribution. Instead, they are bifurcated. There tend to be infrequent but costly incidents, like the contraction of a rare, debilitating disease, which requires long-term treatment. But these kinds of diseases tend to be exceptional. Far more common are frequent yet inexpensive sicknesses such as ear, eyes, nose and throat ailments. Lee thought it worth trying to develop a system which dealt with these two types of ailments separately. He had noticed that the pooling-of-risk approach (insurance) works well for serious and unpredictable medical ailments. But it encourages consumer abuse for treating minor ailments.

Lee then set out five fundamental premises which underpin the Singaporean health care system to this day:

1. Adequate and affordable healthcare is a basic right and a fundamental part of a nation's 'social contract' with its citizens. Society pays for healthcare one way or another, so it is beholden upon the government to design and oversee the system to optimize care and minimize the cost to taxpayers. The system should be tilted in favour of those who need it most and can afford it least.

2. The consumer must become the centre of focus for the healthcare system rather than physicians or insurance companies. To do so, they must have incentives to take responsibility for their own health.

3. Many people by nature are prone to immediate gratification and are bad at postponing benefits. Healthcare costs are in many ways like a pension. During youth, healthcare costs are low; they rise exponentially with age and become payable at a time when the person's ability to earn wages has been exhausted.[11] So mechanisms must be established to encourage, nudge or even force savings while people are younger in order to provide for healthcare needs when they become older.

4. Free markets do not function well for healthcare, so the system needs to be modified to mitigate abuses by those who seek to exploit the inherent weaknesses.

5. Most conditions, especially costly chronic ones such as diabetes, hypertension and obesity, are best avoided altogether or by treating them before complications set in. So considerable effort should be undertaken to educate people to take personal

---

11. In Britain, two-fifths of the NHS budget is spent on those over sixty-five (Robineau 2016).

responsibility for their health through their habits, lifestyles and exercise patterns, and to undergo periodic screening and diagnosis.

The Mechanics of Cost Savings in Singapore

With these premises in mind, Lee Kuan Yew went about building a radically new healthcare system. It is constructed on three pillars and referred to as the 3M system. Here is a brief overview of how the system works:

The first pillar is for rare, costly incidents. These are covered by a low-cost insurance policy, called MediShield Life. Its purpose is to provide coverage against catastrophic sickness or accidents which trigger large, unexpected bills. It is compulsory and universal, regardless of age and pre-existing conditions. The rationale is similar to the origins of insurance against fire for homes. Accidents happen so everyone is insured; but since incidence is relatively rare, the costs can be pooled across the entire population and shared (which is how household fire insurance came about). In this manner, scale advantages and costs benefits are considerable and so premiums can be kept modest. MediShield costs from US$12 a month (S$16) for a twenty-nine-year-old to US$50 (S$68) a month for a sixty-nine-year-old without subsidies (Carroll and Frakt 2017). Premiums rise with age to reflect higher incidence of ailments.

Pricing is also variable based on facilities required. There are five classes of care in hospitals: A, B1, B2+, B2 and C. *A* gets you a private room, your own bathroom, air conditioning and your choice of doctor. *C* gets you an open ward with seven or eight other patients, a shared bathroom and a pre-assigned doctor. While choosing *A* means you pay for all the services, choosing *C* means the government pays up to 80 per cent of the costs. Patients desiring a more exclusive service can do so by purchasing additional private insurance or paying from their own pockets. At the same time, those with the greatest needs receive the greatest assistance (Carroll and Frakt 2017).

The second pillar, and the most innovative aspect of Singapore's model, is its Medisave scheme. There is a deductible on every invoice for healthcare treatment in this category and there is co-payment on every dollar so that the patient always has some interest in watching over their bill. Earlier, Singapore imposed a fifty-cent charge on prescription drugs, even when it was an expensive drug. Lee learned that this token price ensured that people valued the medicine. 'An earlier policy of free medicine showed that people often took the medicine home, took two pills, threw away the rest and went back to ask for more. So the principle that healthcare is not free at the point of consumption was established right from start,' explained Lee's son, Prime Minister Lee Hsien Loong, during the National Day speech in August 2018.

Lee also realized that cost savings alone are not sufficient. Healthcare ailments are linked to age and 75 per cent of our life-long outlays for health are spent during the last five years of our lives. Figure 10.1 shows that healthcare costs increase dramatically as we age. In Canada, for example, the annual healthcare cost for one eighty-year-old is equivalent to that of fifteen children. So there is, analogous to a pension fund, a massive need to stash away savings early for the inevitable and costly hit which awaits us towards the end of our lives.

Health Care Costs are Programmed to Rise Dramatically Due to Ageing

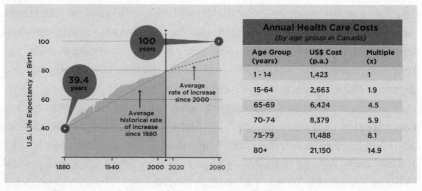

Figure 10.1 Are Social Contracts Ready for 100-Year Lives?

Life expectancy has increased steadily in the US and is expected to reach 100 by 2080. Since the cost of caring for elderly (80+) is 15x the level of children, healthcare costs are programmed to explode, unless checked.

Source: Wikimedia Commons

Medisave is effectively an individual savings account designed to do this. Every Singaporean sets aside a portion of their salaries via salary taxes for their own medical needs and those of their families. Workers up to age fifty-five put 20 per cent of their wages into these accounts, matched by an additional 17 per cent of wages from their employer (after age fifty-five, these percentages go down). The contribution is divided to fund long-term needs for both retirement care and healthcare. About 8 to 10.5 per cent of wages are kept for Medisave, depending on age; the rest is deposited in the individual's social security account. Both are housed in the individual's own bank account and earn interest, which is set by the government (currently at 4 per cent). Once an individual builds up the maximum amount of around US$52,000, additional savings are channelled to augment their retirement account. Sometimes the government even pays bonus contribution to align their interests and provide an incentive. As Prime Minister Lee Hsien Loong once said, 'It's a win–win outcome.'

Medisave is also designed to improve social cohesion by encouraging family support and home care. Holders may use their savings to pay for immediate family members (children, parents, spouses and siblings), which creates a sense of family responsibility for health. An ingenious aspect of the architecture was to permit any unspent portion or unused Medisave allowances to be transferred to an individual's retirement scheme once they reach a certain age. In the event of death, residual benefits are inheritable by the spouse or children. So medical costs and retirement needs are interwoven and work together holistically when a person's ability to earn wages has been exhausted.

For the first time, consumers with 'skin in the game' had a considerable incentive to save. And they did. Savings in Medisave accounts have grown from US$27 billion in 2006 to more than US$55 billion, with average balances of approximately US$16,000 per person (Ministry of Health 2016). The median total savings, or fiftieth percentile of all working-age families in the US is just US$5,000 (Elkins 2018). Professor Phua Kai Hong told me that the combined savings in Medisave plans amount to fifteen years' worth of the annual budget outlay for healthcare.

Figure 10.2: Value Extraction in Healthcare

Source: Banx

The third pillar is the Medifund, or the 'safety net' feature of Singapore's healthcare system. It is an endowment fund set up by the government, designed as a last resort for people who are destitute and cannot afford to pay their medical bills, even after drawing on their Medisave and MediShield benefits. The amount of help someone could get from Medifund depends on the patient's and family's income, condition, expenses and social circumstances (Carroll and Frakt 2017). It is designed to ensure that no one is denied necessary healthcare treatment because they cannot afford to pay.

How to Deal with Monopolies

While each of these pillars contributed to substantial improvements, the issue remained of how to resolve the monopoly problem which plagues healthcare. This rears its head on two fronts – pricing of healthcare treatment and the cost of doctors.

A patent on a drug effectively confers monopoly status so the issue arises about what price is considered a fair reward for a company's research and development efforts. The Ministry of Health, like NICE in the UK and other regulatory agencies in countries which seek to protect consumers from abusive practices, considers the benefits of a drug relative to its costs and then uses a reference system to compare prices of similar drugs in other countries. Typically, this means looking at prices in some twenty countries, throwing out the outliers and then taking the average price.

In instances where there are several drugs producing similar therapeutic benefits, Singapore uses its market power as the biggest buyer of healthcare to bargain for lower prices. The Ministry of Health also decides which drugs are eligible for subsidies and Medisave spending and also publishes a 'standard drug list' of drugs which are provided at subsidized rates to patients. Drugs which don't appear on either list may still be available in hospitals, but at higher prices. The purpose is to provide an incentive to pharmaceutical companies to get onto the standard list at more affordable prices. In the US, Medicare is prohibited, by law, from negotiating down the price of pharmaceuticals. As a result of this disparity in policies, Singaporeans spend about 60 per cent less on drugs than Americans (Haseltine 2013).

To prevent the kind of irrational pricing prevalent in the US, the government regularly publishes hospital bill sizes and selected quality indicators on its website to encourage transparency, consumer knowledge and choice. In contrast, a study in the US found that the cost of a hip transplant varied by more than 1,000 per cent, from $11,100 to $125,798 (Paddock 2013).

The other part of the system which exhibits monopoly characteristics is the doctors, a profession which is highly restricted in terms of who can become a doctor. Economists use the term 'rents' to describe any payment in excess of the cost needed to bring that factor into production. The number of doctors is restricted by universities and state licensing – and it is no secret that the best means to ensure high and steady increases in wages is to curtail supply. Leaders of these institutions lack the incentives to reduce costs which translate to lower rewards for their constituents. So it is hardly surprising that remuneration for doctors has outpaced our ability to pay them (i.e., normal wages) by a vast margin. Moreover, many doctors organize themselves to get an ever-increasing share of the pie. Physicians are often part-owners in clinics so they have a greater interest to collude by referring cases to experts within their 'owned' practice and siphoning off from the most profitable patients.

The average physician income in the US is double what doctors earn in Singapore and other countries like Korea, Germany and Japan, according to *Payscale and Salary Explorer*. This wage differential is even more extreme for specialists like orthopaedic surgeons.

Singapore has managed to temper the cost of physicians, one of the most important components of healthcare costs, through a variety of measures. It has increased the number of universities educating physicians from one to three, including a collaboration with Duke University Medical School. It offers more affordable education, clearing the way for a larger number of applicants. A medical degree from Duke-NUS costs less than half of what it costs at Duke in the US. As a quid pro quo, students are required to undertake a minimum term of service in the public healthcare sector at a lower wage than is offered in the private market. To augment the supply of physicians further, Singapore has been open to accepting doctors from countries which it deems to have acceptable standards of medical education.

Singapore has also managed to control malpractice suits and the price of insurance for doctors. Besides lowering costs, this builds an environment in which the self-confidence of the doctor is higher and so is the trust of the patient. Far from punitive, being a physician in Singapore is considered to be among the most lucrative and attractive professions.

Prevention

Luis Cantarell, the head of Nestlé Health Science, once suggested whimsically that the 'minister of health' should be called the 'minister of sickness'. Setting aside his humour, Cantarell was highlighting an undeniable truth – it is much more cost effective to prevent sickness and disease than to treat them. Trust for America's Health, an organization active in this field, estimates that an investment of $10 per person per year in community-based programmes tackling physical inactivity, poor nutrition and smoking could yield nearly six times this investment in the form of medical savings. This could save the US more than $16 billion annually in five years (Fried 2017).

The need for such investment is immense. Approximately 75 per cent of healthcare spending in the US is on people with chronic conditions like arthritis, diabetes, heart disease and obesity (Centres for Disease Control and Prevention 2017). In 2010, The Centers for Disease Control and Prevention (CDC) reported that one in three Americans could have diabetes by 2050 (Boyle et al. 2010) caused, in part, by poor eating and lifestyle habits. Similarly, more than 80 per cent of lung cancers are due to smoking, which means they are avoidable (Centers for Disease Control and Prevention 2018). Much of this is not rocket science and is largely a function of raising awareness. Reduced intake of table salt goes a long way towards reducing high blood pressure. Exercising 150 minutes per week substantially mitigates the onset of diabetes and obesity. Abstaining from smoking tobacco greatly reduces the risk of lung cancer.

Despite all this evidence, our healthcare systems have primarily focused on discovering treatments rather than preventing or curing disease. Singapore has recognized that the public sector must take the lead in prevention as there is no incentive for the private sector to do so. Healthcare providers like physicians and pharmaceutical companies earn money when patients contract illness, not when they avoid it. There are plenty of Nobel laureates in physiology and medicine for discovering breakthrough drugs, but who in academia is rewarded for preventing the onset of disease in the first place?

Singapore, with its emphasis on pragmatism, is investing appreciable amounts in education to encourage individuals to take personal responsibility for their health through their habits, lifestyle and exercise patterns. Public health campaigns raise awareness of the risks of unhealthy lifestyles; they promote healthier choices for food, regular exercise and stress the importance of avoiding harmful behaviour like smoking. Children's 'health booklets' meticulously record their medical history and keep parents informed and involved in their child's formation of healthy lifestyle habits. During their formative years, young Singaporean men participate in mandatory military training, which helps instil the value of fitness and a proper diet. Even urban planning gets involved. Bicycle paths, parks and exercise corners have been established all over the city to promote exercise and bus routes have been redesigned with fewer stops to encourage more walking. Active ageing programmes encourage senior groups to socialize, be active, go for regular medical checks and take care of their health. The seniors take brisk walks and perform group dancing; some of them even do tai chi.

Absence of Abuse: A Litmus Test

A different way of analysing Singapore's healthcare system is to look at the common abuses which arise elsewhere and see how its system has responded. In Singapore, we see a remarkable absence of the injustices which prevail elsewhere. While unpaid medical bills are a leading cause of bankruptcy in the US, they are a rarity in Singapore. Theft and fraud are rampant in medical systems worldwide, with costs estimated to be some $272 billion in the US alone (*Economist* 2014). Then there are the legal but morally hazardous acts like astronomically raising prices of crucial medicines because, as one pharma executive said, 'I can.' To cite one example, Turing Pharmaceuticals overnight raised the price of Daraprim, a sixty-two-year-old medicine for a deadly parasitic disease, from $13.50 to $750 for a single pill (Pollack 2015). Drug prices in Singapore are 30–70 per cent cheaper than the US due to collective bargaining based on a reference list of prices available in other countries (Wei-Yan 2019). The US is one of only two countries in the world which permit DTC (direct-to-consumer) advertising. Other countries believe that most people are unqualified to judge whether the healthy, energetic and sexually viral lifestyles depicted in late night television advertisements can be achieved with the pop of a few pills. This is despite warnings from the American Medical Association which has called for a complete ban, saying 'Direct-to-consumer advertising inflates demand for new and more expensive drugs, even when these drugs may not be appropriate' (Robles 2015).[12]

Technology

Historically, regulation and innovation have been opposing forces, which may explain why the delivery of healthcare has been so resistant

---

12. 'Pharmaceutical advertising in the US is growing faster than any other leading ad category,' said Jon Swallen, chief research officer at Kantar Media, a consulting firm which tracks multimedia advertising. It exceeded $6 billion in 2016, with television picking up the lion's share, according to Kantar data.

to improvement. But with the development of artificial intelligence and other technical applications, this could very well change. Eric Topol, a cardiologist and the director of the Scripps Translational Science Institute in La Jolla, California, argues in his recent book, *The Patient Will See You Now*, that smartphones will radically change how we solicit, receive and pay for medical care in the future. He cites an example: 'Let's say I have a rash that needs to be examined. I snap a picture of it with my smartphone and download an app to process the image. Within minutes, a dedicated computer algorithm texts me my diagnosis.' It seems our phones are set to become the central hub of our medical records, a means of monitoring and telling us when our bodies are behaving atypically.

These transformations are already under way. British Columbia is at the forefront of telemedicine, enabling patients in remote areas to connect with experts for specialist advice at a fraction of the cost and inconvenience of conventional treatment. CliniCloud already produces a microphone which fits on our phone and turns into a digital stethoscope. Lumify, made by Philips, can conduct head-to-toe ultrasounds via an app which costs $199 for unlimited use. By contrast, an ultrasound machine costs $350,000 (Murgia 2017).

Singapore is well positioned to benefit from these developments for a number of reasons. First, technology is moving towards empowering the patient, which is already a central aspect of Singapore's system. Second, China and most of Asia are lightly regulated regimes, which means they can be expected to welcome new technology—especially those involving AI such as predictive diagnostics. With all of this happening in Singapore's own backyard, they should be early adopters rather than late resistors. Finally, Singapore has a large business consisting of for-profit hospitals such as Raffles, effectively exporting expertise and efficiency in healthcare. Their very survival depends on turning technical innovation into a competitive advantage.

Criticisms

Singapore's healthcare system has its share of critics. The population is getting older, which means they will get sick more often, so the demographic advantage it had at the outset has largely played out. Having dealt effectively with the diseases of poverty, it must deal increasingly with ailments of affluence like arthritis, obesity and Alzheimer's. The Health Promotion Board (HPB) found that Singaporeans were, on average, 3kg heavier than they were fifteen years ago (Lai 2017). And obesity is a harbinger of all sorts of ailments including diabetes, kidney defects and hypertension, which are all expensive to treat. Incentives in the system depend on self-reliance and savings, but this requires discipline and may create a bigger hazard if people forego necessary treatments to save money. Other people argue that Singapore is too small; but smallness should, if anything, be a disadvantage due to absence of advantages of scale through negotiation of prices, or cost advantages of larger facilities which can be amortized across a larger population.

Libertarians have long criticized Singapore as a 'nanny state'. The term, of British origin, is pejorative and suggests that government policies are over protective or that they interfere unduly with personal choice. But, as our chapter 'Critical, but not Urgent' shows, human beings are wired to deal with urgent problems. Sometimes, we need a little nudge to deal with slow-evolving but potentially life-threatening problems, like saving for our pensions or healthcare.

Conclusion

Enabling citizens to live full and healthy lives at a cost which is affordable to all is one of the most important aspects of any nation's social contract. Some do it better than others.

By learning from experience over the years, Singapore married the best of a market-based healthcare system with the best of single-payer models. It started by being candid about the nature of healthcare – that it is more accurately characterized as a pension obligation than a pay-as-you-go expense. It recognized that ears, eyes, nose and throat ailments involve a considerably different care and cost opportunity than chronic diseases such as heart disease, diabetes or multiple sclerosis. It then provided a substantial incentive for people to save, and welded this to each individual's retirement scheme. *The Patient Will See You Now* may stretch the point, but Singapore has succeeded in shifting the fulcrum of power away from physicians and insurance companies to the individual patients, each with a stake and an incentive to hold costs in check. In the future, technology will continue to favour the consumer by reducing information asymmetry and spurring competitive choice.

Singapore is arguably a much more privatized system than even the US. The Singaporean model is consumer driven and requires less government or insurance intervention. Two-thirds of healthcare spending is private and only about one-third is public (Carroll and Frak 2017). This is just the opposite in the US, a fact that should appeal greatly to conservatives keen on reducing the role of the big government.

Kishore's book *Can Singapore Survive?* echoes the spirit of vulnerability in *Too Small to Fail*, and reminds us that, although far from being a utopia, Singapore's healthcare system is a laboratory seeking continuous improvement. He says, 'The task of achieving affordable healthcare is a very challenging one. There is no perfect system and tough choices need to be made about trade-offs. Singapore will need to adapt as it has done since its inception.'

Estimates suggest that global spending on healthcare will increase from $8 trillion currently to $18 trillion in 2040, so for some societies it may become a question of how long they can afford to tolerate the status quo (Georgiev et al. 2018). Just to provide some magnitude of what's at stake, had America replicated Singapore's healthcare system since, say, 1980, it would have theoretically saved an average of $150,000 per American, or more than $4 trillion in what may be fairly described as the largest redistribution of wealth in modern history. Perhaps there is some merit in having some skin in the game, and a 'Singapore lite' version may be worth trying out.

References and Further Reading

Arrow, K.J. 'Uncertainty and the Welfare Economics of Medical Care'. *The American Economic Review*, vol. 53, no. 5 (1963): pp. 941–973. https://www.jstor.org/stable/1812044.

Boyle et al. 'Projection of the year 2050 burden of diabetes in the US adult population: dynamic modeling of incidence, mortality, and prediabetes prevalence'. *Population Health Metrics*, 2010. https://pophealthmetrics.biomedcentral.com/articles/10.1186/1478-7954-8-29.

Brooks, D. 'Do Markets Work in Health Care?' *The New York Times*, 2017. https://www.nytimes.com/2017/01/13/opinion/do-markets-work-in-health-care.html.

Capestany, C. et al. 'How Singapore helped 90% of households to own their homes'. *Bloomberg*, 2018. https://www.bloomberg.com/news/videos/2018-08-30/how-singapore-helped-90-of-households-to-own-their-homes-video.

Carroll, A.E. and A. Frakt, A. 'What makes Singapore's health care so cheap?'. *The New York Times*, 2017. https://www.nytimes.com/2017/10/02/upshot/what-makes-singapores-health-care-so-cheap.html.

Chen, L.C. and K.H. Phua. 'Transferring Lessons from Singapore: An Art or a Science?' *The Lancet*, 2013. www.thelancet.com/journals/lancet/article/PIIS0140-6736(13)61921-2/fulltext.

Chin, M. '1 in 4 Americans refuse medical care because they can't afford it'. *New York Post*, 2017. https://nypost.com/2017/06/07/1-in-4-americans-refuse-medical-care-because-they-cant-afford-it/.

Coughlan, S. 'Pisa tests: Singapore top in global education rankings'. *BBC News*, 2016. https://www.bbc.com/news/education-38212070.

Cox, W.M. and R. Alm. 'How Are We Doing?'. *The American*, 2008. http://www.aei.org/publication/how-are-we-doing/.

Dow, N.T. *A Mandarin and the Making of Public Policy: Reflections of Ngiam Tong Dow* (Singapore: NUS Press, 2006).

Elkins, K. 'Here's how much the average family has saved for retirement at every age'. *CNBC*, 2017. https://www.cnbc.com/2017/04/07/how-much-the-average-family-has-saved-for-retirement-at-every-age.html.

Fried, L.P. 'How investing in public health could cure many health care problems'. *The Conversation*, 2017. https://theconversation.com/how-investing-in-public-health-could-cure-many-health-care-problems-84256.

George, C. *Singapore: The Air-Conditioned Nation Essays on the Politics of Comfort and Control, 1990-2000* (Singapore: Landmark Books, 2000).

Georgiev, P. et al. 'Health system financing: Iips for emerging markets'. *McKinsey & Company*, 2018. https://www.mckinsey.com/industries/healthcare-systems-and-services/our-insights/health-system-financing-tips-for-emerging-markets.

Haseltine, W. *Affordable excellence: The Singapore healthcare story: How to create and manage sustainable healthcare systems* (Washington, D.C.: Brookings Institution Press, 2013).

—— 'Singapore's Health Care Lessons for the U.S.'. *Brookings*, 2013. https://www.brookings.edu/blog/up-front/2013/05/06/singapores-health-care-lessons-for-the-u-s/.

Holmes, O. 'Singapore's ruling party batters opposition in huge election win'. *The Guardian*, 2015. https://www.theguardian.com/world/2015/sep/11/singapore-election-early-count-shows-ruling-party-in-strong-position.

'How Prescription Drug Prices Compare Internationally'. *The Wall Street Journal*, 2015. http://graphics.wsj.com/table/GlobalDrug_1201.

Koh, V. 'SGH to take responsibility, pay for treatment needed by infected patients'. *Today*, 2015. https://www.todayonline.com/singapore/sgh-take-responsibility-pay-treatment-needed-infected-patients.

Lai, L. 'Singapore risks hitting obesity rates of 15% in seven years'. *The Straits Times*, 2017. https://www.straitstimes.com/singapore/singapore-risks-hitting-obesity-rates-of-15-in-seven-years.

Levine-Rasky, C. 'Don't blame seniors for rising healthcare costs'. *Canadian Dimension*, 2018. https://canadiandimension.com/articles/view/dont-blame-seniors-for-rising-healthcare-costs.

Lim, J. *Myth or Magic: The Singapore Healthcare System* (Singapore: Select Publishing, 2013).

Lim. L.Y.C. 'Singapore's success: After the Miracle', in *Handbook of Emerging Economies* ed. R.E. Looney (Abingdon, UK; New York: Routledge, 2014).

Mahbubani, K. *Can Singapore Survive?* (Singapore: Straits Times Press, 2015).

Ministry of Health. 'Medisave Accounts and Balances, Annual', 2016. https://data.gov.sg/dataset/medisave-accounts-and-balances-annual.

Murgia, M. 'How smartphones are transforming healthcare'. *Financial Times*, 2017. https://www.ft.com/content/1efb95ba-d852-11e6-944b-e7eb37a6aa8e.

Nicholls, A. and A. Pannelay, A. 'Health outcomes and cost: a 166-country comparison'. *The Economist Intelligence Unit Healthcare*, 2014. https://stateofreform.com/wp-content/uploads/2015/11/Healthcare-outcomes-index-2014.pdf.

Paddock, C. 'Prices for hip replacement in US vary hugely'. *Medical News Today*, 2013. https://www.medicalnewstoday.com/articles/256222.php.

Ping, H.K. *The Ocean In A Drop: The Next Fifty Years*, Ips-Nathan Lecture Series (Singapore: World Scientific Publishing Company, 2015).

Pollack, A. 'Drug goes from $13.50 a tablet to $750, overnight'. *The New York Times*, 2015. https://www.nytimes.com/2015/09/21/business/a-huge-overnight-increase-in-a-drugs-price-raises-protests.html.

'Preventive Health Care'. *Centers for Disease Control and Prevention, CDC*, 2017. https://www.cdc.gov/healthcommunication/toolstemplates/entertainmented/tips/PreventiveHealth.html.

'Price changes in consumer goods and services in the USA', 1997-2017', *Our World in Data*, 2017. https://ourworldindata.org/grapher/price-changes-in-consumer-goods-and-services-in-the-usa-1997-2017.

Reid, T.R. *The Healing of America: A Global Quest for Better, Cheaper, and Fairer Health Care* (New York: The Penguin Press, 2009).

Robb, G. 'Nobel economist takes aim at rent-seeking banking and healthcare industries'. *Market Watch*, 2017. https://www.marketwatch.com/story/nobel-economist-takes-aim-at-rent-seeking-banking-and-healthcare-industries-2017-03-06.

Robles, P. 'Ban on consumer ads could make pharma's digital shortcomings more costly'. *Econsultancy*, 2015. https://econsultancy.com/ban-on-consumer-ads-could-make-pharma-s-digital-shortcomings-more-costly/.

Schwab, K. et al. 'The Global Competitiveness Report 2018'. *World Economic Forum*, 2018. http://reports.weforum.org/global-competitiveness-report-2018/.

Sims, A. 'Singapore ranked world's healthiest country, UK fails to make top 20'. *Independent*, 2015. https://www.independent.co.uk/life-style/health-and-families/health-news/singapore-ranked-worlds-healthiest-country-uk-fails-to-make-top-20-a6716281.html.

Song, K.B. *Brand Singapore: How Nation Branding Built Asia's Leading Global City* (Singapore: Marshall Cavendish, 2011).

'The Singapore exception". *The Economist*, 2015. https://www.economist.com/special-report/2015/07/18/the-singapore-exception.

Stempel, J. 'Buffet: Health care "tapeworm" drags on economy'. *Reuters*, 2010. https://www.reuters.com/article/us-berkshire-buffett/buffett-health-care-tapeworm-drags-on-economy-idUSTRE62022120100301.

'The $272 billion swindle'. *The Economist*, 2014. https://www.economist.com/united-states/2014/05/31/the-272-billion-swindle.

Topol, E. *The Patient Will See You Now: The Future of Medicine Is In Your Hands* (New York: Basic Books, 2015).

'What are the risk factors for lung cancer?' *Centers for Disease Control and Prevention, CDC*, 2018. https://www.cdc.gov/cancer/lung/basic_info/risk_factors.htm.

Wilson, M.R. 'Lobbying's top 50: who's spending big'. *The Hill*, 2017. https://thehill.com/business-a-lobbying/business-a-lobbying/318177-lobbyings-top-50-whos-spending-big.

Yew, L.K. *From Third World to First: The Singapore Story: 1965- 2000* (New York: Harper Collins, 2000).

——*Hard Truths to Keep Singapore Going* (Singapore: Straits Times Press, 2011).

——*One Man's View of the World* (Singapore: Straits Times Press, 2013).

——*The Singapore Story: Memoirs of Lee Kuan Yew*. Student edition (Singapore: Marshall Cavendish; Straits Times Press, 2015).

Conversations and Interviews

Aloysius Chia Wei-Yan, David Blumenthal, Kishore Mahbubani, Phua Kai Hong, Tommy Koh, Vikram Khanna, Kishore Mahbubani, and Lim Siong Guan.

11

Ireland: The Celtic Tiger

Ireland's ascent as the rising star of Europe

The Bridge of Tears in County Donegal, Ireland

Source: Wikimedia Commons

> But then, once in a lifetime
> The longed-for tidal wave
> Of justice can rise up,
> And hope and history rhyme.
>
> —*Seamus Heaney (The Cure at Troy)*

Across the Irish countryside, a familiar scene played out throughout the nineteenth century. Anxious travellers, many in their teens, travelled to the nearest train station in the company of weeping relatives and neighbours. A long voyage lay ahead, as they set off for distant lands – America, Australia, Canada – in the hope of escaping crushing poverty and famine. Loved ones often trailed behind them as far as a local landmark, such as the small stone bridge in west County Donegal on the road to Londonderry Port. The bridge, located just outside the town of Falcarragh, is called 'The Bridge of Tears' – Droichead na Caointe. This walk had the finality of a funeral. People would leave behind their family and their loved ones; the chances of parents ever seeing their children again were minimal as the journey was long, dangerous and expensive. Many who crossed the bridge never made it to their destinations, dying of sickness and disease on ships transporting them in ghastly conditions.

During most of Ireland's rich yet isolated history, its most popular export was its people. They left not by choice but out of dire necessity. The joke was that the view of Ireland which most Irish knew best was the one looking back from a boat sailing away from places like the Londonderry Port.

Unlike the nascent countries like Israel and Singapore and consistently successful countries like Denmark and Switzerland, the Irish story is different. It is a story of revival, recompense and deliverance. In a short span of time, a country which for hundreds of years was infamous for famines, civil wars, tragic poets and leprechauns, managed to turn its fortunes around and become the 'Celtic Tiger'.

Not very long ago, most observers had written off Ireland as a failed nation – the kind which causes IMF officials sleepless nights, or which features in popular books like *Why Nations Fail*. The country languished in a deadly mix of negligible growth, high unemployment, rampant inflation, heavy taxation and enormous public debt. Ireland is a rare story of a prematurely developed country waking from a deep hibernation and emerging as the European Union's tiger, growing at a pace similar to that of the prosperous small countries in the Far East. Three decades ago, Ireland's GDP per capita was around two-thirds of Britain's. Today, it is more than 57 per cent higher.

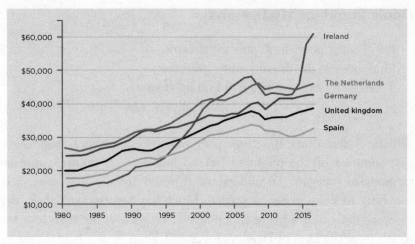

Figure 11.1: The Celtic Tiger: Growth in GDP Per Capita

This graph shows how Ireland has increased its GDP at an incredible rate over the past few years, bypassing its Euro neighbours.

Source: World Bank, 2017

Ireland's sudden economic surge has perplexed researchers, forecasters and sceptics around the world, and has attracted a steady flow of experts from places such as Bratislava, Tel Aviv and Vilnius, who are keen to understand and, more importantly, emulate Ireland's progress. Mapping Ireland's ascent provides valuable data for governments around the globe. How could this nation rise up, and so quickly? Many developed countries, struggling with stagnating wages and increasing youth unemployment – including Ireland's troubled neighbours in western Europe – would love to raise their game as Ireland has. This chapter tries to understand the factors which form the 'beating heart' of the Celtic Tiger. It also discusses the lessons from Ireland's economic boom and offers a method for replication and making it last.

* * *

Don't Tread on My Dreams

> But I, being poor, have only my dreams;
> I have spread my dreams under your feet;
> Tread softly because you tread on my dreams.
>   —W. B. Yeats, *The Cloths of Heaven*

William Butler Yeats, the iconic poet and voice of Ireland, might have best summed up the plight of Ireland before its breakneck journey to modernity began. To understand how far Ireland has come, it is necessary to know where it started. Much has been written about the Irish economy and a lot of it is polemic. For many, the Irish love for words from the likes of Heaney, Joyce and Yeats was only matched by their disdain for action. Many jested that the Irish were best at feeling sorry for themselves and their literary giants provided a steady fodder of tragedy and endless regret.

That Ireland would be an archetype of strong economic growth was never anticipated. On the contrary, the country seemed imprisoned in its own unfortunate legacy and stereotype. Fatalism and resignation prevailed over action and perseverance. While most countries were jolted out of their slumber by the Protestant Reformation, or honed their national pride and expanded their political reach and intellectual curiosity because of colonialization, Ireland remained stubbornly insular and avoided reaping the benefits of modernity. A succession of occupiers from the Vikings to the Elizabethans and the Edwardians stunted the island's economic growth, while the Catholic Church kept its grip on Irish hearts and minds for more than a thousand years.

Increasingly, the nation grew to define itself in terms of victimhood and inferiority in relation to Great Britain. When its much bigger neighbour was not subjecting Ireland to physical domination, it was wounding the nation's fragile pride with arrogance and ridicule.

Like a Four-Act Play

The Irish narrative appears on several fronts like a four-act play. Firstly, there is the height and the speed with which it rose from the ashes. In the 1970s, Ireland was one of Europe's poorest countries. Today, it is more prosperous than the average European Union country, and getting richer.

Secondly, Ireland is for many the poster child of globalization. It emerged as a rising star in the 1980s when globalization was just taking hold. Most countries in a similar state started with low-cost labour industry, such as textiles, and worked their way up the value chain to the more fruitful manufacturing and services industry. Ireland leap-frogged this conventional path by becoming a base for the world's most successful and forward-thinking companies such as Apple Inc., Facebook, eBay and Google. It realized that there was value in attracting multinational companies, providing them with schools, low-cost and well-educated workers, logistic infrastructure and a low-tax regime.

It zeroed in on the most promising sectors. While pharmaceutical and medical devices were obvious choices, others, such as the online retail giant Amazon and India's largest computer software services firm Infosys, showed interest. These big corporates allocate capital and talent around the world as if it were a giant chessboard. Obviously, the corporates don't look at everything with the same intensity and not all decisions are well-vetted. But their criteria are remarkably similar and the Irish single-mindedly set out to meet those criteria. They learned early on that a thirty-three-year-old geek in Palo Alto ticked the same boxes, whether it was Adobe or Zalando evaluating a move.

Martin Shanahan, Chief Executive Officer of the Industrial Development Agency (IDA), Ireland – the branch of the government devoted to attracting investment – believes the key to Ireland's success has been the ability to get an anchor tenant and make it as happy as possible. That company then becomes the best salesperson the country could have, since few foreign companies are likely to make a choice to move without first consulting their peers. If it was good enough for Apple, it would probably be good enough for Amazon, the story went. And these giant corporates came to Ireland in droves. Apple arrived in 1980 followed by Intel in 1989 and Amazon in 2005 (Donnelly 2013), and Ireland was spontaneously beavering away at building clusters. This created a critical mass of services and personnel in the country.

Building new businesses or inventing new products has never been an Irish strength. The country has thrived by attracting well-established companies to use Ireland as a stepping stone to pursue their growth aspirations. By 2016, one out of five workers in Ireland was an employee of a foreign multinational company (Burke-Kennedy 2016). Without these jobs, Ireland's unemployment rate would have been comparable to Spain's 23 per cent.

Indeed, in the 1980s, when globalization began, Ireland's economy resembled Portugal's or Spain's. The part of the economy indigenous to Ireland remained relatively underdeveloped. Comparative statistics suggest that when it comes to patent generation, new business formation and venture investing, the Irish are not especially innovative or entrepreneurial. They may be energetic and enthusiastic but they seem to lack the steadfast work ethic of the Swiss, Scandinavians or Singaporeans. Irish infrastructure is average; the country lacks a train to its main airport and its harbour is sufficient only as a feeder hub, but not more. Spouses of multinational executives prefer to live and raise their children in Switzerland. 'It rains a lot,' commented the wife of one of Apple's Irish production plant managers in Cork.

Thirdly, while Euro-scepticism remains popular, Ireland has thrived on unapologetic euro-enthusiasm. The Sergei Brins and Mark Zuckerbergs of this world saw an entry into Ireland as an easy access to the European single market – the most sizeable one after their home market. Many continental Europeans can be reserved and stiff, and the nonchalant and friendly Irish suited the Californian mindset. Yeats' words – 'There are no strangers, only friends you have not met yet' – fit well into this context.

A well-qualified and English-speaking human capital was yet another significant advantage. Most of the men and women between their late twenties and early thirties had tertiary educational qualifications, which was good to meet the needs of the foreign multinationals. A sound education system no doubt facilitated adaptability and provided impetus to the job market created by the arrival of these multinationals. Consider Intel Ireland, the country's largest employer and a major contributor to its soaring economy. It started in 1989 with a low-cost manufacturing plant. Today, more than 4,500 people work at its Leixlip campus and, in 2014, the company announced a $5 billion investment to upgrade its manufacturing capability to state-of-the-art, making it the largest private investment in the history of the Irish State (Intel 2019).

Fourthly, an important and quite remarkable feat is that Ireland managed to do all this while dealing with the instability brought on by the neighboring conflict in Northern Ireland. Reconciliation and negotiating peace is tough, and yet twenty-five years of painstaking diplomacy by leaders on both sides of the sectarian divide has largely put an end to the violence which disfigured the island since Northern Ireland was created in 1921. Peace has boosted the economy of the whole of Ireland. The leaders of a growing number of countries with intractable geopolitical conflicts may wish to study this.

Punching above Its Weight

So, what has been the secret of Ireland's rags-to-riches story? Brendan Walsh, the distinguished professor of economics at University College Dublin, summed it up succinctly to me over the phone: 'The Irish boom has been led by a favourable tax regime; compelling demographics; a low-cost and educated labour force; and a concentration on attracting industries with genuine growth prospects' (Interview 2015).

Let us examine these factors briefly, one at a time.

Favourable Tax Regime

Ireland's economic progress was fuelled by its robust fiscal policy. The case of its low-tax regime, which was the main attraction for the foreign capital, is indispensable to understanding the country's growth.

Most governments have complex relationships with important companies. They see them as a source of taxes, but also as a source of jobs; so they must be careful not to kill the goose which lays golden eggs. The emergence of large, essentially rootless, multinational companies has changed the dynamics of government–industry relationships – and not in governments' favour. Ever since the supremacy of the shareholder took hold, the interests of multinationals and governments have been diametrically opposite. A dollar of saved taxes means a dollar of increased dividends, or vice versa. So, multinationals employ the world's brightest tax experts and view them as profit centres. They are tasked with scouring the world to reduce the corporation's overall tax burden.

For countries dependent on stable revenues from their industries, it is difficult to attract such companies. But for Ireland, it was easy. It had no indigenous industry to worry about hurting or insulting when it offered newcomers attractive deals. While the corporate tax rate is officially just 12.5 per cent, it is often far lower in practice thanks to bespoke deals with the bigger multinationals. These firms set up subsidiaries in Ireland which own patents, licences and other intellectual property. Subsidiaries in countries with higher tax rates pay royalties to the Irish subsidiary as a means of shifting profits from high to low tax jurisdictions. Since most governments only tax profits earned in their respective countries, this transfer of profits lets big companies avoid paying tax in jurisdictions with higher rates.

Of course, there are other considerations like political stability, language and the need to be close to customers. But a jurisdiction is unlikely to make it through the vetting process and receive approvals from the multinational boards unless it has competitive tax rates.

The results for Ireland were startling. It recorded massive trade surpluses with the rest of the world – about 14 per cent of GDP from 1995 through 2014 (Klein 2016).

This tax competition has become hugely contentious and governments are now trying hard to make pacts not to undercut each other. Donald Trump has made this a focus of policy reforms. In August 2016, the European Commission ordered Ireland to collect €13 billion ($14.7 billion), a sum almost equal to 6 per cent of its annual GDP, in unpaid taxes from Apple (*Economist* 2016). The Commission contended that Apple pursued unacceptable tactics allowing it to shrink its tax rate in Europe to well below 1 per cent. The European Commission is also considering questionable structures set up by several other (mostly American) firms, including Starbucks and McDonald's. While Apple is appealing the case, all this begs the question as to whether such benefits are sustainable for a country in the long term. We will revisit this issue later in this chapter.

Demographics

We opened this chapter by observing that, historically, Ireland was best at exporting its young workers. Ironically, these former exports, or

Irish diaspora, have now become an extended workforce and a source of its comparative advantage. With a population of just 4.8 million, Ireland is a small country, roughly comparable in terms of workforce to Chicago or Sydney. However, for every one of these workers, there are around fifteen people of Irish descent living around the globe. In Australia, 10 per cent of the population claims Irish ancestry. The figure is even higher in Canada, where 13 per cent of the population has Irish roots. In the US, a staggering thirty-five million people claim some Irish ancestry (Haynie 2016). So it is no surprise that American firms advertise in Boston and San Francisco to fill vacancies in their Irish businesses.

A nation's output is a product of its people and productivity. Ireland continues to benefit from several aspects of its demographics compared to its peers in Europe. Unlike most of Europe, which is ageing, Ireland has a young population and one of the lowest proportions of over-sixty-five-year-olds (O'Doherty 2015). Until the 1980s, female participation in the workforce was low by international standards; today it is above average. On the same estimates, youth and women account for half of Ireland's growth since the 1990s (Sherry interview).[13]

With youth comes mobility. The unique feature is the migratory nature of Ireland's workforce, which serves as a kind of economic safety-valve. People leave in bad times and come back in good. A company's workforce is normally a fixed cost, so profits tend to be tied to business cycles as there are both delays and reluctance in adjusting staff levels. Ireland has a considerably more fluid and variable workforce. Between 2000 and 2015, the total size of the workforce was nearly stable, but 80 per cent of workers moved either in or out (National Competitiveness Council 2016, p. 116).

Build and They Will Come

The Industrial Development Agency (IDA) of Ireland is like a marketing machine with nineteen offices around the world and a staff of 250

---

13. In 1981, 30 per cent of the female population (over the age of fifteen) was working. By 2016, the figure had nearly doubled to 56 per cent (World Bank 2017). Women accounted for a considerable portion of Ireland's economic growth over this period.

organized around the five most promising sectors such as healthcare, social media and financial services. It encourages companies to establish their operations in Ireland. As wages rose, IDA was able to attract companies that could offer higher paying jobs, focusing on software, financial services, personal computers, pharmaceuticals and medical devices. Ireland has attracted enormous sums as investments in relation to the size of its economy. According to OECD, direct investment in Ireland from America alone was $10 billion at the end of 1994, that is, $3,000 per head. American investment in France and Germany was $500 per head. In Spain, it was just $200 per head (*Economist* 1997).

When Dr Vishal Sikka, the Chief Executive Officer and Managing Director of Infosys, announced that Infosys would establish its first overseas R&D centre in Dublin, he stated in grandiose terms, 'With an ecosystem of like-minded partners in Ireland, we will pursue new ideas and new ways to solve the greatest challenges of our times – the important things that only human imagination and ingenuity can achieve' (Infosys 2015). The decision made by Infosys was noteworthy, not because it would create 250 high-end innovation jobs, but for the message it sent.

Infosys' story, strange as it might seem, is comparable to that of Ireland. Narayana Murthy started Infosys in 1981, about the same time that Ireland woke from its slumber. Roll the clock forward and Infosys is now the poster child of Indian pride and prosperity with over $11.54 billion in annual revenues and more than 225,000 employees (Infosys 2019). This has been achieved largely by working smarter than Western companies. So, choosing to deploy capital and talent in Ireland is an important step for anyone seeking efficiencies in either or both of them.

Infosys was just one in a long line of computer companies which chose Ireland as a beachhead to the Eurozone. IBM, Intel, Gateway, Dell, Fujitsu, Motorola and other leaders of the computer and electronics industries built new facilities in Ireland (Donnelly 2013). IDA claims that nearly a third of the personal computers sold in Europe are now made in Ireland and that the country has received 40 per cent of all American investment in European electronics since 1980 (*Economist* 1997). New investment has also poured into other sectors of the economy, especially food processing, pharmaceuticals and telemarketing.

Ireland has about 300 foreign biopharma companies. Thirteen of the top fifteen global biopharma companies – including Amgen, Eli Lilly, Merck and Roche – operate in Ireland (*Silicon Republic* 2016). The pharma sector makes up over 50 per cent of all exports and provides a steady supply of well-paid, skilled jobs. In 2014, this was valued at $64 billion, making Ireland the largest net exporter of pharmaceuticals in the EU (Shahid 2017). Merck has, for example, invested more than $2.5 billion (Burke 2017). Ireland has become a base for a new class of drugs called biologics which have an attractive potential as the first generation of products using biotechnology come off patent.

Ireland has also attracted international banks and other financial institutions. Dublin's International Financial Services Centre is home to back-office data processing operations of many banks and brokerage firms such as Citibank, Merrill Lynch, Daiwa, ABN Amro and 400 others.

To the Brink and Back

Recognition was late in coming. In 1988, the *Economist*, in its characteristically patronizing fashion, published a survey about Ireland entitled 'The poorest of the rich'. And in 1997, Ireland featured on the *Economist*'s cover as 'Europe's shining light' (*Economist* 2004). But just as prosperity was lightening the burdens of history, and Irish diaspora and those at home started walking with a swagger, the classic Irish tragedy yet again reared its head. Ireland faced the worst economic crisis of its history.

We have heard the same refrain so many times. Banks, industrialists and politicians became overconfident and megalomania and greed set in, feeding a speculative frenzy driven by irresponsible banks and real estate developers, all in a cosy relationship with leading politicians. This orgy was all financed with huge borrowings by Irish banks, largely dependent on funding from banks in other European nations. Banks threw money to consumers with great laxity. Private sector debt increased from €135 million (US$151 million) in 2003 to nearly three times that level in 2008 (*Irish Times* 2018). Banks saw their balance sheets swell and collateral equity ratios decline, so even a minor correction in asset value could wipe them out.

And that is just what happened. By late 2010, property prices had collapsed and banks were teetering on the brink of disaster. Jobs were haemorrhaging, with almost 20 per cent of private sector employment wiped out. Yields on Irish ten-year bonds rose to over 15 per cent, with speculation that the country might be forced to default or even leave the Euro (Kenny 2015). Locked out of the bond markets, Ireland was forced into a humiliating acceptance of a €67.5 billion (US$75.3 billion) EU-International Monetary Fund rescue in 2010 (Kenny 2015).

As in other parts of the world, bank managements and boards of directors were not held accountable or subjected to any fines or jail terms due to impropriety or failure to exercise proper diligence as stewards. The Irish government was forced to step in to guarantee the banks' debts, turning private losses into public obligations.

Before the bank collapse, Ireland had little public debt. It had spent the previous decade reducing public debt by nearly half, from 120 per cent to 68 per cent of GDP while converting a budget deficit of 32 per cent of GDP to a small surplus (*Trading Economics* 2018). But with taxpayers suddenly responsible for the huge bank losses, the nation's creditworthiness was in doubt. Ireland tried to reassure the markets by undertaking a draconian programme of spending cuts. From 2008 to 2014, successive Irish governments took $38 billion spending out of the economy, or nearly 17 per cent of GDP (*Economist* 2013). Lacking its own currency, it was unable to devalue to become more competitive.

The country, so close to ruin, has since come a long way. Unlike most countries which chose, in similar circumstances, to kick the can down the road, Ireland embraced austerity and succeeded. Zombie banks were closed, and those that remained were restructured. Public sector wages were cut, services rationalized and new taxes introduced to broaden the revenue base. In total, Ireland delivered a fiscal consolidation of over 18 per cent of GDP (Kenny 2015). Along with other measures, this helped reassure investors, markets and the Irish people that the government was serious about fixing its economic problems.

And it worked. Per capita GDP has increased some 40 per cent since the crisis and now exceeds the 2007 level (CEIC Data 2018). The country can raise funds in the markets at record low interest rates. During the past three years, Ireland was one of the fastest-growing countries in the

Eurozone and unemployment has fallen by a third, bringing it below the Eurozone average (Whelan 2018).

Nevertheless, legacies from the crisis remain. Government debt to GDP is burdening the next generation and offers the country little room to manoeuvre if it confronts a new crisis. During the housing bubble, too many homes were built in the wrong places thanks to sloppy urban planning. As the recovery builds, commercial space and housing are in short supply, putting pressure on prices. Transportation also reflects a certain short-sightedness – from unconnected tramlines to an on-and-off plan for a metro and the absence of a train connection between Dublin airport and the city.

Following Ireland's trampoline-like rebound, investors and its people have regained confidence in the country's prospects and its leadership. But many observers remain cautious. Ireland's past provides several painful reminders of how hard-won economic progress and credibility can be easily reversed by policy errors or external potholes. In the past, Ireland's growth trajectory was thwarted by the two oil shocks of the 1970s, and even more by the unsuitable policy response when the government sought to offset the cut in living standards imposed by higher oil prices through fiscal and monetary expansion. The result was the high inflation, high unemployment, slow growth and even electoral instability which marred the 1980s.

Happily Ever After

The fourth and final act of the classic Irish play is the scene when the hero, now unencumbered by his or her flaws and fully exposed to the audience, metaphorically climbs into the ring to duel with the opponent to see who will triumph in the end. Few will disagree that Ireland's development has been both transformational and spectacular. If any country lends substance to the cliché that the global economy is an opportunity and not a threat, it is Ireland. Ireland is proof that globalization is the fastest road to prosperity. Could an open, creative Ireland be an example to follow at a time when other countries are beginning to turn inwards?

Sceptics might say that its success is built on a fragile substrate of tax dodges for multinationals and subsidies from Europe. Some might argue that the country is prone to hiccups and that it is only a matter of time before it blunders again. How much longer will the Irish model deliver such striking success? It is difficult to say.

After thirty years of boom, Ireland has lost a good bit of its low-cost advantage. The benefits of emancipating women and including them in the work force have largely played out. There are many of Silicon Valley's greatest successes in its burgeoning industrial base, but technology can be fickle. Polaroid and Digital Equipment invested in Ireland during the 1960s, lured by the country's low costs and zero corporate tax. But by the 1990s they were gone.

Finally, there appears to be a global attack on tax havens from all sides, including OECD, European Union and the US, so an industrial strategy which depends largely on low taxes would seem inappropriate. While Ireland will fight this, it seems a matter of time before the playing field regarding taxes is levelled. Dan O'Brien, author of *Ireland, Europe and the World*, warns that without Ireland's foreign companies, it would be as closed and poor as Greece.

Herein may lie Ireland's opportunity. Ireland's economic success is a tale of two economies – a still-backward, unproductive and labour-intensive one owned by the Irish, and a modern, exceptionally productive and capital-intensive one owned by foreigners. To prolong Ireland's success, higher productivity will be needed from the poorer half of its economy. Ireland must play to its strengths. Its economy is exceptionally open to trade and investment. It has a young, English-speaking population and a remarkably flexible labour market. It has a star-studded cast of foreign industrial investors for locals to work with, raise its education standards and even learn the jargon and vernacular of its investors.

The dislocation caused by the UK's departure from the EU may throw up opportunities. Ireland has a solid cluster of financial service companies, such as Citigroup, JP Morgan and Northern Trust. It offers a more cost-effective substitute to London for those concerned about being a part of the European Union. 'There isn't going to be a new London, but Ireland will win new business,' says Susan Dargan, country head in Ireland of State Street, the US bank which employs 3,000 people in Ireland (Boland 2017). After all, wages are much lower than in London. Average wages at Google Ireland are **£72,000** (US$90,600) compared with an average of £160,000 (US$201,000) in London, and Cushman and Wakefield reports that office costs are 75 per cent lower (Bowers 2016).

We should recognize that Ireland's success did not happen by accident. Successive governments have stayed the course and presented Ireland as a stable, dependable partner with coherent and sensible policies. Ireland looks, probably for the first time in its history, politically attractive. As large countries with dominant two-party systems lurch radically from one side to the other with successive elections, Ireland appears more grounded. Unlike most countries, there does not seem to be much debate between 'left' and 'right'. In Ireland, those labels mean nothing. The two main parties, Fine Gael (which leads the ruling coalition) and Fianna Fail (in opposition), draw their identity not from any alignment with social or economic classes, but from the fact that their founders fell out with each other over the treaty with Britain in 1921.

Figure 11.2: The Pot of Gold

Source: Banx

Conclusion

For all of Ireland's progress, it is still too early to conclude whether its prosperity can last. Obviously, higher productivity is needed. The lowest hanging fruit has been plucked and there is intense competition for new foreign investment from many other countries. The relative costs and benefits are continuously calculated. A low tax policy, one of the four pedestals of the Irish model, looks to be distinctly out of favour.

Ireland would do well to raise the performance of its indigenous economy and reduce the dependence on decisions made in Palo Alto. It has an excellent ecosystem of the world's best companies competing in the most attractive sectors to show it the way. So, Ireland still has wind in its sails. If only it could learn to spawn off companies in a manner which California does, or could devise a way to genetically clone the likes of Elon with Irish stem cells. Part of the country's future success depends on developing its own home-grown technology rather than merely serving as a landlord for others. The Collison brothers from rural Ireland developed a novel payment technology called 'Stripe' used by the likes of Amazon and Apple to settle online purchases. The company, now worth $9.2 billion, makes Patrick, 29, and John, 27, two of the world's youngest billionaires (Metcalf 2016). But Stripe is an American company and not an Irish one. The Irish diaspora has returned, but real progress awaits the day when Irish ingenuity follows the same path.

Ireland has set the stage for the Irish to pursue their futures at home. It is now a place where people are 'crossing the bridge' to return rather than to leave. Far from being insular, it is outward-looking with the highest percentage of exports amongst the European countries. The country has earned the respect of those who used to poke fun at it and, as the *Economist* summarized in 2004, 'has far more clout than its small population might suggest'. Mary Robinson was its first woman President (1990–1997) and she then served as the United Nations High Commissioner for Human Rights. Europeans were impressed by the Irish presidency of the European Union in 1997, which oversaw not only the eastward expansion of the EU and the choice of a new commission president, but also a deal on a new EU constitutional treaty, brokered by the Irish Taoiseach (prime minister) (*Economist* 2004).

Who would have predicted twenty years ago that Ireland would be led by an openly gay prime minister of Indian extraction, barely forty years old, who championed same-sex marriage and abolished the nation's rigid law against abortion? In just one generation, Ireland has morphed into a forward-thinking nation that leads, rather than lags behind, its peers in Europe.

Remnants of condescension have faded with every strain of progress. Less concerned about political or geographical constructs, the country has realized that its lifeline is its ability to attract the best and brightest companies competing in the most promising sectors of technology. In this sense, it looks at Singapore, Israel and Switzerland as its competitors more than members of the EU.

Yeats, in his infinite Irish wisdom, once said, 'We are happy when we are growing.' If Ireland can continue to grow as it has during the past generation, this would truly be a miracle. And if the Irish spirit is any indication, grow it will. Today, Ireland feels like a proud, redeemed and respected nation that defines itself in relation to the EU, an association of nations in which it is recognized by some as an equal and by others even as a superior.

References and Further Reading

Boland, V. 'Ireland braced for economic uncertainty of Brexit'. *Financial Times*, 2017. https://www.ft.com/content/5b039b18-e1a6-11e6-8405-9e5580d6e5fb.

Bowers, S. 'Google Ireland staff paid much less than London colleagues'. *The Guardian*, 2016. https://www.theguardian.com/technology/2016/feb/07/google-ireland-staff-paid-less-than-half-their-london-colleagues.

Burke, E. 'Ireland is a home for 24 of the world's top biotech and pharma companies'. *Silicon Republic*, 2017. https://www.siliconrepublic.com/careers/biotech-pharma-companies-ireland.

Burke-Kennedy, E. 'One-in-five now employed by foreign multinationals'. *The Irish Times*, 2016. https://www.irishtimes.com/business/economy/one-in-five-now-employed-by-foreign-multinationals-1.2486929.

Donnelly, P. 'How foreign firms transformed Ireland's domestic economy'. *The Irish Times*, 2013. https://www.irishtimes.com/business/how-foreign-firms-transformed-ireland-s-domestic-economy-1.1593462.

'Female labor force participation rates, 2016 vs 1980'. *Our World in Data, World Bank*, 2017. https://ourworldindata.org/female-labor-force-participation-key-facts.

'Figure 6.3.6. Net Migration (000s), 2000-2015'. *Ireland's Competitiveness Scorecard 2016, National Competitiveness Council*, 2016. http://www. competitiveness.ie/publications/2016/ics-2016.pdf.

'GDP per capita growth (annual %)'. *The World Bank*, 2017. https://data. worldbank.org/indicator/NY.GDP.PCAP.KD.ZG.

'Green is good'. *The Economist*, 1997. https://www.economist.com/ special/1997/05/15/green-is-good.

Haynie, D. '10 countries with the most Irish emigrants'. *U.S. News*, 2016. https://www.usnews.com/news/best-countries/articles/2016-03-17/10-countries-with-the-most-irish-emigrants.

'Infosys Banks on Ireland for FinTech Expertise'. *Infosys*, 2015. https://www. infosys.com/newsroom/press-releases/Pages/fintech-research-development. aspx.

'Infosys Digital Navigation Framework'. *Infosys*, 2019. https://www.infosys. com/about/pages/index.aspx.

'Intel Leixlip'. *Intel*, 2019. https://www.intel.ie/content/www/ie/en/company-overview/intel-leixlip.html.

'Ireland GDP per capita'. *CEIC, CEIC Data*, 2018. https://www.ceicdata.com/ en/indicator/ireland/gdp-per-capita.

'Ireland Government Debt to GDP'. *Trading Economics*, 2018. https:// tradingeconomics.com/ireland/government-debt-to-gdp.

Kenny, E. 'How Ireland pulled back from the brink'. *World Economic Forum*, 2015. https://www.weforum.org/agenda/2015/01/how-ireland-pulled-back-from-the-brink/.

Klein, M.C. 'Placing Ireland's economic "recovery" in context'. *Financial Times*, 2016. https://ftalphaville.ft.com/2016/07/14/2169550/placing-irelands-economic-recovery-in-context/.

Metcalf, T. 'Stripe Founders Are Youngest Irish Billionaires with Funding'. *Bloomberg*, 2016. https://www.bloomberg.com/news/articles/2016-11-28/ stripe-founders-are-youngest-irish-billionaires-on-new-valuation.

O'Brien, D. *Ireland, Europe and the World: Writings on a New Century* (Dublin: Gill and Macmillan, 2009).

O'Doherty, C. 'Ireland's population is youngest in the EU'. *Irish Examiner*, 2015. https://www.irishexaminer.com/ireland/irelands-population-is-youngest-in-the-eu-369301.html.

'Outstanding private sector loans'. *The Irish Times*, 2018. https://www.irishtimes.com/business/economy/the-crash-10-years-on-from-wreckage-to-recovery-of-sorts-in-six-charts-1.3346380?mode=sample&auth-failed=1&pw-origin=https%3A%2F%2Fwww.irishtimes.com%2Fbusiness%2Feconomy%2Fthe-crash-10-years-on-from-wreckage-to-recovery-of-sorts-in-six-charts-1.3346380.

Shahid, A. 'Ireland's Economic Backbone: The Pharmaceutical Industry'. *University Observer*, 2017. https://universityobserver.ie/irelands-economic-backbone-the-pharmaceutical-industry/.

'The eighth austerity budget'. *The Economist*, 2013. https://www.economist.com/europe/2013/10/19/the-eighth-austerity-budget.

'The luck of the Irish'. *The Economist*, 2004. https://www.economist.com/special-report/2004/10/14/the-luck-of-the-irish.

'13 biopharma companies making their own luck in Ireland'. *Silicon Republic*, 2016. https://www.siliconrepublic.com/jobs/biopharma-companies-ireland-list.

'Upsetting the Apple cart'. *The Economist*, 2016. https://www.economist.com/europe/2016/09/08/upsetting-the-apple-cart.

Whelan, S. 'Ireland fastest growing economy in European Union again with growth of 7.8%'. *RTE*, 2018. https://www.rte.ie/news/business/2018/0315/947638-cso-gdp-figures/.

Conversations and Interviews

Professor Brendan Walsh, Kevin Sherry, Denis O'Brien, Colm McLoughlin, Michael Smurfit, Dermot Desmond, Michael O'Leary, and Martin Shanahan.

12

Denmark: Copenhagenization

Denmark's bold attempt to redefine living while preserving its environment

The Bicycle Capital

Source: Banx

For one year now, he had been sitting in the same spot every day, from morning to noon, carefully observing, measuring and mapping how people used the space around them. Children chasing runaway balls, elderly people looking for their next place to rest, shopkeepers rearranging their windows to entice those passing by. The street, known to Copenhageners as 'Strøget', used to be a main thoroughfare for car traffic but was turned into the world's first pedestrian zone – perfect for people watching. The young man's name was Jan Gehl, an

202

up-and-coming Danish architect, and an unconventional professor at Copenhagen's Royal School of Architecture. Little did he know that his studies of people would become the foundation for urban development around the world.

On one of those chilly mornings in 1967, Gehl came to realize that cities had been increasingly designed and engineered to accommodate cars rather than people. People drove to the same place of work, usually alone, parked their cars in the same garage, took the same lift to their office, ate at the same cafeteria and then reversed the procedure on the way home, only to repeat the routine each day. Meanwhile, more time was spent sitting idly in traffic as the number of cars grew. New or wider roads sprung up to reduce congestion and buildings were erected to accommodate more parking. 'Copernicus should have said that it was cars, not the sun, that our lives revolved around,' Gehl thought.

In the 1960s, Copenhagen was a dreary city – heavily polluted and congested, with sulphur dioxide levels to rival London, New York or Stuttgart. At the same time, Denmark imported all of its energy and was coughing up the highest CO_2 emission rate in the developed world. By the 1980s, the city was on the brink of bankruptcy, the unemployment rate was above 17 per cent and the city was on the verge of losing its social cohesion and vitality (Katz and Nowak 2018, p. 121). A failed attempt to move families outside the city had left Copenhagen with mainly students and pensioners, which devastated the city's tax base.

Copenhagen's road to recovery and success was neither linear, nor without controversies along the way, but the local and national powers eventually rallied behind Jan Gehl's then radical urban planning ideas. He called cars the bete noir of humanistic city living, a battle that would become his life's work.

This chapter describes how Gehl, Copenhagen and Denmark went against the tide, how they took some bold choices about their future and stuck to them, and how those actions have ultimately paid off. The 2017 Smart Cities Index, which evaluates how prepared cities are to face the future through integrated planning, ranked Copenhagen first among 500 cities (Garfield 2017). And the city is set to become the world's first carbon neutral capital by 2025 (Københavns commune, no date). If this study is correct, Copenhagen has arrived at the future first. So how did it get there?

This is not a razzle-dazzle story about a novel, miraculous technology designed by iconic entrepreneurs like Steve Jobs, Jack Ma or Elon Musk. This is a fairly low-tech story about bikes, blades and batteries. As with most things in Denmark, it began with modest, blue collar workers. Characteristic of Danish achievement, it is a story of collective effort where the community has been the hero rather than an individual. In a world full of political divisiveness, it is a story about cohesion. Finally, and remarkably, it is also a story of how a government can be innovative and how the right policies can help create a profitable industry.

It begins with Gehl, pedestrians and bicycles.

* * *

Gehl's first maxim for restoring urban vitality was to re-design the city for people and not for cars. To succeed, he had to reduce the need and desirability of cars. A substitute was needed so he turned to bicycles. Little has changed in technology since the bicycle was invented in 1817 and nick-named the 'hobby horse'. Two wheels, a chain, a couple of pedals and a plastic seat – sometimes the best inventions are really that simple, and sometimes they are discovered by taking one technological step backwards.

Anyone who visits Copenhagen today can't help but notice the rivers of cyclists which fill the main arteries of the city and flow continuously through its many bike lanes. It is probably the closest one comes across on land to swimming in a vast school of fish. In a city of 613,000 people, 62 per cent pedal to work each day; together, they pedal 1.4 million kilometres a day (Weihe 2017).

On my visit there, I hired a bike and soon realized that everything seems to be within a brisk ten- to fifteen-minute ride. There is state-of-the-art infrastructure such as dedicated lanes, bridges exclusively for cyclists and special garages to park bikes in shopping centres. The traffic lights are synchronized to the average speed of cyclists so that motion is uninterrupted. As I painfully learned, deviations from an intricate code of hand signals and etiquette bring immediate reprimands. There are bikes for carrying children, others for hauling goods, tandem bicycles for lovers – all in an infinite variety of shapes, sizes, colours and styles. Shops feature stylish bells, which vary in sound and design to personalize fashion statements and individualize warnings. Many riders even don their favourite hats to ride in style while keeping their heads warm and dry.

Pedestrians and bikes were the foundation for Gehl's radical new form of humanistic urban planning. He realized that more life takes place at 3–15 kmph (i.e., walking or riding) than in a motor vehicle. Social life is about meeting people, about chance encounters and short greetings on the way to somewhere. Studies show that much of any trust has to do with reciprocity, and reciprocity is a function of repetition and the frequency of human interaction. If you only deal with someone once in your life, or don't have to look at them in the eye and face their scorn, the incentive to deal fairly is vastly diminished. Try short changing a customer who trusts you with their business regularly every week. In *The Theory of Moral Sentiments* Adam Smith wrote that a person 'feels horror at the very thought of exposing himself to the disgrace which attends upon the detection of falsehood.'

Gehl believed that the litmus test of a good city is the number of children on the street. In Denmark, kids fill city spaces, knowing they are safe. It is hardly surprising that Danes rank among the highest in the world with regard to trust (McArdle 2018); where else do you see unsupervised ten-year-old children on buses or subways? Or that 'fake news' doesn't thrive there to the extent it does in larger, more anonymous societies.

Life is also about chance and spontaneity, according to Jane Jacobs in *The Death and Life of Great American Cities*. Not much of this happens in garages or lifts, or when sitting in a vehicle in traffic jams. Gehl recognized the value of casual, unplanned public interactions, from a nodding hello to a passer-by, or a quick, superficial chat with a grocer.

However, along with the carrots, there had to be sticks to wean people from their dependency on automobiles. Copenhagen was re-zoned to promote pedestrian areas, and special bike lanes were commissioned. With 450 km of dedicated bicycle lanes and bridges, the city is the most bicycle friendly city in the world (Cycling Embassy of Denmark 2009; Fleming 2018). Since Copenhagen is land-constrained, more walking and biking meant less roads needed for cars. More congestion at the outset was part of the solution to dissuade drivers from commuting.

Other incentives have helped to steer behaviour. Car prices in Denmark are treble those in some other countries; and this special tax has helped to discourage car usage. Parking is also expensive and, as a general rule, the closer you are to the city centre, the more expensive it is to park.

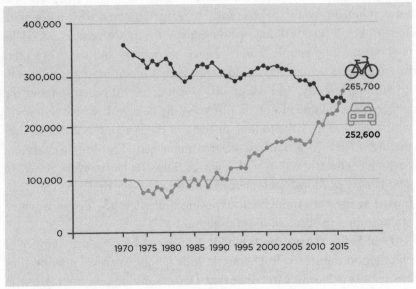

Figure 12.1: Bikes Replacing Car Usage

In 2016, the number of bicycles entering Copenhagen city centre exceeded the number of cars for the first time.

Source: Copenhagenize Design Co.; Colville-Andersen, 2018

Street parking is restricted or prohibited, so the risk of someone opening their car door while a bike passes by or a car driving into an oncoming cyclist is minimized. Today, nine out of ten Danes own a bike, while only four out of ten own a car (Cycling Embassy of Denmark 2017). The estimates (from energy, health, insurance and transportation costs) suggest that for each 1 km a resident of Copenhagen rides, society earns 4.8 krone or 75 US cents; driving a car the same distance costs 10.09 krone or $1.58 (Fleming 2018). What has traditionally been a cost has become a source of gain.

It wasn't only about money. The Danes care deeply about their environment. They realized that 30–40 per cent of CO_2 emissions come from vehicles and that cars cause unnecessary fatalities. So in 2018, the government announced a ban on sales of all fossil-fuel guzzling cars from 2030 (Levring 2018). Danes also care about quality of life. The TomTom Traffic Index, which measures the congestion levels in 390 cities around the world, estimates that the congestion level in Los Angeles (ranked the worst in the US) is twice as high as in Copenhagen. To put that into perspective, drivers in Los Angeles waste over a week sitting in traffic every year (TomTom 2017). Who wouldn't prefer to spend that time on a holiday?

And Danes are also healthier. Thanks in part to daily exercise, Denmark has one of the lowest obesity rates in Europe (Smith 2017). Studies estimate that Copenhagen has 1.1 million fewer sick days compared to other cities due to cycling (Cycling Embassy of Denmark 2017). In fact, the Copenhagen case demonstrates how savvy, long-term urban planning is the cheapest way to boost health and city welfare.

For all these social victories, Gehl became something of a rock star. 'Copenhagenization' came to be known in urban planning circles around the world for an approach to city design which focused on the needs of both individuals and society. The mayor of Melbourne commissioned Gehl to advise on improving the city's liveability, as did Michael Bloomberg when he was mayor of New York; cities like Moscow and São Paulo are next in line.

Companies are also beginning to recognize the value in Gehl's approach to urban planning. John Zimmer and Logan Green, founders of the car-sharing start-up Lyft, shared their vision of how car-sharing could benefit society and echoed Gehl's quest to transform Copenhagen forty years ago. They wrote, 'Over the last fifty years, urban development has centred around the automobile, but imagine for a minute what our world could look like if we found a way to take most of these cars off the road. It would be a world with less traffic and less pollution. A world where we need less parking – where streets can be narrowed and sidewalks widened. It's a world where pedestrians, bikers and children can navigate a city just as quickly and safely as an automobile. That's a world built around people, not cars' (Eadicicco 2019). Gehl and Copenhagen have taught us that such a world is possible. Perhaps Zimmer and Green should take a trip across the seas to see for themselves.

From Bikes to Blades

In rural Jutland, tractors are more common than bicycles. About the same time when Gehl was scratching his head about how cities could be redesigned, Denmark plunged into another, not totally unrelated crisis. And once again, the country placed a big bet on a radical solution.

Until OPEC imposed an embargo on its members' oil exports in 1973 in retaliation to the Western support for the Yom Kippur war, crude oil price had fluctuated between $1.50 and $2.00 per barrel for decades. In 1974, it climbed precipitously to $11 (Amadeo 2019). Denmark had no sources of natural energy and it was completely dependent on coal and oil for heating and fuel.

Denmark covers 43,000 square kilometers of land across 1,419 islands and peninsulas, resulting in one of the highest ratios of coastline to territory in the world. The highest point in the country is only 170 meters above sea level, so nothing separates it for thousands of kilometers from the persistent strong northwesterly winds.

After the oil crisis hit them, Danes knew things had to change. For a modest, rural farming society in a cold climate, a tank of fuel and winter heating made up a decent chunk of the average person's income. Efforts to subsidize energy costs to ease the pain brought the government to a point of financial collapse. It was time to go back to the drawing board.

People have harnessed the wind's energy for thousands of years. In the 1950s, the Danes invented the Gedser wind turbine, a robust 200kW, three-bladed turbine with such remarkably low operating costs that it is still used today. But the cost of energy produced by wind has historically been uneconomical compared with fossil fuels so there was no incentive to invest in or operate windmills to produce power.

In an act of desperation, a cottage industry emerged, started by unemployed metal workers and farmers who constructed makeshift blades forged from derelict automobile bodies, mimicking the vintage Gedser turbine.

Danish politicians were quick to recognize the significance of these ventures, crafting a bold strategy to secure full energy independence. The first national energy plan, published in 1976, set out two priorities – discover and extract oil reservoirs thought to be in the North Sea, and explore the possibility of large-scale electricity generation from wind power.

In retrospect, the plan was speculative, bordering on the illusionary. The first part of the plan was not sufficient. Petroleum and gas discoveries in the North Sea were relatively meagre (they peaked much later, in 2005). The second was initially worse. Studies revealed that the cost per LCOE (levelized cost of energy) for generating power from wind was extremely high – 500 per cent higher than the cost today (Lantz, Wiser and Hand 2012). Even the most optimistic experts doubted that wind could ever compete against traditional fossil fuels or nuclear energy, which was considered at the time to be the front runner to rescue the world from energy dependency.

But never mind the odds. What ensued was a concerted effort from metal workers, the government, industry, education and even pension funds to end the nation's dependency on costly and dirty fossil fuels.

To facilitate the wind energy sector's emergence, the government set up a capital grant programme in the 1980s to cover 30 per cent of the installation cost of new turbines (IRENA 2013). The government policy held its course despite changes in prime ministers and the vagaries of energy prices which radically altered calculations of return on investment for long-term projects.

Denmark's multi-party political system, where no party has had a majority since more than a century, has been an important factor in the country's ability to carry out long-term plans. Parties have an incentive to work together in coalitions to achieve reforms, knowing that no single party is likely to emerge with the power to reverse a widely accepted policy unlike what happens in Britain and the US. The government energy agreement of 2018, which is looking towards 2030, was unanimously supported by all parties in parliament.

Coalitions also formed elsewhere in the society. Jørgen Abildgaard, climate director of the municipality of Copenhagen, told me, 'Businesses have one motive – profit – and local authorities another, and so on.' But Denmark is different. He continued, 'When I travel just a few hundred kilometres south from Denmark, people are often baffled by the informal tone we use here, which tends to be light on formality and high in substance. Businesses, local authorities, civil societies, all sit down and bash out a common solution within the guidelines set by city authorities. So we actually have to listen to each other.'

Listening to each other proved effective. Danish industry, another coalescing force, seized the incentives the government provided. Wind turbines popped up like mushrooms throughout Denmark. Around 8,000 were erected between 1977 and 2000 (Quartz+Co 2015, p. 6–7). In 1991, Denmark started offshore construction. By 2009, they had built the largest offshore wind farm in the world at that time, Horns Rev 2 (D'Armagnac 2010). Thanks to its shallow bays and inlets, most turbines are anchored offshore, out of sight and mind for most Danes. Denmark now generates more than 40 per cent of its electricity from wind, the highest proportion in the world (Neslen 2016). Its vast spread of windmills can produce up to 140 per cent of Denmark's electricity on particularly windy days (Neslen 2015). Excess power (on those windy days) is sold to neighbouring Sweden, Germany and Norway through a state-of-the-art grid, showcasing the magnificent potential of Denmark's wind farms.

Danish manufacturers, along with many component suppliers, are global market leaders, supplying to both California and China, the two fastest growing markets in the world, with turbines for their wind farms. Seven of the world's top ten wind turbine manufacturers have a presence in Denmark and equipment to generate wind power accounts for 3.7 per cent of all Danish exports (Ministry of Foreign Affairs of Denmark 2018; Danish Wind Industry Association 2018). Over 9 per cent of all Danish industrial employees work one way or another in the green sector (*Gate 21* 2017, p. 7). Vestas, a leading global manufacturer of wind turbines, had a revenue of over ten billion euros (US$11 billion) in 2017 and over 23,000 employees globally (Vestas 2017). With 8,000 components in the entire value chain, dense clusters of small and medium enterprises have formed throughout Denmark to service the global opportunities.

The education sector has also played an important role. The Technical University of Denmark (DTU) was the first university to offer degrees in the design and engineering of wind energy equipment. It is the only place in the world where turbines up to 250 metres in height (current limit) can be tested (IRENA 2017). DTU has unsurpassed expertise in this specialized sector. There is a close interaction between academia and industry. Vocational training in Denmark is based on the dual education system, which combines class-based learning with apprenticeships. Excellence in turbines requires this combination of craftsmanship and engineering.

Danish citizens were encouraged to have a stake by investing a portion of their savings in wind farms through their pensions funds. The decision has paid off, as returns from investments in wind infrastructure have provided large returns in a low interest rate environment.

More growth is planned. Denmark plans to increase wind's share of its power deliveries to 60 per cent by 2025 (State of Green 2017). Now that the cost of wind power has declined by 80 per cent and is projected to fall to around 0.30 krone/kWh (US$0.045/kWh), it has become the most economic option (Danish Ministry of Energy, Utilities and Climate 2018). Choosing renewable energy over fossil fuels is also the best option for preserving the environment.

The Sky Is the Limit (Cloud Storage)

As we have seen, Denmark's commitment to the only natural resource at its disposal has enabled it to approach its target of self-sufficiency in clean energy much quicker than anyone expected. Combined with an aggressive programme to improve reliability of delivery through underground cabling, the country has created one of the most reliable power grids in the world.

It probably did not occur to anyone involved in the project forty years ago that electricity reliability might become a competitive advantage. And you would have been laughed at if you had said that Denmark's climate, with temperatures varying between freezing and 16°C through the year, could become a crucial advantage for its industry.

Enter the new cloud storage industry. Most of us don't think about what happens to our photos and documents when we upload them, with a click of a button, to iCloud, Dropbox or Google Drive. Data must be stored somewhere and the demand for cloud storage appears to be on an unstoppable growth path. The annual growth rate of the cloud storage market is projected to be 29 per cent, with the sector expected to reach $113 billion in revenues by 2022 (*News Wire* 2017). About 90 per cent of the world's data was created in the last two years, and it is estimated that there will be around forty trillion gigabytes (40 zettabytes) of data by 2020 (Petrov 2019).

In its search for secure and reliable storage sites, Apple turned to Denmark. They began the construction of a 166,000 square metre hyperscale data centre near Viborg in Jutland, among the largest in the world. The data centre will support cloud storage for services like iCloud for photos, files, messages and Siri for millions of European users. A second data centre, near Aabenraa in southern Denmark, has also been announced (Hamilton 2017).

Other companies quickly followed suit and Denmark is well on its way to becoming a kind of Fort Knox for cloud storage. Google has acquired land in Fredericia and Aabenraa for data centres. Facebook chose Odense for a 55,000 square metre data centre and also plans to build a 250,000 square metre data centre near Esbjerg – that's the size of thirty-five football fields (Smolaks 2018).

The sizes and costs of these projects are significant. Apple has allocated $1 billion for its data centre in Viborg (Wienberg 2019). Its centre in Aabenraa is expected to attract other businesses and create up to 10,000 jobs. (Friis Mikkelsen 2017).

So why do all these companies choose a small country like Denmark?

Denmark has several competitive advantages. Some are fortuitous, like the cool climate. Data centres emit vast amounts of heat because they use large amounts of power. Just as we take measures to prevent our laptops from overheating, data centres have to be kept cool to ensure maximum efficiency. In a city like Viborg, where temperature averages 16°C in the summer and just above freezing in winter, the environment helps to reduce cooling costs.[14]

Since cloud storage increases carbon emissions, companies such as Apple are struggling to prove that they are environment friendly. Having Danish data centres which will run entirely on renewable energy enables them to comply with their commitment to run on 100 per cent renewable energy.

---

14. Located between the North Sea and the Baltic Sea, Denmark has an abundance of cold ocean water on its doorstep. As ocean water is increasingly being used to cool data centres, Denmark could find itself with another advantage.

Erik Stannow, Nordic manager for Apple, mentioned a third reason: 'The reliability of the Danish grid is one of the main reasons we will operate two sites in Denmark' (Gronholt-Pedersen 2017). Denmark's state-of-the-art power grid has an uptime of 99.99 per cent and 80 per cent of its power lines are underground, so they are protected from the vagaries of weather or natural disaster (State of Green 2018). While thousands, or even millions, of Californian residents are affected by regular power outages, older citizens in Jutland are hard pressed to remember a single incident.

Progress often means taking two steps forward and one step back. Despite leading the fight against climate change, Denmark's carbon footprint is set to increase dramatically once these data centres are built (O'Sullivan 2018). Moreover, thermal pollution will go up due to the vast amounts of heat emitted by these huge data centres. This could have a significant and lasting impact on the local weather. Danes need to pedal faster to meet their CO_2 targets and not sacrifice their progress when attracting global companies. As they have adapted in the past, they will need to do so again. Perhaps radically.

Figure 12.2: Big Architects

'Amager bakke' is a combined heat and waste-to-power plant that doubles as a ski slope—all with considerable aesthetic appeal.

Source: Bjarke Ingels Group

Getting to Denmark

In our chapter 'Fallacy of Scale', we described Denmark as a bumble bee which defies all theory. It should not be able to fly because its wings are too tiny in proportion to its body mass. But it does. However, replication of its success may be difficult. Trust, modesty and a sense of belonging, we have argued, are strong but overlooked parameters for competitiveness, but how and where are they measured? You won't find them in OECD or GDP statistics. Critics remain sceptical whether growth, demographics and productivity will be able to maintain the liberal Danish social contract. At 46 per cent of GDP, its total tax burden on residents is the second highest in the OECD (OECD, no date). Adrian Wooldridge of the *Economist*, in his survey of Nordic nations, encouraged the desire to 'get to Denmark' but warned that there is also a challenge for Danes just to stay there (*Economist* 2013).

What lessons might we draw from this chapter on Denmark?

Virtues can be created from vulnerabilities. In an interview, Erik Rasmussen, founder of Scandinavia's leading independent think-tank *Monday Morning*, told me that the Danes have a knack of managing to make money out of things which are necessary for political reasons or 'welfare solutions'. In addition to wind powered energy, Denmark is among the leading producers of hearing aids for the ageing (William Demant) and insulin for diabetics (Novo Nordisk).

Governments can and should be innovative. We may not look to them to create the latest products – a Nespresso machine, a post-it note or an iPhone – but, as the Danes have demonstrated with energy and urban planning and the Finns have taught us with primary education, governments can be bold and forward-looking. Of course, policy-making is a risky business and there was undoubtedly a little luck involved in most of the cases we have reviewed. Few believed that the cost of wind energy would ever be economical and the Danish government would have looked very foolish had its wager not paid off. But it did.

Good things usually take time so there is something to be said about stable and enduring policies. Collaboration is more effective at intermediating compromise than confrontation. The Danish experiment with wind power would not have worked without a political consensus. Ove Kaj Pedersen, professor emeritus in political science at Copenhagen Business School, summarizes, 'After a crisis, Danes start to collaborate.' It's a mantra we should all follow.

Free markets are optimal for allocating scarce resources across a vast spectrum of goods and services, but they don't engender sharing and are not especially suited to solving long-term, slow-burning problems, as our chapter 'Critical but Not Urgent' explains. What happens to a corporation in twenty-five years doesn't really matter to today's CEO. Which Silicon Valley venture capitalist would have had the risk appetite and stamina to take the chance the Danish government took? Denmark, not California, became the world leader in wind energy industry because of a decision it took which California's private sector is not geared or incentivized to take.

And finally, myths can be busted. The Danes have proved false the established belief that industrial growth must necessarily be coupled with growth in pollution. Denmark has doubled its GDP since 1973 and has reduced greenhouse gasses by almost 40 per cent since 1990 (Nørtoft 2018). While people around the world consider politics and economics as adversaries, Denmark has shown that politics can be profitable. The consumer's love for their automobile, once inviolable, is like many other loves which can fade over time, especially in the face of superior alternatives. Before Gehl, the human aspect of cities was virtually ignored in urban planning; now, it is gaining popularity around the world.

In the course of a generation, Copenhagen has gone from a highly unattractive place to live to one of the most desirable, and is well on its way to becoming the world's first carbon neutral capital by 2025. During this period, Denmark has gone from a wholly dependent and costly importer of dirty energy to a lucrative producer of highly reliable electricity and an exporter of clean energy.

Perhaps most importantly, the Danes have taught us an invaluable lesson. There is no other earth. It's high time we manage the one we have right.

References and Further Reading

Amadeo, K. 'OPEC Oil embargo, Its Causes, and the Effects of the Crisis'. *The Balance*, 2019. https://www.thebalance.com/opec-oil-embargo-causes-and-effects-of-the-crisis-3305806.

'Bicycle Statistics from Denmark'. *Cycling Embassy of Denmark*, 2009. http://www.cycling-embassy.dk/wp-content/uploads/2009/03/Fact-sheet_English.pdf.

Campbell, J.L. and O.K. Pedersen. 'The Varieties of Capitalism and Hybrid Success: Denmark in the Global Economy'. *Comparative Political Studies*, 40(3) (2007): pp. 307–332.

Campbell, J.L., J.A. Hall, and O.K. Pedersen. *National identity and the varieties of capitalism: The Danish experience* (Canada: McGill-Queen's University Press, 2006).

Colville-Andersen, M. 'Copenhagenize your city'. *The Guardian*, 2018. https://www.theguardian.com/cities/gallery/2018/jun/11/copenhagenize-case-urban-cycling-graphs.

——'Danish 180% Tax on Cars is Rather Irrelevant'. *Copenhagenize.com*, 2012. http://www.copenhagenize.com/2012/10/danish-180-tax-on-cars-is-rather.html.

'Danish wind power breaks all records in 2017', *Ministry of Foreign Affairs of Denmark*, 2018. https://investindk.com/insights/danish-wind-power-breaks-all-records-in-2017.

D'Armagnac, B. 'Danish wind farms show sustainable attitude to renewable energy'. *The Guardian*, 2010. https://www.theguardian.com/world/2010/aug/10/denmark-renewable-wind-farm-energy.

'Denmark best in class for security of supply in the EU'. *State of Green*, 2018. https://stateofgreen.com/en/partners/state-of-green/news/denmark-best-in-class-for-security-of-supply-in-the-eu/.

'Denmark is heading towards 60% wind energy'. *State of Green*, 2017. https://stateofgreen.com/en/partners/state-of-green/news/denmark-is-heading-towards-60-wind-energy/.

'Denmark, Sweden still the highest-tax OECD countries'. *OECD*. http://www.oecd.org/general/denmarkswedenstillthehighest-taxoecdcountries.htm.

Eadicicco, L. ' "We were told we were crazy" – Lyft's founders describe how far the company has come in a new letter in its IPO filing'. *Business Insider*, 2019. https://www.businessinsider.com/lyft-ipo-founders-letter-2019-2?r=US&IR=T.

'Energiindustriens Historiske Omstilling og Betydning for Danmark'. *Quartz+Co*, 2015. https://www.danskenergi.dk/sites/danskenergi.dk/files/media/dokumenter/2017-07/150224Energiindustriens_historiske_omstilling_QuartzogCO.pdf.

'Facts about Cycling in Denmark'. *Cycling Embassy of Denmark*, 2017. http://www.cycling-embassy.dk/facts-about-cycling-in-denmark/statistics/.

Fleming, S. 'What makes Copenhagen the world's most bike-friendly city?'. *World Economic Forum*, 2018. https://www.weforum.org/agenda/2018/10/what-makes-copenhagen-the-worlds-most-bike-friendly-city/.

Friis Mikkelsen, P. 'Viborg mærker allerede effekten af byggeri af datacenter'. *DR*, 2017. https://www.dr.dk/nyheder/regionale/midtvest/viborg-maerker-allerede-effekten-af-byggeri-af-datacenter.

Garfield, L. 'These 10 cities are the most prepared for the future'. *Business Insider*, 2017. https://www.businessinsider.com/smart-cities-ranking-easypark-group-2017-11?r=US&IR=T.

Gehl, J. *Life Between Buildings: Using Public Space* (Washington: Island Press, 2011).

Gerdes, J. 'Copenhagen's ambitious push to be carbon-neutral by 2025'. *The Guardian*, 2013. https://www.theguardian.com/environment/2013/apr/12/copenhagen-push-carbon-neutral-2025.

'Global Cloud Storage Market is Expected to Reach $112.73 Billion by 2022'. *News Wire*, 2017. https://www.newswire.com/news/global-cloud-storage-market-is-expected-to-reach-112-73-billion-by-2022.

'Grøn vækst i Greater Copenhagen'. *Gate 21*, 2017. https://www.gate21.dk/wp-content/uploads/2017/05/GrønVækstiGreaterCopenhagen_web.pdf.

Gronholt-Pedersen, J. 'Apple to build second renewables-powered data center in Denmark'. *Reuters*, 2017. https://ca.reuters.com/article/idCAKBN19V0MJ-OCATC.

Hamilton, B. 'Google buys second plot in Denmark as speculation grows it will establish data centre'. *CPH Post*, 2017. http://cphpost.dk/news/google-buys-second-plot-in-denmark-as-speculation-grows-it-will-establish-data-centre.html.

Jacobs, J. *The Death and Life of Great American Cities* (London: Pimlico, 2000).

Katz, B. and J. Nowak. *The New Localism: Or How Cities Can Thrive in Age of Populism* (Washington, D.C.: Brookings Institution Press, 2018).

Lantz, E., R. Wiser and M. Hand. 'Figure 3. IEA Wind Task 26: The Past and Future Cost of Wind Energy, Work Package 2'. *NREL*, 2012. https://www.nrel.gov/docs/fy12osti/53510.pdf.

Levring, P. 'Denmark to Ban Sale of Fossil Fuel Cars in 2030, Boost EV Sales'. *Bloomberg*, 2018. https://www.bloomberg.com/news/articles/2018-10-02/denmark-plans-2030-ban-on-fossil-fuel-car-sales-premier-says.

McArdle, M. 'You Can't Have Denmark Without Danes'. *Bloomberg*, 2018. https://www.bloomberg.com/opinion/articles/2018-02-23/you-can-t-have-denmark-without-danes.

Neslen, A. 'Denmark broke world record for wind power in 2015'. *The Guardian*, 2016. https://www.theguardian.com/environment/2016/jan/18/denmark-broke-world-record-for-wind-power-in-2015.

——'Wind power generates 140% of Denmark's electricity demand'. *The Guardian*, 2015. https://www.theguardian.com/environment/2015/jul/10/denmark-wind-windfarm-power-exceed-electricity-demand.

Nielsen, V.V. 'The Danish Wind Cluster: The Microeconomics of Competitiveness'. *Harvard Business School*, 2017. https://www.isc.hbs.edu/resources/courses/moc-course-at-harvard/Documents/pdf/student-projects/Denmark_Wind_2017.pdf.

Nørtoft, M. 'Energiforbruget er lavere end for ti år siden (opdateret)'. *Danmarks Statistik*, 2018. https://www.dst.dk/da/Statistik/bagtal/2018/2018-04-04-2016-bryder-otte-aars-trend-med-faldende-energiforbrug.

'Note on technology costs for offshore wind farms and the background for updating CAPEX and OPEX in the technology catalogue datasheets'. *DK, Danish Ministry of Energy, Utilities and Climate*, 2018. https://ens.dk/sites/ens.dk/files/Analyser/havvindsnotat_translation_eng_final.pdf.

O'Sullivan, F. 'Denmark's carbon footprint is set to balloon – blame big tech'. *Wired*, 2018. https://www.wired.com/story/denmarks-carbon-footprint-is-set-to-balloonblame-big-tech/.

Petrov, C. 'Big Data Statistics 2019'. *Techjury*, 2019. https://techjury.net/stats-about/big-data-statistics/.

Preetish. 'Want to ensure business growth via big data? Augment enterprise data with web data'. *PromptCloud*, 2017. https://www.promptcloud.com/blog/want-to-ensure-business-growth-via-big-data-augment-enterprise-data-with-web-data/.

'Renewable energy benefits: leveraging local capacity for onshore wind'. *International Renewable Energy Agency*, IRENA, 2017. https://www.irena.org/-/media/Files/IRENA/Agency/Publication/2017/Jun/IRENA_Leveraging_for_Onshore_Wind_2017.pdf.

'Revenue Statistics 2018 – Denmark'. *OECD*, 2018. https://www.oecd.org/tax/tax-policy/revenue-statistics-denmark.pdf.

'Smart Cities Index'. *Easypark*, 2017. https://easyparkgroup.com/smart-cities-index/.

Smith, A. *The Theory of Moral Sentiments* (London, Penguin Books, 2010).

Smith, O. 'World Obesity Day: Which countries have the biggest weight problem?'. *The Telegraph*, 2017. https://www.telegraph.co.uk/travel/maps-and-graphics/the-most-obese-fattest-countries-in-the-world/.

Smolaks, M. 'Facebook is planning second hyperscale campus in Denmark'. *Data Center Dynamics*, 2018. https://www.datacenterdynamics.com/news/facebook-planning-second-hyperscale-campus-denmark/.

'Statistics'. *Danish Wind Industry Association*, 2018. https://en.windpower.org/wind-in-denmark/statistics.

'The CPH 2025 Climate Plan', *Københavns commune*. https://urbandevelopmentcph.kk.dk/artikel/cph-2025-climate-plan.

'30 Years of Policies for Wind Energy: Lessons from 12 Wind Energy Markets', *IRENA*, 2013. https://www.irena.org/publications/2013/Jan/30-Years-of-Policies-for-Wind-Energy-Lessons-from-12-Wind-Energy-Markets.

Thoreson, M. *Hygge: The Danish Secrets of Happiness: How to be Happy and Healthy in Your Daily* (Copenhagen: Life CreateSpace Publishing, 2017).

'TomTom Traffic Index: Measuring Congestion Worldwide'. *TomTom*, 2017. https://www.tomtom.com/en_gb/trafficindex/list?citySize=LARGE&continent=ALL&country=ALL.

Verge, J. 'Apple to Spend $2B on Two Massive European Data enters'. *DataCenter Knowledge*, 2015. https://www.datacenterknowledge.com/archives/2015/02/23/apple-spend-2b-two-massive-european-data-centers.

'Vestas Annual Report'. *Vestas*, 2017. https://www.vestas.com/~/media/vestas/investor/investor%20pdf/financial%20reports/2017/q4/2017_annual_report.pdf.

Weihe, C.P. 'Copenhagen City of Cyclists – facts and figures 2017'. *Cycling Embassy of Denmark*, 2017. http://www.cycling-embassy.dk/2017/07/04/copenhagen-city-cyclists-facts-figures-2017/.

Wienberg, C. 'Apple, Facebook, Google asked to pay for wind parks in Denmark'. *Fin24*, 2019. https://www.fin24.com/Companies/apple-facebook-google-asked-to-pay-for-wind-parks-in-denmark-20190413.

Wiking, M. *The Little Book of Lykke: The Danish Search for the World's Happiest People* (London: Penguin, 2018).

'Windmill History', *The Danish Windmill Corporation*, no date. http://www.danishwindmill.com/danish_windmill_history/history_overview.asp.

Wooldridge, A. 'Northern Lights'. *The Economist*, 2013. https://www.economist.com/special-report/2013/02/02/northern-lights.

Conversations and Interviews

Anders Dons, Austin Salisbury, Claus Meyer, Erik Rasmussen, Finn Junge-Jensen, Flemming Besenbacher, Henrik Tvarnø, Jan Gehl, Jesper Nygård, Jesper Uttrup, John A. Hall, John L. Campbell, Jørgen Abildgaard, Karin Klitgaard, Karsten Dybvad, Kristian Jensen, Lars Fruergaard Jørgensen, Lars Rebien Sørensen, Lykke Friis, Mads Nipper, Margrethe Vestager, Morten Dyrholm, Niels Christiansen, Ove Kaj Pedersen, Peter Katzenstein and Peter A. Hall, Søren Skou, Steen Thomsen, Tom Larsen, Ulrik Vestergaard Knudsen and Vilhelm Vig Nielson.

13

The Nordics: The Theory
of Love

An Impossible Climb

Source: Wikimedia Commons

Around noon, Heikki Tiittanen became a bit impatient when his son did not want to sleep. Usually, the trained engineer had all the time in the world for his small child. He was on paternity leave for six months, a completely normal thing in Finland, where not only mothers but also fathers are offered generous leave around the time their child is born.

While Junior slept, Tiittanen busied himself with household chores and office work for his new company, Finnish Baby Box, which he had founded with two colleagues, also engineers and new fathers. Fortunately, this all took place in his living room, so he could give the attention demanded by his little boy whenever he woke up.

Tiittanen and his friends, Anssi Okkonen and Anton Danielsen, came up with the idea for their new company through drawing on the origins of Finland's efforts to liberate women. The Tiittanens, like all Finnish couples expecting a child, received the popular Finnish maternity package, 'Kela Maternity Box' (äitiyspakkaus). When Tiittanen saw this box for the first time and removed its lid, it hit him: 'I will soon be a father!' Consisting of fifty items, the box contains just about everything a young family needs – clothes, pacifier, nipple cream, a thermometer to measure fevers or bath water, a portable bed and even a child's first book. Finnish Baby Box grew out of a desire to make these baby boxes available to families across the world.

Figure 13.1: The Finnish Baby Box

Source: Wikimedia Commons

Figure 13.2: Inside the Box

Source: Wikimedia Commons

Social contracts are usually forged through adversity. The remarkable drive for gender equality in Finland has been no different. After the Great Depression, Finland had among the highest child mortality rates in Europe (Lee 2013). The government initiated the Kela Maternity Box scheme in 1938 as part of an education programme designed to reduce infant deaths; it also included a complimentary doctor's appointment. At first, it was directed at the poorer sections of the population, but later it was extended to all expecting couples, based on the egalitarian belief that all children deserve the same start in life.

Nobody imagined at that time that a simple cardboard box designed to prevent infant deaths was the first move in what would become the most effective push for gender equality in the world. The unleashing of female talent has been celebrated across the world over the last few generations, but nowhere has there been greater success than in the Nordics.

Denmark, Finland, Norway, Sweden and Iceland consistently rank among the best countries for women, mothers and children. In Save the Children's 2015 Mothers' Index, which calculates the world's best countries for mothers using UN data, the Nordics took the top five spots (Jones 2015). This is partly because balancing a career with parenthood is made easier by excellent and affordable day care. The child's school day bears a closer resemblance to the parent's working day and paid parental leave improves the security of the parent's paycheck. Part-time and flexible work has enabled fathers and mothers to work in tandem as common breadwinners and spend more free time with their children (Working remotely is a common practice in many Nordic workplaces for at least one day per week). According to an Oxford University study, men perform a larger share of the housework in Nordic countries than elsewhere (Oxford University 2016).

Thanks to these simple but revolutionary measures, female participation in the labour force is higher and pay gaps are narrower (Schwab 2018). A woman no longer has to choose between the career she wishes to pursue and the mother she wants to be. Marriage has become unmoored from parenthood. Even interracial and unisex marriages have lost their power to shock.

As a result, women matter more in Nordic societies. They score better in entrance examinations, receive the majority of university degrees and earn higher salaries.[15] With high participation in the workforce and high wages, the economy runs at greater potential. Women after all control 65 per cent of global spending and more than

---

15. It's important to note that a high number of female graduates does not necessarily lead to more opportunities post-university. In the US, for example, women earn substantially less than men despite being better educated (Hess 2017).

80 per cent of US spending, so companies should pay more attention to them (Continuum, 2011). The gender pay gap in these countries is much narrower, and Iceland became the world's first country to force companies to prove they pay their employees the same (Zalis 2018). Women make up close to 40 per cent of members of parliament and have served as prime ministers in each of the Nordic nations save Sweden (World Bank 2018). With greater economic clout and a growing political voice, they are able to pursue fulfilling lives as esteemed members of society. No wonder these nations consistently rank among the happiest and most meritocratic societies.

It has been a long and bumpy ride since the Kela Maternity Box. In this chapter, we attempt to explain this journey. It is the story of how millions of Nordic women, who were once dependent on men, have taken control of their economic, political and maternal lives. And it is the story of how men adapted to them. Most of all, it is the story of how men and women together have managed to remain different while becoming more equal. We close with some serious concerns about the unintended consequences of success.

1. Norway

2. Finland

3. Iceland

4. Denmark

5. Sweden

6. Netherlands

7. Spain

8. Germany

9. Australia

10. Belgium

Figure 13.3: The World's Best Countries to be a Mother

Of the top ten best countries in the world to be a mother, eight are small countries.

Source: The Mother's Index

* * *

Towards Gender Blindness

Progress has been neither uniform nor linear. New policies are one thing, but a new mindset is quite a different matter. Since the dawn of civilization, the gender bargain had been about co-dependency and subordination. Women were physically vulnerable, so they placed a premium on protection. With the unpredictability of childbirth and agrarian sustenance, the traditional social contract of a family, in which the man was the breadwinner and the woman was responsible for the children and domestic chores, was followed for thousands of years. Preachers, elders and grandparents urged that marriage was the crucial bond holding together the nucleus of society.

Women bore, on average, five children as recently as 1960.[16] This meant they had little time or energy for anything else. 'Tips to Look After Your Husband' from a 1950s US home economics textbook is sprinkled with advice such as, 'Most men are hungry when they come home, so have a delicious meal prepared on time' and 'Your husband has just been through a tough day, so touch up your makeup, put a ribbon in your hair and be gay; his boring day may need a lift (Tips to Look After Your Husband 2017). Aside from demonstrating their best behaviour, women worked hard. But their work was unpaid and often under-appreciated.

Technology changed all of this, starting with the birth control pill, which became an instant hit in the 1960s. Women were no longer sexually restrained by the fear of an unwanted pregnancy. Families became a matter of planning, not accident. Hans Rosling, the late Swedish intellectual, felt the washing machine may have had more impact on democracy and economic growth than any invention in history as it freed up women from the drudgery of countless hours of washing clothes manually (Rosling 2010). Then came the dishwasher, coffee maker, microwave oven, vacuum cleaner and a multitude of other gadgets which freed women up from traditional women's work, such as cooking and cleaning, so they could undertake more satisfying endeavours. Having more children wasn't one of them.

---

16. The average number of children per woman has always been low in Nordic countries (Roser 2017).

Childbirth per woman has declined massively from over 5 in 1960 to 1.5–1.9 in most developed nations (Roser 2017). A birth rate of 2.1 is required to maintain population equilibrium. Fewer children meant that motherhood didn't require the single-minded focus it had in the past, so women had considerably more time for education, work and personal enrichment. No longer were they confined to the perfect, submissive, stereotypical housewife which society historically expected them to be.

Where brute strength mattered more than brains, men had an inherent advantage. But jobs that required knowledge and imagination levelled the playing field. The relentless automation of much of manufacturing and the strong growth of service sectors in most advanced economies has meant that women qualified in disproportionately higher numbers for a growing number and variety of attractive jobs.

And women took advantage of this. In 1960, 18 per cent of mothers in the US had some college education; today that figure is close to 70 per cent (Livingston and Cohn 2013). An OECD report found that more than half of today's graduates are women (Nygård 2016). The Nordics surpass that average, with women taking the top spot in Sweden, where they make up 69 per cent of undergraduates (Nygård 2016). No wonder the percentage of Nordic women participating in the workforce ranks among the highest in the world.

The traditional gender roles became way out of sync with reality, and had to be recalibrated. This required a radically different mindset. The Nordic response, at first glance, sounds romantic. But it's not.

The Swedish Theory of Love

In 2016, Erik Gandini directed a cynical documentary film called *The Swedish Theory of Love*. The film reveals how the Nordics overhauled their social welfare systems and mindsets to pave the way towards gender fairness.

One of the most fundamental Nordic values is self-sufficiency. From this derives the basic theory that to truly love someone you must be independent. If one partner is dependent on another's income, they tend to behave in a subordinate manner, providing the wrong foundation for a healthy and lasting relationship. In this sense, achieving a reasonable measure of financial independence is central to expanding the opportunities available to women. This has been the compass which has been used to steer Nordic policy-making, following the introduction of the Kela Maternity Box.

Policies went beyond women. Gandini's film was based on a book by historians Henrik Berggren and Lars Trägårdh which had a provocative title, *Is the Swede a Human Being?* The book's core idea is that 'the Swede' (Nordic) contribute large chunks of their income to fund the welfare state out of self-interest. They can concentrate better on individual goals because they are freed from burdensome dependencies and anxieties about the future.

Bloomberg estimates that the cost of raising a child in the US is $233,610 (Bjerga 2017). If we include private school and university, this number could easily double. In Nordic countries, the most important components – education, child care, health care and transportation – are outsourced and largely paid for by the state, freeing people to choose partners they really love and concentrate their energies and resources on developing careers and raising families. As a gauge of magnitude, families in Britain spend an average of 33.8 per cent of their net income on childcare, compared to 4.4 per cent in Sweden (Luxton 2016).

A child's formation, as our chapter on education points out, is the most precious gift society offers, and Nordic society is far ahead in this respect. PISA scores in Nordic countries are considerably higher than in Britain and the US and the level of children's education is remarkably uniform, irrespective of the parents' status (Jackson and Kiersz 2016). University education is free. By contrast, student loans in the US have overtaken credit card loans and are now the second largest source of consumer debt (Friedman 2018). Harvard's David Laibson observes, 'The variability of educational opportunity in the US is so enormous – why should we then be surprised if thirty years later we have such high degrees of inequality?'

While a child's school day bears hardly any resemblance to an adult's working day in many places, the Nordics have re-engineered the puzzle so there is a better fit. Full-time childcare costs 85 per cent of the median cost in the US and the Nordics see this as a part of their society's social contract (Zarya 2016). Over 90 per cent of Swedish children from ages one to five attend government subsidized day care facilities, often conveniently located close to home (Himmelstrand 2015). Flexible work is more common, so juggling a career with a child's student activities is easier. Part-time work comes with its own rights. Most people finish work at 5 p.m. and take twenty-fives days on holiday every year, so there is time for life after work and restoration.

Career interruptions are also facilitated. In the 1970s, the Nordic countries were the first to offer parental leave, to be shared as parents wish. The total paid leave available to mothers is fifty-six weeks in Sweden and up to 161 weeks in Finland, compared with zero in the US and thirty-nine in Britain (OECD Family database 2017). And paid leave begins five weeks before the delivery date. Leave for fathers is offered and taken. In Norway, a ten-week leave is reserved for fathers, which cannot be transferred to the mother. As a result, 90 per cent of fathers choose to take at least ten weeks off (Chemin 2011). All told, Nordic governments spend four times more per capita on support for childcare compared to the US (OECD Family database 2016).

Child care is also an example of the importance of how policies are framed in *TSTF* countries. In places like the US, elected officials treat child care as a cost which must be funded by reducing benefits to other programmes in what economists describe as a zero sum game. By contrast, *TSTF* nations, and particularly Nordic societies, have recognized that working women pay more in tax than the state spends on child care. This means child care schemes more than pay for themselves, and it's a win–win outcome for all sides.

Figure 13.4: Evolution of Child Care

Source: Banx

There are laws on discrimination, equal pay, property rights, sexual abuse, violence and a host of other issues traditional to society with antiquated gender norms. And Sweden even has its own 'Minister for

Children, the Elderly and Gender Equality' to show that they mean business, and that it's a priority. And a lot of the progress is achieved bottom up. As an example, the Photographic Museum in Stockholm teasingly advertised entry prices for women at 145 Kronor, or 13 per cent less than the price for men, as a protest against the gender wage gap. It is this kind of relentless public deliberation which grinds away at resilient stereotypes and paves the way towards a level playing field. The results speak for themselves.

The *Economist* publishes its annual 'glass-ceiling index', measuring progress with respect to a variety of parameters such as education, pay, childcare costs, maternity rights and representation in senior jobs. This data is compressed into a single measure of where women have the best and worst chances of equal treatment. Nordic nations currently occupy the top four spots (and Denmark is sixth), as they have done consistently (*Economist* 2018).

American and British mothers often seem stuck between two disagreeable options – being stressed out super moms or retreating from the workforce. Many parents spend so much money on education and day care centres that they are constantly on the brink of financial collapse. Nordic nations developed a system which eliminated these deficiencies almost thirty years ago. It is difficult to fathom that a 2014 International Labour Organization report found that only two of 185 nations do not offer paid maternity leave: Papua New Guinea and the US (Walsh, 2017) This is yet another example of the radical variability of social contracts provided around the world and, hence, the scope for improvement.

At the corporate level, being able to recruit the best talent from the entire universe of candidates (rather than only 50 per cent) also has its advantages. Studies show that companies promoting gender empowerment are also considerably more profitable.[17] At the collective level, the nations most advanced in gender empowerment are also the world's most competitive nations, demonstrating that all citizens can be beneficiaries from victories for women.

---

17. Companies with 30 per cent female executives have as much as six percentage points more in profits, according to a study which surveyed 22,000 publicly traded companies in ninety-one countries (Worstall 2016).

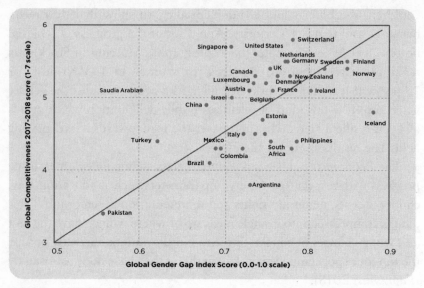

Figure 13.5: Global Competitiveness Index Vs Global Gender Gap Index

This graph suggests that closing the gender gap leads to a more competitive economy.

Source: World Economic Forum

Glitches

The Nordics are in a league of their own with regard to gender equality, but this is not to say that they have reached the pinnacle of achievement. In recent years, families in Sweden and Finland have found their single salaries insufficient to bring up a family, meaning both parents have to work, which takes away from the joys of parenthood.

There are some Nordic paradoxes. Studies show, curiously, that the greater the gender equality, the less likely women are to pursue STEM (science, technology, engineering, mathematics) subjects (Khazan 2018). *Hjernevask* (Brainwash), a popular Norwegian science documentary series, shows how women still cling to traditional female professions despite having the freedom to pursue other careers.

The Nordics have also not succeeded in converting gender empowerment into more women in the C-suite as heads of departments. Women in large corporations account for only 3 per cent of CEOs compared to 5 per cent globally (Zander 2014). In 2008, Norway introduced a quota which required listed companies to reserve at least 40 per cent of their director positions for women. Despite this, a study found that the quota failed to benefit women at lower levels of the corporate hierarchy (*Economist* 2018).

Balancing the demands of family and career is still difficult. This could perhaps be seen by looking at Europe's leaders – many of them, such as Merkel, Macron and May, are childless. The so-called 'motherhood penalty' persists. There is no market for part-time CEOs, and prejudices die hard, so senior positions can remain out of reach. Employers anywhere view long hours as a sign of commitment, so all things being equal, those who work longer hours have better career prospects. People who want to spend time with their children are, sadly, at a disadvantage. Think of any competitive 'up or out' style law or consulting firm. The opportunities at big firms for critical early promotions often coincide with wanting to start a family. Even the Nordics have difficulty crafting policies which counteract these inherent limitations. There is a need for role models for young, working women who strike this balance.

Almost half the marriages in Nordic countries end in divorce, and half the children are born outside wedlock, figures which are slightly higher than other Western nations (Chamie 2017). Indeed, Denmark has the highest divorce rate in Europe (Lebowitz 2018). Gandini's film may have sounded romantic, but one of its key messages was that there is something to be said about love and co-dependency, and that an unintended and undesirable consequence of growing dependency on the state is loneliness. Men, in particular, suffer in this respect, triggering the publication of popular 'How to' books about how to cope with the plight of manhood like *Who Stole My Spear?* by Tim Samuels.

So, while gender equality is a commendable objective, it remains an uphill battle even in the Nordics. Changing 200,000 years of habits is not easy.

The Delights of Staying Single (and its Unintended Consequences)

Have societies achieved short-term victories on gender equality at the cost of collective and long-term defeat? Population in most industrialized countries, and many others, is dropping drastically. Nordic nations boast higher reproduction rates than the European average, but at 1.74, Denmark's population atrophies by 20 per cent per generation (Roser 2017). To maintain equilibrium would mean either a sharp increase in native births or quadrupling the number of immigrants over the next fifty years, to a point where foreigners would exceed native Danes – not the most politically palatable prognosis.

Singapore's reproduction rate is 1.24, and foreigners already constitute 46 per cent of residents, which would seem to be tantamount to gradual extinction unless corrected. In just two decades, the proportion of women who remain childless in Singapore has almost tripled (Lee 2016). Advertisements in Singapore's subway system like 'Women are born with a finite number of eggs' haven't arrested the disturbing decline in reproduction. There are few countries who can claim to have been as good at devising and implementing public policies to achieve the desired ends as Singapore. Despite having thrown virtually everything but the kitchen sink at improving fertility rates, little has worked. Confucian values mean that women are expected to take care of ageing parents. So, if a single-child woman marries a single-child man, she would be expected to take care of four grandparents, in addition to mothering her own children.

Women have educated themselves and economies have thrown out such an enormous range of opportunities that the cost of motherhood looks increasingly unattractive, especially as they see their peers climbing career ladders. Raising children is incredibly demanding and a life-long commitment. The statistics seem to suggest a 'why bother?' attitude. The figures mentioned here are aggregate and disguise the fact that the higher the qualifications of the woman, the more likely she will be to remain childless, so there is a qualitative deterioration which may be more disturbing than the quantitative one.

Johanna Wallenius, a professor at the Stockholm School of Economics reiterated this in an interview, arguing that Sweden's reproduction rate of 1.91, still below equilibrium, is vastly superior as it has also created fairness for women. Without question, Sweden and other Nordics have lowered costs of having children, but these policies do not appear to be sufficient to restore population stability.

The issues raised by declining birth rates are all difficult. Japan's population, with a birth rate of 1.44 per woman, is set to fall to eighty-eight million by 2065, which is a decline of 31 per cent (Harding 2017). This, with Singapore's crisis, should be a wake-up call about the huge social changes resulting from declining fertility in developed countries and should encourage us to think about how to cope with their far-reaching consequences. But this is beyond the scope of this book.

Maybe the Finns could design a box with fifty enticing items that improve reproduction, as it did for combatting child mortality.

References and Further Reading

Bjerga, A. 'Children Don't Come Cheap: Cost of Raising One Hits $233,610'. *Bloomberg*, 2017. https://www.bloomberg.com/news/articles/2017-01-09/children-don-t-come-cheap-cost-of-raising-one-hits-233-610.

Boycott, R. 'Strings attached: why women's sexual liberation came at a price'. *The Financial Times*, 2019. https://www.ft.com/content/012d4edc-40ee-11e9-9499-290979c9807a?accessToken=zwAAAWmRpHywkc8BLU7cQ O4R6dOUmSkJecmAeg.MEUCIQCPfyKYupkL7XwkYgisOIWyXOofLQ s4y-wt6bZLQrjX-gIgP2wwFNT0ju1d9xn4sIHpivN8qheqq3dn7Fb_P2rgb 7w&sharetype=gift?token=2ed0f521-7090-42f8-90f9-2f1e221917e5.

Chafetz, J S. and J. Hagan. 'The gender division of labor and family change in industrial societies: A theoretical accounting'. *Journal of Comparative Family Studies*, vol. 27, no. 2. (1996): pp. 187–219.

Chamie, J. 'Out-of-Wedlock Births Rise Worldwide'. *YaleGlobal Online*, 2017. https://yaleglobal.yale.edu/content/out-wedlock-births-rise-worldwide.

'Chart PF3.1.A. Public spending on early childhood education and care'. *OECD*, OECD Family database, 2016. https://www.oecd.org/els/soc/PF3_1_Public_spending_on_childcare_and_early_education.pdf.

Chemin, A. 'Norway, the fatherland'. *The Guardian*, 2011. https://www.theguardian.com/money/2011/jul/19/norway-dads-peternity-leave-chemin.

'50-year study pinpoints countries where women are doing the least housework'. *Oxford University*, 2016. http://www.ox.ac.uk/news/2016-09-02-50-year-study-pinpoints-countries-where-women-are-doing-least-housework-0.

'Figure 33: Global Competitiveness Index Vs Global Gender Gap Index 2015'. *World Economic Forum*, 2015. http://reports.weforum.org/global-gender-gap-report-2015/the-case-for-gender-equality/.

Friedman, Z. 'Student Loan Debt Statistics in 2018: A $1.5 Trillion Crisis'. *Forbes*, 2018. https://www.forbes.com/sites/zackfriedman/2018/06/13/student-loan-debt-statistics-2018/#2a988abf7310.

Gandini, E. *The Swedish Theory of Love* (Stockholm, documentary film 2016).

Ghodsee, K. *Why Women Have Better Sex Under Socialism: And Other Arguments for Economic Independence* (London: Bodley Head, 2018).

Harding, R. 'Japan's population set to fall to 88m by 2065'. *Financial Times*, 2017. https://www.ft.com/content/00df659e-1dcf-11e7-a454-ab04428977f9.

Hess, A. 'For the first time in history, women are better educated than their husbands—but men still earn more'. *CNBC*, 2017. https://www.cnbc.com/2017/11/21/women-are-better-educated-than-their-husbands-but-men-still-earn-more.html.

Himmelstrand, J. 'Swedish daycare: International example or cautionary tale?'. *eReview*, 2015. http://www.imfcanada.org/archive/1107/swedish-daycare-international-example-or-cautionary-tale#_edn2.

Ibe, C. 'The Nordic Paradox: Gender Equity and Sexual Assault'. *Harvard Politics*, 2017. https://harvardpolitics.com/world/the-nordic-paradox-gender-equity-and-sexual-assault/.

Jackson, A. and A. Kiersz. 'The latest ranking of top countries in math, reading and science is out – and the US didn't crack the top 10'. *Business Insider*, 2016. https://www.businessinsider.com/pisa-worldwide-ranking-of-math-science-reading-skills-2016-12?r=US&IR=T.

Jones, R. 'The best and worst places in the world to be a mother'. *The Telegraph*, 2015. https://www.telegraph.co.uk/women/womens-life/11576970/The-best-and-worst-places-in-the-world-to-be-a-mother.html.

Khazan, O. 'The More Gender Equality, the Fewer Women in STEM'. *The Atlantic*, 2018. https://www.theatlantic.com/science/archive/2018/02/the-more-gender-equality-the-fewer-women-in-stem/553592/.

Lebowitz, S. 'One of the happiest countries has one of the highest divorce rates – but new rules may change that'. *Business Insider*, 2018. https://www.businessinsider.com/denmark-new-rules-parents-divorce-2018-4?r=US&IR=T.

Lee, H. 'Why Finnish babies sleep in cardboard boxes'. *BBC News*, 2013. https://www.bbc.co.uk/news/magazine-22751415.

Lee, P. 'Tackling Singapore's baby shortage'. *Straits Times*, 2016. https://www. straitstimes.com/singapore/tackling-singapores-baby-shortage.

Livingston, G. and D. Cohn. 'Record Share of New Mothers Are College Educated'. *Pew Research Center*, 2013. http://www.pewsocialtrends. org/2013/05/10/record-share-of-new-mothers-are-college-educated/.

Luxton, E. 'These are the countries where parents spend the most on childcare'. *World Economic Forum*, 2016. https://www.weforum.org/agenda/2016/12/ childcare-cost-oecd/.

Mullainathan, S. 'The Hidden Taxes on Women'. *The New York Times*, 2018. https://www.nytimes.com/2018/03/02/business/women-hidden-taxes.html.

Nygård, G. 'More than half of graduates are women'. *Statistics Norway*, 2016. https://www.ssb.no/en/utdanning/artikler-og-publikasjoner/more-than-half-of-graduates-are-women.

'Proportion of seats held by women in national parliaments'. *The World Bank*, 2018. https://data.worldbank.org/indicator/SG.GEN.PARL.ZS?year_high_ desc=true.

Rosenberg, M. 'How Total Fertility Rate Affects a Country's Population'. *ThoughtCo*, 2018. https://www.thoughtco.com/total-fertility-rate-1435463.

Roser, M. 'Fertility Rate'. *Our World in Data*, 2017. https://ourworldindata. org/fertility-rate.

Rosling, H. 'The magic washing machine'. *TEDWomen*, 2010. https://www. ted.com/talks/hans_rosling_and_the_magic_washing_machine.

Schwab, K. et al. 'The Global Competitiveness Report 2018'. *World Economic Forum*, 2018. http://reports.weforum.org/global-competitiveness-report-2018/.

'Special Report on Marriage'. *The Economist*, 2017. https://ukshop.economist. com/products/special-report-on-marriage?redirect=International.

Stone, L. 'American Women Are Having Fewer Children than They'd Like'. *The New York Times*, 2018. https://www.nytimes.com/2018/02/13/upshot/ american-fertility-is-falling-short-of-what-women-want.html.

'Table PF2.1.A. Summary of paid leave entitlements available to mothers'. *OECD, OECD Family database*, 2017. https://www.oecd.org/els/soc/ PF2_1_Parental_leave_systems.pdf.

'Ten years on from Norway's quota for women on corporate boards'. *The Economist*, 2018. https://www.economist.com/business/2018/02/17/ten-years-on-from-norways-quota-for-women-on-corporate-boards.

'The glass-ceiling index'. *The Economist*, 2018. https://www.economist.com/graphic-detail/2018/02/15/the-glass-ceiling-index.

'The Power of Parity: How Advancing Women's Equality Can Add $12 Trillion to Global Growth'. *McKinsey & Company*, 2015. https://www.mckinsey.com/~/media/McKinsey/Featured%20Insights/Employment%20and%20Growth/How%20advancing%20womens%20equality%20can%20add%2012%20trillion%20to%20global%20growth/MGI%20Power%20of%20parity_Full%20report_September%202015.ashx.

'Tips to Look After Your Husband – Excerpts from a 1950s Home Economics text book'. *Facebook*, 2017. https://www.facebook.com/notes/bring-back-some-memories/tips-to-look-after-your-husband-excerpts-from-a-1950s-home-economics-text-book/378717735874795/.

Worstall, T. 'Business Gender Diversity Solved: More Women Means More Profits'. *Forbes*, 2016. https://www.forbes.com/sites/timworstall/2016/02/10/business-gender-diversity-solved-more-women-means-more-profits/#3031a818170f.

Zalis, S. 'Lessons From the World's Most Gender-Equal Countries'. *Forbes*, 2018. https://www.forbes.com/sites/shelleyzalis/2018/10/30/lessons-from-the-worlds-most-gender-equal-countries/#4c4d9ebe7dd8.

Zander, C. 'Even Scandinavia Has a CEO Gender Gap'. *The Wall Street Journal*, 2014. https://www.wsj.com/articles/how-sandvik-scania-are-addressing-the-ceo-gender-gap-1400712884.

Zarya, V. 'Think College Is Expensive? In Most States, Child Care Costs Even More'. *Fortune*, 2016. http://fortune.com/2016/09/28/child-care-costs/.

Conversations and Interviews

David Laibson, Johanna Wallenius and Melanne Verveer.

14

Israel: Start-Up Nation 2.0

Many countries have long admired and even tried to emulate Silicon Valley. Everyone has failed, save Israel. How did Israel become one of the foremost entrepreneurial hotspots of the world?

Female Soldiers Take a Break in the Desert Sun

Source: Israel Defence Forces

It's 7 p.m. on Allenby Street, a fashionable part of Tel Aviv with a breezy, carefree spirit. Young people getting off work are gathering at their favourite watering hole for a drink to unwind before going their ways home for dinner. Several eighteen-year-old girls in identical Israeli military uniforms are sporting guns slung over their shoulders. They are the age when many girls elsewhere dress to entice rather than frighten, to be different rather than the same. But we are in Israel, and it would take only seven minutes for a missile launched from Tehran to reach Tel Aviv, so everyone has to be perpetually alert.

As I sit nursing a drink, sirens roar as police cars, motorcycles and special forces block the road. Special forces looking like Michelin Men in their uniforms peel out of the vehicles. They move quickly yet fluidly. My heartbeat races but as I gaze beyond the periphery of the road, there is a surprising sense of calm. Far from being panic-stricken, onlookers appear more bored than afraid. A certain distance is kept, a cigarette is smoked, children continue to skip rope. The episode lasts about thirty minutes – a false alarm, yet again. For days now, the neighbourhood will be more tense than usual with heightened vigilance, but gradually the mood will change – until the next incident. I learn later that this happens almost every other month. Such is the pulse of life in Tel Aviv.

As the old saying goes, necessity is the mother of invention. And no nation in the world has grasped necessity, especially that of fighting terror, as intensely as Israel. It is a country on constant alert. Frisking at most public places is commonplace, and purses are rigorously checked at entrances to supermarkets and shopping malls. Going through a security check at Ben Gurion Airport is probably the closest one comes to being interrogated as a possible spy. Forget political correctness – people are suspected based on their colour and ethnicity using sophisticated algorithms or by sharp-eyed detectives. Questions are asked to expose the slightest pattern of deceit and answers are cross-examined.

This chapter provides an insight into how Israel has had a burst of technological innovation, despite considerable loss of peace and individual freedom. It is the story of a country which has experienced the worst geopolitical conflict of modern times and yet emerged prosperous. It is also a story with universal implications.

***

The Jewish people are one of the most ethnically diverse people in the world. Over six million Jews from countries all over the world are settled in Israel and nearly eight million are dispersed around the world, their largest numbers being in the US and France (Maltz 2018). The first wave of Jews to Israel came from Germany and eastern Europe, with the same lineage which dominates the American Jewish population. Then came the Sephardic Jews, migrants from Africa and the Middle East, originally expelled during the 1492 Spanish Inquisition. A number of Russian Jews migrated following the fall of the Soviet Union. In between, Jews from every part of the world settled in Israel by design or accident.

After the destruction of the Second Temple in 70 CE and the expulsion of Jews from ancient Israel, Jews dispersed throughout the world and transformed the concept of Israel into an ideal which passed from generation to generation and reinforced with each passing persecution. Wherever Jews went, they were subject to evictions, massacres and prohibitions. During times when agriculture was the dominant industry, Jews were prevented from owning land. Later, they found themselves excluded from craft and merchant guilds during the Middle Ages. They were confined to ghettos and denied their own names.

'Rothschild', meaning 'red shield' in German, was an arbitrary sign posted on the door of a Jewish ghetto shack in Frankfurt. Never mind that it would later become the world's central bank for over a century and the quintessence of the ultra-wealthy. In many places, Jews were unable to vote or hold office until well into the nineteenth century. Benjamin Disraeli could become prime minister in Britain in 1868 because he renounced his allegiance to Judaism and took Christian oaths. Unable to cast their votes at the ballot, Jewish political voices were silenced.

Theodor Herzl, an Austro-Hungarian writer, lit the torch and set the tone for Israel's renaissance after more than a thousand years of homelessness. In 1897, at the First Zionist Congress in Basel, Switzerland, he proclaimed the utopian form of Zionism, set out in his seminal book, *Der Judenstaat* (Jewish Nation). He said, 'The Jews who wish for a State will have it. We shall live at last as free men on our own soil, and die peacefully in our own homes. The world will be freed by our liberty, enriched by our wealth, magnified by our greatness.'

Herzl never lived to see the formation of Israel. It would take World War II and the Holocaust, in all its tragic severity, to overcome entrenched opposition and win international backing for the establishment of a new nation state. Even then, the formation of Israel proved easier said than done. In *Israel Is Real: An Obsessive Quest to Understand the Jewish Nation and its History*, Rich Cohen argues that the notion of Israel was much easier to inculcate and maintain compared to the establishment and governance of the actual nation. Chemi Peres, son of the late President Shimon Peres, recounted to me his father's recollection of his arrival: 'I came to Israel as a child and recall the disappointment of what I saw compared to what I hoped it would be. Dry land, barren, empty, nothing. We were allotted a parcel of land on the edge of a dessert carved out of a territory arbitrarily defined by the British mandate and surrounded by hostile neighbours, who all wanted to see us dead.'

So much for the 'Promised Land'.

Turn the clock forward by two generations and Israel has become one of the world's foremost entrepreneurial hotspots. With a thousand new firms launched every year, the country has far more high-tech start-ups per capita than any other nation in the world (TLVC 2015). Israel has the third-largest number of companies listed on Nasdaq, behind only the US and China (Williams 2018). With a population of 8.5 million people, it attracts more venture capital per capita than any other country, roughly two times as much as the US and five times as the UK (Dibner 2018). It leads the world in civilian R&D spending per capita (Cocco 2017). Trade with China exceeded $10 billion halfway through 2015, starting from zero, when diplomatic relations were established in 1992 (Yarowsky 2015). Israeli people have reaped the benefits. At $38,900, GDP per capita has raced past South Korea and increased eleven times since 1980 (OECD 2017). The unemployment rate is 3.7 per cent, a record low (Heruti-Sover 2018). Public debt has decreased to 61.2 per cent of GDP (Waksman 2019). Its current account is in surplus and foreign currency reserves are high.

Founded in 1948, Israel is actually a country in its adolescence. Its success story follows the familiar script used by other *TSTF* countries. This includes – a small, adaptive and ambitious population; a geopolitical struggle which hardens resolve; a lack of natural resources;

a tiny domestic market and hence the need to export; a dominant culture with homogenous values; stable, pro-business politics; considerable value placed on education and work ethic; and a vast, well-connected and resourceful diaspora.

Despite these advantages, the flowering of Israel's economy has been a relatively recent phenomenon. The country had to overcome many significant challenges since its inception. Its first step was to populate the nation and then to feed and defend itself. Herzl's utopian vision of Israel was a country of common values and egalitarian ideals. Early Israel was based on a network of kibbutzim – agricultural communities which symbolized and embodied these principles. Between 1940 and 1950, the number of kibbutzim in Israel nearly tripled from eighty-two to 214, with those living in them increasing from 26,550 to 67,550. Today, the number of kibbutzim is at 270 (Jewish Virtual Library, no date).

However, it takes more than utopian beliefs to spur prosperity; agriculture as a driving economic force has its limits. Large numbers of Jewish refugees from Europe, Africa and the Arab world presented challenges in both number and kind for kibbutzim. Until the 1950s, nearly all kibbutzniks were established by members from eastern Europe (Ashkenazi kibbutzim). Jews from Ethiopia, Iraq, Morocco and Russia may have practised the same religion, but they were considered culturally different. So, membership was often restricted. Also, the sheer numbers of new immigrants overwhelmed the fledgling infrastructure of a new, fragile nation.

A visitor to Israel in the 1970s would have landed in a relatively poor country by the standards of the US and developed European nations. Israel's near defeat in the Yom Kippur War in 1973 was a severe blow to the economy and triggered a spiral of high inflation which lingered until the mid-1980s. The war caused the nation to increase defence spending to a lofty 30 per cent of GDP in 1975 (*Economist* 2017). By 1984, public debt had reached nearly 300 per cent and hyperinflation peaked at 450 per cent per annum (*Economist* 2017). There were stringent restrictions on foreign exchange during this period and the shekel was an unstable and unreliable currency. In the early 1980s, the current account deficit was so large that many wrote off Israel as a failed political experiment. There was an increasing chorus of naysayers, revelling in the country's failure and reminding everyone that Israel never should have been permitted to exist in the first place.

It was during this crisis that Israel did some soul-searching and decided to radically shift emphasis from socialist ideals to a free market policy. It was only in 1988 that per capita GDP scraped by and surpassed $10,000 – still a meagre subsidence level by any standard at the time (Cerier 2017). David Shulman of the *New York Review* summed it up when he quipped that Israel was, at the time, a 'mildly Mediterranean version of a modern European social democracy'. The problem was that Israel's economy was in a structural cul-de-sac. It consisted of remnants of agriculture modelled after the kibbutz system and a clutch of businesses and banks effectively controlled by a close circle of oligarchs who collaborated to optimize rents. Israel's oligarchs owed their position not to innovation or entrepreneurship, but to their families' success in gaining control of businesses which the government privatized in the 1980s as a part of its move towards free markets (Ben-David and Wainer 2010).

Then, a couple of stars aligned to unleash the 'Israeli Tiger'. The first star was the failure of the Israeli government to fund the aerospace firm, Israel Aerospace Industries (IAI), which was working at the time on building a fighter jet, Lavi. IAI was forced to lay off thousands of highly-qualified engineers, who then flooded the private sector. These engineers set the stage for the initial wave of start-ups in Israel. The second star was an unlikely source. Between 1989 and 2006, following the collapse of the former Soviet Union, nearly one million Russian Jews migrated to Israel, bringing in thousands of talented engineers and scientists in what is referred to as the 'brain gain' (Maital 2013).[18] They propelled the sudden 20 per cent increase in Israel's population. Rather than the meek-mannered farmers living in communes, or sedate bankers eking

---

18. According to a study by Sarit Cohen of Bar-Ilan University and Chang-Tai Hsieh from Princeton University, '57,000 [Russian immigrants] had worked as engineers and 12,000 as medical doctors; in contrast, there were only 30,000 engineers and 15,000 medical doctors in Israel in 1989' (Maital 2013).

out monopoly-like rents, these people were engineers, scientists, doctors and researchers desperate to survive and keen to make a mark.

Additionally, the internet radically enhanced Israel's ability to compete on a global scale. Since Israel's inception, its defining resource was oil and the focus was regional. Suddenly, data-mining became more important and the internet widened the nation's horizon. Almost overnight, the cost of distance was significantly reduced and Israel was no longer a remote economy stuck within the desolation of the Middle East. The internet was unregulated, yet still accessible as it was not controlled by oligarchs. The opportunities were limitless; anyone could use the World Wide Web to their advantage.

The environment welcomed small teams not needing large amounts of capital and offered an incredible range of improvisation. This platform suited the Israeli mindset – one has to think outside the box and disrupt the status quo. Until this point, 'made in Israel' had a bad reputation for quality; Israeli workers were seen as unreliable when it came to manufacturing, an area which requires routine and repetitive tasks. But software programming is different altogether. There is no routine. An idea once formulated can be implemented effortlessly multiple times. The capital required was modest compared to biotech, medical devices and electronic equipment. Israel Inc. could focus on its strengths in the supply chain, that is, R&D and product development. It could then partner with companies, mainly in the US, leaving them to do the monotonous yet essential metal bashing, logistics and sales.

Tel Aviv fortunately had all the necessary ingredients to become a start-up mecca. It was an attractive place for people in their twenties who were willing to take risks. It was an inexpensive and cool place to live, considering its vibrant culture and nightlife. The city was rife with hungry and talented young engineers and scientists desperate to succeed. The impact of the brain gain made it reminiscent of Palo Alto of the 1980s or Seattle of the 2000s. The factors which have and continue to drive Israel's innovation machine are unique to its journey. The recipe has several home-grown ingredients including religion, military and diaspora.

Chutzpah and Moms

In *The Chosen Few*, Zvi Eckstein, Dean of the Tiomkin School of Economics at IDC Herzliya, and Maristella Botticini, a professor at Bocconi University, explain that one of the keys to Israel's success was education. For over a millennium, all Jewish men were required to learn to read the *Torah*, so basic literacy was achieved long before other cultures (It wasn't until the Protestant Reformation that Christians of protestant denominations were encouraged to read). Knowledge was encouraged, and so was curiosity.

The ancient Jewish sages of the *Talmud* had a tradition of constantly questioning everything and looking for new answers, a tradition which has not faded over time. A rabbi in Jerusalem joked to me that 'the *Talmud* is 600 years of argument "codified"'. There is a popular word in Hebrew to describe constructive defiance – chutzpah. While there is no exact translation, its synonyms are 'gall', 'brazen nerve', 'effrontery' and 'incredible guts'. Chutzpah has permeated into Israeli society, generating intolerance of hierarchy and encouragement of constructive criticism. The military is the quintessence of authority and great military leaders around the world espouse the importance of the chain of command, ranks and following orders. But subordinates in the Israeli military are permitted to challenge and contradict their superiors, as long as it is meant to lead to understanding or improvement.

Another well-known Jewish trait is that people feel a perpetual lack of satisfaction. Shimon Peres, former president of Israel, who immigrated in 1934 and was considered the protégé of Israel's founding father David Ben-Gurion, felt that it was the innate dissatisfaction coupled with defiance among Jews which have been the fundamental drivers for innovation in the country (Peres 2017).

Yossi Vardi credits the concept of the 'Jewish mother' for this never-ending dissatisfaction. Vardi, a gruff venture capitalist who invented ICQ, the first standalone instant messaging service, is widely considered one of the fathers of the Israeli start-up scene. Stroking his thick unkempt moustache, he told me, 'Jewish mothers are our secret sauce. From birth till death, they tell us we must succeed, that we must be better than our cousins, or her friend's son, or whoever.' Vardi says that this mother figure is not strictly gendered and can be embodied in a father or even a grandmother. In any case, it is engrained in the Jewish mindset. 'There is a culture of success in Israel driven by a need to prove yourself, if only to meet the expectations of our mothers,' he adds.

Figure 14.1: Mother

Source: Banx

Unit 8200

Israel's second secret sauce is its military. It is an elixir for social cohesion, a flywheel which generates constant technical innovations and a rigorous and no-nonsense training ground for future entrepreneurs and industry leaders.

At its inception in 1948, Israel studied the Swiss military system and borrowed the concept of mandatory military service. It went one step further from Switzerland by including women in positions involving combat. Most recruits are drafted, psychologically screened and receive weapons training right after high school. Three years of service gives the military an opportunity to systematically identify, recruit and develop the nation's brightest talent. From eighteen years of age, young men and women learn how to assume responsibility, set and achieve goals, and lead subordinates irrespective of their social class or level of education. Shlomo Yanai tells me, 'It's intensive and free management training of the most effective kind.' He's a former commanding general in the Israel defence force and CEO of Teva, Israel's largest company.

The pantheon of Israel's military elite divides into two categories – officers in the Israeli air force and members of Unit 8200, the Israeli forces' electronic-intelligence wing. The top priority of Israel's defence is early recognition of dangers and rapid response. The former depends on competences developed in Unit 8200 and the latter on the air force. Most of the nation's great entrepreneurs and innovators are from the air force and the technical branches of the Israeli Defence Force (IDF), especially Unit 8200.

The most capable people are admitted to Unit 8200 and according to someone who ran this unit for a number of years, '90 per cent of the secret intelligence from the IDF comes from it.' Moreover, IDF is the most respected institution in Israel, enjoying even more respect than its Supreme Court, and vastly more than politicians. This is clear from the fact that the common feature of political leadership under the Likud or the Labour Party and its predecessor, the Mapai Party, has been unconditional support of the military.

Ohad Bobrov, vice president and chief technology officer at Check Point Software Technologies, explained to me how it works. A third generation Israeli of a mixed Russian and Yemeni lineage, Bobrov was talent-spotted by his teachers as a child and encouraged to take computer programming classes. He was then recommended for Mamram, an elite software development course of the Israeli army. 'It's a highly selective programme and my mother was very happy to learn of my acceptance,' says Bobrov. 'Joining Unit 8200 was the most significant event in my life. We were asked to solve problems we knew others were unable to solve, so the notion of failure is not only acceptable but good. It means you are trying to do a very hard thing so the bar is very high. We are taught that failure is a building block for success because we learn much more failing than succeeding. But we must stand up to mistakes, study them, extract the lessons and then move on.'

Bobrov, a veteran of the Rolling Sword Squadron, a helicopter attack unit of the Israeli air force and CEO of his third start-up, told me how they routinely debrief and analyse what is right or wrong: 'I am regularly surprised to see how many American companies, large or small, don't sit down as a team and be critical. Not for assigning whose fault it was, but for figuring out how to do it better next time.'

After Bobrov completed his military service and before he moved on to his third start-up, he sold his second start-up to Check Point, the largest cyber security company in Israel and one of Israel's most successful start-ups. Gil Shwed, co-founder of Check Point, is also from Unit 8200; he invented the firewall for PCs, as did the founder of Waze and Mobileye, both among Israel's most successful start-ups. For Bobrov and other graduates of Unit 8200, it is a path to a rewarding life, conferring a huge competitive advantage. 'Every kid who leaves Unit 8200 thinks he's going to be a cyber-millionaire,' says Yigal Erlich, one of the pioneers of Israel's venture-capital scene. Shlomo Yanai agrees, 'There is no better credential. A PhD from Technion or a Masters from the Harvard Business School don't compare in value.'

The defence industry, start-ups, technology, research and innovation are all part of the same ecosystem. Universities, companies, military and secret services thrive based on tight co-dependence and cohabitation. Chemi Peres told me that one third of the high technology firms have a member from Unit 8200. Professors at Technion served in the technical branch of the military and still maintain contacts and receive research contracts. While most militaries have compliance units, regulations and fines for conflicts of interest, the Israeli military's operative word is 'synergies'. For example, an Israeli officer helped start Israel's drone programme in the late 1960s by buying battery operated, remote-controlled airplanes at FAO Schwarz, a toy store in Manhattan, and sending them back to Israel in the embassy's diplomatic pouch. According to a recent study by PWC, the market for drones is now estimated to be nearly $130 billion with all sorts of applications (PWC 2016). Israel's drone programme would not have been possible without the remarkable support of many people.

While the developed countries were doing away with their voluntary militias and shifting to permanent paid personnel, Israel was building up and extending its system of conscription, spurred by frugal means. Israel decided to invest in brains while other military systems continued to stress brawn. It also helps that Israel is small. Small armies and small companies are suitable for free-form organizations. But organizational experts say that once units exceed fifty, these methods of management become counterproductive.

Diaspora

Israel's third home-grown advantage is its potent and widespread diaspora. David Ben-Gurion once said, 'Suffering makes a people greater and we have suffered much.' This shared suffering has helped define the acute sense of belonging of the Jewish diaspora. Ben-Gurion engaged Jewry anywhere as partners in the enterprise of Israel's resurgence in the ancient homeland, going so far as to say that 'their faith is their passport.' Israel is a country built more by people than by territory. Countries such as Ireland, India, Greece and China may have vast diasporas, but Israel is the only country which was formed by its diaspora. The Jews in Israel came from Ethiopia, France, Russia, America and Yemen. Over half the world's Jewish population are Israeli-born to at least one parent who was also Israeli-born. Around 46 per cent of the Jewish population resides in Israel, a country which has nearly nine million citizens. At the same time, one in four Jewish individuals live in a country different from where they were born, which makes Jewish people 'the world's top migrants' (Jewish Virtual Library 2018). This combined coefficient of migration in Israel is high by global standards and common with other *TSTF* countries such as the Netherlands, Ireland, Singapore and Switzerland.

For Israel, the diaspora has been a valuable source of growth, talent, capital and start-ups. Jim Sherwin, who used to be Bobby Fisher's sparring partner in chess (both Jewish), and later with Hunter Douglas, once told me that the Jews were like other prosperous communities around the world including the Huguenots, Parsis, Mormons and offshore Chinese – smart, well connected, tribal and hungry for success. While Israel's population has come in waves, its annualized growth has averaged 5.3 per cent since its inception (World Bank 2017). GDP equals people times productivity and Israel has leveraged both fronts. Immigrants have provided impetus for development of infrastructure and job growth, benefiting the economy enormously. Immigration has also helped to keep Israel's demographic composition young and vibrant. Around 51 per cent of Israelis are below thirty compared to 30 per cent in Germany, 28 per cent in Japan and 40 per cent in the US (Senor and Singer 2011).

Studies show that immigrants have lower risk aversion and are more likely to start a new business because they are out of their comfort zones and eager to achieve recognition. This is not unique to Israel. Elon Musk of Tesla, Sergey Brin of Google, Steve Jobs of Apple, Jeff Bezos of Amazon and Pierre Omidyar of eBay were immigrants or children of immigrants (Roberts 2017). More than half of America's start-ups worth at least $1 billion have at least one immigrant founder, and seven of these were founded by Israeli immigrants (Anderson 2016).

Many Israelis also migrate to foreign countries and serve as outposts to spot opportunities or threats. Some come back loaded with valuable experience and relationships. The diaspora has also been an important source of capital. Almost all the venture capital invested in Israel over the past thirty years has come from overseas investors, with Israeli institutions notably absent (a source of consternation among many). In addition, successful Jews abroad have been generous benefactors. Michael Steinhardt, a famous hedge fund manager, almost single-handedly established and funded Birthright.[19]

Most of all, the diaspora provides an extraordinary source of connections and talent. As David Brooks notes, 'Jews are a famously accomplished group' (Brooks 2010). Choose an epoch or field at random and you will find them pushing the frontiers of achievement. Think of Bohr, Einstein, Freud, Marx, Mahler, Spinoza or even Levi Strauss. The genius of Jews doesn't seem to be waning, judging from recent contributions from the likes of Bernanke, Brin, Lauder, Spielberg and Zuckerberg. They make up 0.2 per cent of the world population, 27 per cent of the Nobel physics laureates, 31 per cent of medicine laureates, 21 per cent of the Ivy League student bodies, 38 per cent of those on *Business Week*'s list of leading philanthropists, and 51 per cent of the Pulitzer Prize winners for non-fiction (Brooks 2010). Among the Jewish diaspora, a kind of 'We will try to help you if we can' attitude is palpable. It is no wonder that this list is so impressive.

---

19. Taglit-Birthright Israel, also known as Birthright Israel or simply Birthright, is a not-for-profit educational organization which sponsors free ten-day heritage trips for young adults of Jewish heritage, aged 18–26, to visit Israel generally for the first time.

Challenges

While Israel has rightly earned accolades for its success in developing its enviable entrepreneurial ecosystems, there are still many challenges ahead.

Teva Pharmaceutical Industries, Israel's most valuable company, is ranked only 704th in Forbes's Global 2000 list (Forbes 2018). This is also the only Israeli firm which appears in the world's 500 largest companies list by market cap. Other countries studied in *Too Small to Fail* have ecosystems which are much better at producing successful multinationals. Denmark, for instance, has a smaller population than Israel (5.8m versus 8.97m) but three companies in the top 500. Sweden (10.2m) has nine, Switzerland (8.6m) has seventeen, while the Netherlands (17.1m) has twelve (*Economist* 2014). Critics say that Israeli entrepreneurs are better at starting businesses than growing them and are eager to sell out when $5 or 10 million is waved under their noses. Making these early exits is like selling seeds before the fruits ripen. Chemi Peres explained to me, 'Jews have been subject to so much loss and uncertainty that the prospect of becoming financially independent is a huge temptation.' Indeed, Israeli start-ups rarely go public. According to the Milken Institute think tank, from 2002 to 2012, only 9 per cent of exits were IPOs (rather than being bought by a bigger firm) and these IPOs had an average size of just $32 million. In the US, the numbers were 20 per cent and $237 million (*Economist* 2014).

If start-ups grow into big firms, this can generate greater benefits for society. Eugene Kandel, professor at the Hebrew University of Jerusalem, agrees: 'Opportunities at R&D centres tend to be constrained to high-end developers while larger companies hire more sales staff, accountants and the like.'

Chemi Peres thinks the trend is changing as the second generation of successful or serial entrepreneurs take charge. Entrepreneurs now realize that they sacrificed too much value selling out early and are keen to build more valuable businesses. Waze, a car navigation service, for instance, waited a few years before Google acquired it in 2013 for $966 million. Wix, which helps people create websites, turned down several acquisition offers and went public in 2013 (*Economist* 2014). In 2014,

Mobileye, which makes software which helps drivers avoid car accidents, raised $890 million, a record for an Israeli company going public in the US (*Economist* 2014).

There is a list of other growing concerns on the horizon. Former Intel Israel president, Mooly Eden, feels Israel has a shortage of workers in engineering, maths and science training.[20] Israel also runs the risk of pricing itself out of the start-up market unless it can keep a lid on cost increases. Young people are more willing to take chances if living costs are low. But rents and food prices have both spiralled upwards. Israel has attracted considerable venture capital to establish a vibrant start-up community, but returns have thus far been disappointing. To maintain this lifeline, investors will need to be rewarded more generously.[21] It would also help if Israel's pension funds and insurance companies, which should be able to bear the risk of venture investing and invest for the long term, started to invest and support their country's start-up activities.

Most disturbing of all may be the remarkably high level of inequality in Israel. Average figures are misleading as the benefits are limited to the few who are winners in the start-up space and others increasingly feel left behind. There are three main reasons for the beneficiaries being limited in number – the ultra-orthodox often live on public subsidies to pursue a life of religious (Talmudic) studies; Arab citizens struggle to participate in higher wage occupations or as entrepreneurs; and the low-probability–high-impact nature of start-ups benefits only a small number of exceptionally rich (and fortunate) entrepreneurs.

---

20. The number of high school students taking five units of maths has declined from 13,000 in 2007 to around 9,000 in 2013, a 30 per cent drop (Arlosoroff 2014).

21. Start-up investing normally produces only 2–3 payoffs out of 20–30 investments, with a high failure rate. Israeli start-ups have been unable to scale and constantly exit early to foreign buyers, so most portfolios are missing these big-impact winners. This has also been compounded by entrepreneurs who circumvent venture capital funds and raise money directly on the basis of their reputations and networks, such as with arguably Israel's most successful start-up, Mobileye.

Too Important to Fail

Israel at once impresses, captivates, frustrates and infuriates. In a short period, it has emerged as an oasis of prosperity in a deeply troubled region. Robert Solow, a Nobel laureate, demonstrated that rising incomes are largely attributable to technological progress and not to capital accumulation or cost improvements.

Israel's GDP per person was last recorded at $40,258 and set to increase. Its standard of living is on par with Europe's most-developed economies (CEIC 2018). In 2015, Israel was ranked among the five happiest countries in the world according to the Better Life Index published by the OECD, just behind other *TSTF* countries, Denmark, Switzerland and Finland. Over 300 multinationals have set up R&D centers in Israel to mine and invest in Israeli innovations so growth is programmed to continue. Delegations from Brazil, China, Ireland and Singapore visit Israel in hordes trying to understand its success formula, which comes as no surprise.

Figure 14.2: 300 Multinational R&D Centres

Israel has become a mecca for MNC research centres.

Source: Start-up Nation Central

Israel also attracts with its breezy informality. Its lack of hierarchy provides a solid base for meritocracy and accepting mistakes as stepping stones.

Cohesion, belonging and placing community above self-interest is important for stability in any society. The team-spirited life agriculture offers is clearly fading, but a little bit of kibbutz seems to be present in every Israeli I met. Psychologist Tal Ben-Shahar suggests, 'The number-one predictor of happiness is the time we spend with people we care about and who care about us' (*Octavian Report* 2015). He feels Israelis are happier because friends and family are very important to them. Professor Shlomo Maital of Technion, Israel's equivalent of MIT, adds that children also matter: 'Israel has the highest fertility rate among OECD countries. When there are lots of babies and children around, they give hope for the future' (Collins 2016).

This may sound like the 'land of milk and honey' from 'Exodus 3:8' of the *Torah*. It is what Herzl envisaged on the establishment of Zionism in Basel in 1897. But Shimon Peres reminds me of the problems ahead: 'Leading the Jewish people is not easy – we are a divided, obstinate, highly individualistic people who have cultivated faith, sharp-wittedness and polemics to a very high level' (Peres 1986). Indeed, Israel is bursting with polemics and contradictions. It has more R&D researchers per capita, but its youth score below the OECD average on maths tests administered by PISA. It may have among the most intricate and cohesive social norms in the world, but it is among the worst countries when it comes to contract enforcement and has the highest per capita number of lawyers in the world.

Most disturbingly, while Israel ranks among the twenty most-competitive countries and the ten most-innovative countries in the world, it has one of the most unequal income distributions among Western nations. Professor Maital told me, 'For a society that needs internal social cohesion when facing external threats, such inequality is a clear and present danger.' Tamir Pardo, ex-chief of the Mossad, Israel's national intelligence agency and someone uniquely trained to assess looming dangers of all sorts, agrees: 'The most pressing threat to Israel is not Iran, but rather the increased polarization within Israeli society' (Whitman 2016).

Further, Israel must resolve its conflict with Palestine. It would be difficult to find a country which receives more press per capita. This would be fine if it were positive. But much of it isn't. Most of the world wants the Israeli–Palestinian conflict resolved rather than just living with it. This is possible. As our chapter on Ireland points out, even Sinn Féin and the IRA agreed to put their swords down.

All these challenges appear daunting and would seem to justify a good deal of pessimism. But if Israel teaches us anything, it is that it remains full of people who are full of hope while others around them despair. Shimon Peres, Israel's perennial beacon of confidence, famously said, 'Optimists and pessimists die the exact same death, but they live very different lives!' (Zapesochny 2016). What Peres failed to add was that pessimists are often wrong because they assume a world where there is no change or innovation. They simply extrapolate from the present, failing to recognize the new developments and insights which might alter the current trends. Anyone who had plotted Israel's trajectory in 1973 would have predicted that it would have self-destructed by now. But it hasn't – Israel is among the most innovative countries in the world.

Israel 2.0 has a far stronger base compared to 1973, when it was given up for dead. There are 344 R&D centres firmly planted in Israeli soil, funded by the likes of Google, Intel and Samsung (Marker 2018). However, 653 start-ups which had been in business for at least four years wound up operations in 2014, so there is a cumulative treasure of wisdom extracted mainly from failure (Orpaz 2017). There are also cheap, direct flights which connect San Francisco and Shanghai to Tel Aviv. There are clusters of companies and expertise around biotech, blockchain, artificial intelligence, food technology, driverless cars and cyber security.

More importantly, the mindset has changed. Innovation and start-ups have become a national sport. Eyal Niv, a partner of Pitango, a leading venture capitalist, told me that his ten-year-old son said, 'When I grow up, I want to run a start-up.' Similarly, Ohad Bobrov of Unit 8200 told me, 'Mothers used to want their children to grow up to become officers in the military, medical doctors or professors. Now they want them to become entrepreneurs.'

Israel 2.0 has much of what the world yearns for, but it needs to build companies and not just start them. It must also figure out a way to allow the less privileged to participate in the spoils, or risk losing the social cohesion which has built its Noah's Ark. As Yossi Vardi summarizes, 'Society is a boat and if it sinks, the next big start-up won't save it.' But it is worth having some Israeli optimism. And who among us would not benefit from a bit more chutzpah?

References and Further Reading

'About us'. *Tel-Aviv Capital*, 2015. http://www.tlvc.co.il.

Anderson, S. 'Immigrants and Billion Dollar Startups'. *National Foundation for American Policy*, 2016. http://nfap.com/wp-content/uploads/2016/03/Immigrants-and-Billion-Dollar-Startups.NFAP-Policy-Brief.March-2016.pdf.

Arlosoroff, M. 'What's Threatening the Future of Israeli High-Tech? A Shortage of Math Students'. *Haaretz*, 2014. https://www.haaretz.com/israel-news/business/.premium-the-fuzzy-math-behind-matriculation-exams-1.5261700.

Bassok, M. 'Israel Cut Public Debt to Record Low 62.1% of GDP in 2016, Marking Seventh Annual Drop'. *Haaretz*, 2017. https://www.haaretz.com/israel-news/business/israel-cut-public-debt-to-record-low-62-1-of-gdp-in-2016-1.5489409.

Ben-David, C. and D. Wainer. 'The Controversy Over Israel's Business Elite'. *Bloomberg*, 2010. https://www.bloomberg.com/news/articles/2010-10-07/the-controversy-over-israels-business-elite#p1.

'Better Life Index 2015', *OECD*, 2015. https://www.oecd-ilibrary.org/social-issues-migration-health/data/oecd-social-and-welfare-statistics/better-life-index-2015-edition-2015_493ca5e9-en.

Brooks, D. 'The Tel Aviv Cluster'. *The New York Times*, 2010. https://www.nytimes.com/2010/01/12/opinion/12brooks.html?mtrref=en.wikipedia.org&gwh=B234E221F3FFB1495980575A202FD0CA&gwt=pay.

Cerier, S.E. 'Israel's economy has flourished only recently'. *Financial Times*, 2017. https://www.ft.com/content/e3117cd8-4c3f-11e7-919a-1e14ce4af89b.

Cocco, F. 'How Israel is leading the world in R&D investment'. *Financial Times*, 2017. https://www.ft.com/content/546af0b2-ede5-11e6-930f-061b01e23655.

Cohen, R. *Israel is Real: An Obsessive Quest to Understand the Jewish Nation and its History* (New York: Picador, 2010).

Collins, L. 'My word: population density, people power and blessings'. *The Jerusalem Post*, 2016. https://www.jpost.com/Opinion/My-Word-Population-density-people-power-and-blessings-469139.

Dibner, G. 'European & Israeli Venture Data 2017'. *Medium*, 2018. https://medium.com/angularventures/european-israeli-venture-data-2017-45510d40c5f1.

Eckstein, Z.M. and Botticini. *The Chosen Few: How Education Shaped Jewish History, 70-1492* (Princeton, N.J.: Princeton University Press, 2012).

'Faith on the Move – The Religious Affiliation of International Migrants'. *Pew Research Centre*, 2012. http://www.pewforum.org/2012/03/08/religious-migration-exec/.

'GDP growth (annual %)'. *The World Bank*, 2017. https://data.worldbank.org/indicator/NY.GDP.MKTP.KD.ZG?end=2017&locations=IL&start=1961&view=chart.

'Global Market for Commercial Applications of Drone Technology Valued at over $127 bn'. *PWC*, 2016. https://press.pwc.com/News-releases/global-market-for-commercial-applications-of-drone-technology-valued-at-over--127-bn/s/ac04349e-c40d-4767-9f92-a4d219860cd2.

'Gross Domestic Product (GDP)'. *OECD Data*, 2017. https://data.oecd.org/gdp/gross-domestic-product-gdp.htm.

Heruti-Sover, T. 'Israel's Unemployment Rate Drops to 3.7%, Part-Time Jobs on the Rise'. *Haaretz*, 2018. https://www.haaretz.com/israel-news/business/israel-s-unemployment-rate-drops-to-3-7-part-time-jobs-on-the-rise-1.5865222.

Herzl, T. *The Jewish State* (New York: Dover Publications, 2008). http://www.gutenberg.org/files/25282/25282-h/25282-h.htm.

'Israel'. *Better Life Index 2017, OECD*, 2017. http://www.oecdbetterlifeindex.org/countries/israel/.

Israel Defence Forces. 'Female Soldiers Take a Break in the Desert Sun'. *Flickr*, 2011. https://www.flickr.com/photos/idfonline/6005011659/.

'Israel forecast: nominal GDP per capita'. *CEIC Data*, no date. https://www.ceicdata.com/en/indicator/israel/forecast-nominal-gdp-per-capita.

'Israel's economy is a study in contrasts'. *The Economist*, 2017. https://www.economist.com/special-report/2017/05/18/israels-economy-is-a-study-in-contrasts.

Maital, S. 'The debilitating brain drain'. *The Jerusalem Post*, 2013. https://www.jpost.com/Magazine/Opinion/The-debilitating-brain-drain.

Maltz, J. 'World Jewish Population on Eve of New Year – 14.7 Million'. *Haaretz*, 2018. https://www.haaretz.com/jewish/.premium-world-jewish-population-on-eve-of-new-year-14-7-million-1.6464812.

'#704 Teva Pharmaceutical'. *Forbes*, 2018. https://www.forbes.com/companies/teva-pharmaceutical/#25ef6b013915.

Orpaz, I. 'For Every Mobileye, 600 Israeli Start-ups Crash'. *Haaretz*, 2017. https://www.haaretz.com/israel-news/business/for-every-mobileye-600-israeli-start-ups-crash-1.5450822.

Peres, S. 'In Homage to Ben-Gurion'. *The New York Times Magazine*, 1986. https://www.nytimes.com/1986/10/05/magazine/in-homage-to-ben-gurion.html.

Peres, S. *No Room for Small Dreams: Courage, Imagination and the Making of Modern Israel* (London: W&N, 2017).

Roberts, J.J. '7 Well-Known Tech Firms Founded by Immigrants or Their Children'. *Fortune*. 2017. http://fortune.com/2017/01/30/tech-immigrant-founders/.

Senor, D. and S. Singer. *Start-Up Nation: The Story of Israel's Economic Miracle* (New York; Boston: Twelve, 2011).

Shulman, D. 'Israel's Irrational Rationality'. *The New York Review of Books*, 2017. https://www.nybooks.com/articles/2017/06/22/israels-irrational-rationality/.

'The Art of Happiness: an interview with Tal Ben-Shahar'. *Octavian Report*, 2016. https://octavianreport.com/article/tal-ben-shahar-on-how-to-be-happy/.

'The Kibbutz & Moshav: History & Overview'. *Jewish Virtual Library*, no date. https://www.jewishvirtuallibrary.org/history-and-overview-of-the-kibbutz-movement.

The Marker. 'Multinationals Open More Than 20 R&D Centers a Year in Israel'. *Haaretz*, 2018. https://www.haaretz.com/israel-news/business/multinationals-open-over-20-r-d-centers-a-year-in-israel-on-average-1.6436189.

'The scale-up nation'. *The Economist*, 2014. https://www.economist.com/business/2014/12/11/the-scale-up-nation.

'Unemployment rate, Total, % of labor force, 2006-2012'. *OECD Data*, 2016. https://data.oecd.org/chart/5oLd.

'Vital Statistics: Latest Population Statistics for Israel'. *Jewish Virtual Library*, 2018. https://www.jewishvirtuallibrary.org/latest-population-statistics-for-israel.

Waksman, A. 'Israel's Public Debt Grows for First Time Since 2009'. *Haaretz*, 2019. https://www.haaretz.com/israel-news/business/israel-s-public-debt-grows-for-first-time-since-2009-1.6895665.

Whitman, A. 'Ex Mossad chief: Israel's biggest threat is potential civil war, not Iran'. *The Jerusalem Post*, 2016. https://www.jpost.com/Israel-News/Politics-And-Diplomacy/Ex-Mossad-chief-Israels-biggest-threat-is-potential-civil-war-not-Iran-466415.

Williams, S.M. 'How Israel Became the Startup Nation Having the 3rd Most Companies on the Nasdaq'. *Seeking Alpha*, 2018. https://seekingalpha.com/article/4151094-israel-became-startup-nation-3rd-companies-nasdaq.

Yarowsky, M. 'With Strong Tech Ties, Is Israel China's New Best Friend?' *NoCamels*. 2015. http://nocamels.com/2015/05/china-israel-tech-relations/.

Zapesochny, R. 'The Quintessential Israeli Optimist'. *The American Spectator*, 2016. https://spectator.org/the-quintessential-israeli-optimist/.

Conversations and Interviews

Chemi Peres, Eugene Kandel, Eyal Niv, Jim Sherwin, Mooly Eden, Ohad Bobrov, Saul Singer, Shlomo Maital, Shlomo Yanai, Yigal Erlich and Yossi Vardi.

15

Australia: Lay Down Your Weapons

Lessons from Australia on how to eradicate firearms atrocities

The Gun Buy-back Programme

Source: Wikimedia Commons

'If more guns made [America] safer, we'd be the safest country on earth'

– Pete Buttigieg, Mayor of South Bend, Indiana

On 28 April 1996, Carolyn Loughton was enjoying lunch with her fifteen-year-old daughter, Sarah, at the Broad Arrow Café near the waterfront in Australia's historic Port Arthur. They were at their

259

table when Martin Bryant, a psychologically disturbed man, entered the restaurant and began shooting. Carolyn threw herself on top of her daughter and was shot in the back. Carolyn survived her injury, but Sarah – who was shot in the head, did not. So began a nine-hour killing spree which left thirty-five dead and twenty-three wounded, the worst mass shooting in the nation's history. Bryant's weapons, a semiautomatic Colt AR-15 and a .308 FN rifle, had been legally purchased – despite the fact that Bryant had qualified for a disability pension on psychiatric grounds.

Twelve days after the Port Arthur attack, the public outcry spurred Australia's then prime minister, John Howard, to enact a sweeping package of gun reforms. The reforms prohibited automatic and semi-automatic assault rifles and required licensees to take a gun safety class and demonstrate a legitimate need other than self-defence for a particular type of gun. The most innovative and effective aspect of the reforms, however, was the gun buy-back programme, in which taxpayers paid $250 million for the purchase and destruction of over 650,000 privately owned guns (Wahlquist 2016).

Today, more than two decades since Carolyn Loughton lay helplessly with her lifeless daughter in her arms, few Australians would deny that their country is safer as a consequence of the reforms. In the eighteen years before the 1996 reforms, Australia suffered thirteen gun massacres (Grubel 2013). Since then, there have been just two.

How did Australia succeed in passing these reforms, and what can the US and other countries learn from them today?

* * *

Howard's Choice

John Howard was sitting in his residence at Kirribilli House, in a quiet suburb of Sydney, when he received a call from his chief of staff informing him of the massacre. After four and a half years leading the conservative Liberal Party in opposition, Howard was finally the prime minister. Only two months earlier, he had been swept into office with a forty-five-seat majority, the second largest in Australian history. Gun control had not featured in Howard's campaign, although as head of the Liberal Party, he was expected to support the status quo on guns, which was largely a hands-off policy. But the killings forced him to choose – should he stake his hard-earned and scarce political capital on something which had nothing to do with the reason he was elected? Should he pass up the opportunity to achieve long overdue progress?

Howard likened the situation to the moment in rugby when a player must decide whether to tackle a burly oncoming opponent. There is a split second to decide, and then there is no looking back. The opponent senses the determination of the tackler and chooses whether to shift from a collision to a compromise mode. This was Howard's moment, and he decided to engage. Australia had experienced multiple mass killings in the past, but their reaction soon blew over. Why was it different this time?

Tipping the Scale

Howard's legislative push was successful for a number of reasons. One was the clever design of the gun buy-back programme. Regulations are normally about punishment, not reward. But in this case, people were getting paid for handing in their guns, most of which were lying idle in their basements. Moreover, the price offered by the government was based on the value of a new gun, which was considerably more money than one could get at a pawnshop. As the duration of the offer was limited, gun holders faced the prospect of missing the opportunity to cash in and then being caught with an illegal gun once the law was enacted. So fear of missing out as well as getting into trouble contributed to the scheme's popularity.

The scale of the atrocity also helped to tip the scales and convince the public that something had to be done. William Cox, the judge who presided over Martin Bryant's trial, told me, 'It was the sheer magnitude of the atrocity that shook the foundations of Australian society.' Since the beginning of the twentieth century, all of Australia's previous mass shootings had fewer than fifteen casualties, except for two massacres of indigenous Australians in the late 1920s. Port Arthur's thirty-five deaths and twenty-three injuries, by contrast, left the country in shock.

Another factor was speed. Howard and the Liberals responded almost immediately. Philip Alpers, associate professor at the University of Sydney, told the *Guardian*, 'At that stage the gun lobby was the ruling lobby in Australia. What happened at Port Arthur is that they were outpaced, outflanked and outwitted by a man who had the power to move in twelve remarkable days' (Wahlquist 2016). This deprived the gun lobby of crucial time to organize and delay the action. Howard had the goodwill of his landslide election on his side and he decided to put it to work. 'Progress in politics is 90 per cent about timing,' he told me.

As a conservative politician pushing a left-wing policy, Howard was able to garner support from his conservative base as well as from the opposition. Guns were regulated by the states, so Howard needed to convince them all to back his proposal. Two of the most powerful states, Queensland and Western Australia, initially baulked. They only came around after Howard threatened to hold a referendum on making gun registration the responsibility of the federal government. Since surveys showed that 90 per cent of Australians, including vast majorities in these two states, were in favour of the measures, this threat had teeth (Wahlquist 2016). Howard also appeased state governors by allocating generous funding for the buy-back program to the tune of US$57 million per state.

Women were the final, and arguably the most important, reason for the buy-back scheme's success. Daughters, wives, mothers and grandmothers rallied together and persuaded, even hounded, their fathers, husbands, sons, brothers and grandsons to cash in their weapons. Some even joked that the debate was triggering sex moratoriums among couples. 'Women made up 52 per cent of the voters, but more of the nation's voice,' Howard said. He recalled how an elderly woman from Brisbane told him, 'I've never voted for you and don't think I ever will, but my hat's off to you for what you've proposed to control guns.'

Lessons Learned

The Australian story is instructive for a number of reasons – factual, emotional and political. Australia demonstrated how a nation's sense of identity can change to suit the times. The Australian mindset, as we have seen, is not dissimilar to the American one. As the myths of the frontier and the Wild West have done in the US, the Australian Outback has bred a sense of rugged self-reliance among many Australians. However, other elements in the Australian reform, particularly the speed with which a new consensus could overpower sharp divisions, highlight some of the advantages of a country being small.

Figure 15.1: Gun Control

Source: Banx

Policy-making is always about trade-offs between individual interest groups and the collective interest. In the case of firearms regulation, the collective interest is very compelling. Apart from the peace of mind which comes from the absence of guns, the number and scale of crimes, such as suicides, robberies, break-ins and incarcerations, impose huge costs on society. On the other hand, the interests of people who are interested in guns must, as with any other significant minority group in a democracy, be respected as far as possible. There is no doubt that this balance is badly out of kilter in countries like the US, and most analyses would ascribe the situation to the same forces of inertia and nostalgia which were prominent in Australia.

Australia proved that compromise for greater community benefit is something which can go beyond individual power blocs and unite a country. Australia had many of the makings of political obstinacy –

a strong pro-gun lobby group, seemingly intractable views between rural and urban voters, a decentralized federal system in which states exercise considerable control and a long history of attempted reforms being thwarted owing to powerful interest groups. More often than not, discussions regarding contentious policies resulted in divisive standoffs between these opposing interest groups. Under Howard's leadership, the Australian government was able to mediate smoothly between competing interest groups and power blocs in order to permit the broader public interest to prevail.

Many other countries have managed to reform their regulation of guns to reflect the transformation of societies from their rural and dangerous beginnings to being largely urban and peaceful. In some cases, such as Canada, reform came after the kind of shock which stunned Australia. Canada's Firearms Act 1995 followed the massacre of fourteen university students at the École Polytechnique in Montreal. Subsequent Canadian gun regulations went further by banning more than half of all registered guns and requiring owner licensing and registration of all long guns (Harinam and Mauser 2018). Norway has long had tough gun laws, which explains why the country has such low gun homicide rates, but they were tightened even further following a 2011 massacre which killed seventy-seven people.

Following the terrorist attack in March 2019 in Christchurch which killed fifty people, Jacinda Ardern, the prime minister of New Zealand, faced a similar choice as John Howard. While mourners around the world offered thoughts and prayers to the victims, Ardern and her government chose action. And like Howard, Ardern knew she had to move fast in the wake of tragedy. It took just six days for New Zealand to ban semi-automatic rifles and announce a mandatory gun buy-back programme, which was hailed as the 'fastest response ever by a government after a tragedy' (Beckett 2019). No doubt, Howard's swift response following the Port Arthur massacre provided New Zealand with the inspiration to enact such reforms and a script to follow in terms of the gun buy-back program. Ardern only had to look across the waters to realize that gun reform was the most effective way to prevent further attacks.

Asian countries tend to have a more dirigiste approach, creating massive disincentives to abuse by doling out harsh punishments in response to irresponsible gun use. Singapore assigns the death penalty to anyone who discharges a gun in the course of committing a serious offence, even if no one is injured or killed. The country has one of the lowest gun ownership rates, either licit or illicit, in the world. Between 2000 and 2015, there were only two gun homicides in Singapore (Alpers and Picard 2018). Japan also has negligible incidences of gun abuse due to similar punitive consequences for abuse.

Norway, Switzerland, Israel and Singapore have militia armies, which means they are made up of able-bodied, trained citizens ready and equipped (with firearms in their homes) to serve at any moment. Paradoxically, these countries, while they show high gun usage, have low incidences of gun abuse. Israel has among the highest number of guns owned by civilians, yet the number of gun-related deaths is only about two per 100,000 people, among the lowest in the world (Kershner 2018). The key seems to be that proper training in firearms at a young age helps instil the proper respect for them.

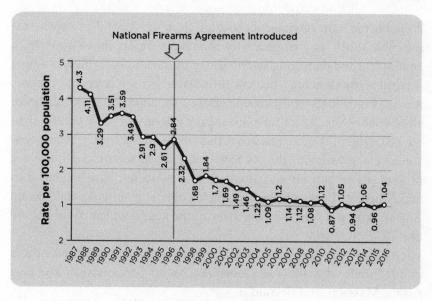

Figure 15.2: Gun Deaths Decline

Gun deaths (per capita) have declined by two thirds since the gun buy-back plan was introduced.

Source: Alpers & Rosetti, 2016; cited in *Medics for Gun Control*

Whether it is conscription or legislation, a nation's policies are always about trade-offs between the individual interest and the interest of the society at large. Think of the collective ledger of costs linked to gun abuse, such as peace of mind, suicides, robberies, break-ins, incarcerations and the impact on the morale of the police force. The US has nearly four times the number of convicted criminals as Australia (OECD 2019). A study in the *American Law and Economics Review* found that gun-related suicides have declined in Australia by about 74 per cent since its gun buy-back programme was initiated (Leigh and Neill 2010). Robberies and burglaries have also fallen significantly.

Bill O'Reilly, formerly of Fox News, once called mass shootings 'the price of freedom' (Roy 2017). Australia shows us that they may actually be an enormous cost of ignorance, but one which can be avoided with the right leadership.

Conclusion

Probably the most obvious observation from the Australian case is that a terrible shock may be necessary to make a society move away from an obsolete and damaging system. It seems obvious that this movement is particularly difficult when the jurisdiction is very large and diverse. Australia only had to turn around about six million adult voters, almost all of them white. In contrast, no society is larger or more diverse than the US, with all the complications this brings to the legislative process. Some very severe gun shocks have occurred in recent years, but the proponents of gun liberty, although in a minority, have managed to make their will prevail. Perhaps the answer is to remove the Second Amendment and turn the issue over to the states, which could behave like *TSTF* countries.

(An abbreviated version of this chapter appeared in *Foreign Affairs* in 2017 under the title 'How Australia Passed Gun Control: The Port Arthur Massacre and Beyond'.)

References and Further Reading

Alpers, P. and M. Picard. 'Singapore – Gun Facts, Figures and the Law'. *GunPolicy.org*, 2018. https://www.gunpolicy.org/firearms/region/singapore.

Altmann, C. *After Port Arthur* (Crows Nest, N.S.W.: Allen & Unwin, 2006).

Bachmann, H. 'The Swiss Difference: A Gun Culture That Works'. *TIME*, 2012. http://world.time.com/2012/12/20/the-swiss-difference-a-gun-culture-that-works.

Beckett, L. 'New Zealand's swift change to gun laws highlights 25 years of US inaction'. *The Guardian*, 2019. https://www.theguardian.com/world/2019/mar/21/new-zealand-shooting-swift-gun-law-changes-contrast-us-inaction.

Breiding, R. J. 'How Australia Passed Gun Control: The Port Arthur massacre and beyond'. *Foreign Affairs*, 2017. https://www.foreignaffairs.com/articles/australia/2017-10-13/how-australia-passed-gun-control.

'Buttigieg: 'If More Guns Made Us Safer, We'd Be the Safest Country on Earth.' *NBC Washington*, 2019. https://www.nbcwashington.com/news/politics/Buttigieg-If-More-Guns-Made-Us-Safer-Wed-Be-the-Safest-Country-on-Earth-511931742.html.

Friedman, M. 'Why Not a Volunteer Army?'. *New Individualist Review*, 1967. p. 825. https://oll.libertyfund.org/titles/raico-new-individualist-review.

Grubel, J. 'Australia's gun controls a political template for the U.S'. *Reuters*, 2013. https://www.reuters.com/article/us-usa-guns-australia-idUSBRE9320C720130403.

'Gun Deaths in Australia'. *Medics for Gun Control*, no date. https://www.medics4guncontrol.org/gun_deaths_in_australia.

Harinam, V. and G. Mauser. 'Canada's Impending Gun Ban: Three lessons for the U.S.' *National Review*, 2018. https://www.nationalreview.com/2018/12/canadas-impending-gun-ban-three-lessons-for-the-u-s/.

'Incarceration rates in OECD countries as of 2018'. *Statista OECD*, 2019. https://www.statista.com/statistics/300986/incarceration-rates-in-oecd-countries/.

Kershner, I. 'Fact check: is Israel a model when it comes to guns?'. *The Seattle Times*, 2018. https://www.seattletimes.com/nation-world/fact-check-is-israel-a-model-when-it-comes-to-guns/.

Leigh, A. and C. Neill, C. 'Do Gun Buybacks Save Lives? Evidence from Panel Data'. *American Law and Economics Review*, vol. 12, no. 2 (2010): pp. 509–57. https://doi.org/10.1093/aler/ahq013.

Masters, J. 'US Gun Policy: Global Comparisons'. *Council on Foreign Relations*, 2017. http://www.cfr.org/society-and-culture/us-gun-policy-global-comparisons/p29735.

Roy, J. 'Bill O'Reilly calls mass shootings "the price of freedom"'. *Los Angeles Times*, 2017. https://www.latimes.com/nation/la-las-vegas-shooting-live-updates-bill-o-reilly-calls-mass-shootings-the-1506980448-htmlstory.html.

Wahlquist, C. 'It took one massacre: how Australia embraced gun control after Port Arthur'. *The Guardian*, 2016. https://www.theguardian.com/world/2016/mar/15/it-took-one-massacre-how-australia-made-gun-control-happen-after-port-arthur.

Zhang, L. 'Firearms-Control Legislation and Policy: Singapore'. *Library of Congress*, 2015. https://www.loc.gov/law/help/firearms-control/singapore.php.

Conversations and Interviews

John Howard and William Cox.

Part C
The Future of Nations

16

Citizenship à la Carte

How citizens are becoming more mobile, and why
nations increasingly compete for foreign talent
and wealth

Global Traveller

Source: Wikimedia Commons

'Are YOU a Global Citizen? Let us help you become one.'

So shouted an advertisement in an in-flight magazine, seeking to lure first-class passengers dreaming of travelling without restrictions. Obviously, a lot of people want to become global citizens and, not surprisingly, a whole new industry has emerged around residence permits and citizenship to serve them.

Christian Kälin, chairman of Henley & Partners, the world's leading consultancy group specializing in residence and citizenship planning, estimates that several thousand people spend a combined $2 billion or more a year on acquiring another citizenship and even more on alternate residences. Between thirty and forty countries now have active economic citizenship or residence programmes and another sixty have provisions for one in law (Valencia 2017).

In this chapter, we examine the use of residence permits and citizenship as tools for nations competing to attract the most desirable immigrants, such as top scientists, executives and very rich people. We do so from an admittedly narrow perspective, arguing that it improves the competitive position of small countries more as compared to big countries. Many difficult moral and ethical issues have arisen regarding human migration in our times. We do not, by avoiding them, mean to understate their importance in any way; but they are not the subject of this book.

People have been migrating for centuries, seeking a better future for themselves, but in the past few decades there has been a marked increase among the wealthy, talented and knowledgeable seeking to trade up, or obtain a second residence. Probably the first widely noticed instance of competition among nations for talent in the modern era was in the 1930s and 1940s when the US, the UK and Russia fought over the best nuclear scientists needing or wanting to leave Germany. This activity grew slowly and discreetly, as both the potential immigrants and the recipient countries, for many reasons, didn't want to publicize what they were doing.

Today, however, this is out in the open, and the competition is no less fierce than that which pits top European football (soccer) clubs against one another, as they compete for the best players in the world. The analogy with professional sport is particularly apt, as the aim of all concerned, especially the countries, is to win. And negotiations between potential buyers and sellers are governed by certain rules and gamed by armies of agents.

In 'A Passport of Convenience', Judith Gold and Ahmed El-Ashram, economists at the IMF, describe the new phenomenon of nations 'catering to a small but rapidly growing number of wealthy individuals interested in acquiring the privileges of visa-free travel or the right to reside across much of the developed world, in exchange for a significant financial investment'. I will build on their research and show that citizenship is yet another example of how globalization has redefined many aspects of our lives.

To understand where we are, let us first look back at where we have come from.

Genesis

Historically, nationhood has been a largely monogamous affair. The concept of citizenship originated in Athens in 600 BCE under jus soli, meaning 'right of the soil'. The concept gives anyone born in a particular state the right to nationality. Citizenship based on 'right of the soil' later gave way to the principle of jus sanguinis, or 'right of blood'. In this instance, citizenship is inherited through parents rather than established by birthplace. This became the foundation of Roman law, and later, Common Law, and is still the most prevalent basis for citizenship in most countries today.

From the outset, citizenship was considered exclusive, static and permanent. Gaining access to a new citizenship required renunciation of the previous one. Attorney General Jeremiah Sullivan Black explained the American rationale in 1859: 'No government would allow one of its subjects to divide his allegiance between it and another sovereign; for they all know that no man can serve two masters' (Kälin, no date).

Citizenship entitles the holder to certain legal rights, but it also exacts certain duties and responsibilities. For most of us, citizenship also means common allegiances and loyalties, even a shared sense of belonging. It is what codifies social norms which regulate the vast expanse of our behaviour. As such, it is most likely absorbed through experience than bought with money. Purchasing citizenship can be a source of opprobrium, as Harvard's Steven Pinker pointed out to me: 'There has been a widespread and long held perception that citizenship had a sacred value, like belonging to a family, and buying it is as taboo as selling one's child, or one's vote.'

The concept of acquiring an additional nationality may have been uncommon, but it is not necessarily new. This form of citizenship dates back to Roman law under the concept of ius pecuniae or 'right of money'. This refers to countries granting citizenship to foreign individuals based on contributions, usually in the form of investments. German and Italian merchants who helped Britain in empire building were granted British citizenship in the eighteenth century as a quid pro quo for their contributions. For more than 150 years, Switzerland has attracted the rich and famous. Lord Byron composed poetry overlooking Lake Geneva. Charlie Chaplin, Audrey Hepburn and Freddie Mercury sought Switzerland's pristine air and stunning views once they retired from the spotlight. But there was a price to be paid.

Granting citizenship on the basis of financial contributions has often been given bad press. The perception is that it may also offer a back door to criminals but, as with any offshore activity, it spans a wide ethical spectrum. St. Kitts and Nevis in the Caribbean were among the first to launch these programmes back in 1984, soon after achieving their independence from Great Britain. Their primary appeal was that they conferred citizenship with minimal or no residency requirements. To many, this was as an obvious attempt to create a legalized black market for superfluous citizenships for human rights violators, money launderers or other fugitives from justice.

But the reality is very different. Perceptions have changed and the business of providing residence permits and citizenships has flourished in the wake of insatiable demand. As with any market, there are buyers and sellers. Let us look at them.

Consumer Citizenship

'Billionaires from third world countries can be treated like third class citizens when they visit the developed world,' Judith Gold of the IMF told me, which identifies the most obvious and robust source of demand for citizenship by foreigners. The rapid growth of private wealth, especially in emerging market economies, has led to a significant increase in affluent people interested in greater global mobility and fewer obstacles to travel, such as those posed by visa restrictions (El-Ashram and Gold 2015). However, their countries are likely to be among those, such as China, India and Brazil, which offer their citizens the most restricted passports.

Dimitry Kochenov, a constitutional law expert at Groningen University who works closely with Henley & Partners, maintains a 'Quality of Nationality Index'. For Travel Freedom, India ranks 140 out of 171 countries on the list, as it permits citizens visa-free travel to only forty-nine countries. The Chinese passport is only marginally better, ranking 116th with easy travel to sixty countries (Kälin and Kochenov 2017). Understandably, the wealthier among their citizens are less inclined to let the world's bureaucrats limit their global manoeuvrability.

Countries featured in *TSTF*, unsurprisingly, rank among the highest with regard to automatic visa permissions, which could be seen as an index of connectivity with the world. Singapore and Switzerland have automatic visa arrangements with 176 countries. Citizens of Denmark, Finland, Norway and Sweden are permitted to travel to 175 countries. Only Germany fares slightly better with 177 countries (Kälin and Kochenov 2017). This explains why many wealthy Chinese and Indian citizens seek to acquire these flexible passports – even if it means losing citizenship in their respective home countries.

There are other reasons for demand. Many people feel their countries are politically unstable or threatened by climate change – the so-called 'doomsday preppers'. Others choose to acquire a new citizenship simply because they can. Take, for example, Peter Thiel, the billionaire co-founder of PayPal. He was granted New Zealand citizenship despite spending only twelve days in the country (Roy 2017). Julian Robertson and John Griffin, well-known American hedge fund managers, have also secured New Zealand residency.

Historically, youth has been the largest source of migrants but this may be changing. Ageing societies and shortfalls in pension savings mean that older citizens may look to live in countries where they can stretch their dwindling savings further. Applications for Australian residence from UK citizens doubled following the Brexit vote and the Australian passport ranks as the most popular among British nationals – with the UK having just sixty-two days of sunshine annually compared to 200 in Australia, it's no wonder. Portugal is becoming a haven for middle-class French pensioners and so is Thailand with its unique Thailand Elite Residence programme.

The attraction for a second or alternate nationality may be because it gives something money simply cannot buy. Reaz Jafri, a partner focused on immigration at the law firm Withers Bergman, remarked to me, 'Being rich in China does not give you clean air, and a wealthy Argentine or Brazilian is constantly at risk of being kidnapped.' Tina Turner once told me she likes living in Switzerland because of the absence of paparazzi, and because 'people don't stare at me or bother me for autographs as they do in other countries.' Hans-Joerg Rudloff, the former chairman of Barclays Capital and of Swiss descent, echoes this sentiment: 'Switzerland is one of the few places where rich and famous people can safely walk the streets and live normal lives.'

Unfettered mobility has also become more valuable in the corporate world. Samuel Huntington introduced the concept of the Davos Man in his great book, *The Clash of Civilizations*, decades ago. He premised this lofty appellation on three beliefs – markets are more efficient than governments, the supremacy of shareholder value and nations matter little in a globalized world. The notion of the nationless Davos Man, working for a ubiquitous multinational, has grown in importance. Multinationals increasingly share a common language, values and cultures. Today, the cosmopolitan C-suite folks view their companies like aircraft carriers where they can land, refuel, get supplies and educate their children before flying off to the next destination in their career journey.

The word 'cosmopolitan' comes from Greek meaning 'kosmo' (world) and 'polite' (citizen). Languages, religions, cultures and ethnicities no longer define societies as they once did. A significant increase in international marriages has blurred traditional lines of demarcation and spurred family migration. Migrants in the eighteenth and nineteenth century had little contact with those they left behind, so the decision to leave the country was usually terminal. But twenty-first century migrants can easily communicate with their families by phone, internet, e-mail and can visit them for holidays. I recall the former head of the Swiss Banking Association from an old Basel family telling me about someone working at Roche: 'She was born in Hong Kong to immigrant parents from Taiwan. She was educated in the US, married a Canadian and worked in seven countries before she transferred to Basel. This is a very different person from those I grew up with in my village.' But in order to do this effectively, that Hong Kong native and others of her kind need a full portfolio of permissions.

For many, the world has become much more multicultural, so it is hardly surprising that attitudes towards nationhood and citizenship have changed. By necessity, these people are breaking away from family, community and local beer. They may be fed up with political trends in their native countries. They may be impelled by the fear of missing out. Surveys by Mercer, The Economist Intelligence Unit (EIU) and Monocle entice them with rankings of the 'most liveable cities'. While these surveys produce markedly different results, what is common is that cities in large countries, such as the US, the UK and China, rank very poorly, and cities in *TSTF* countries rank, on balance, very high.

The Mercer Quality of Living Survey ranks 231 cities, from Vienna to Baghdad, on quality of life, using qualitative and quantitative criteria, such as healthcare, education and infrastructure. This ranking is dominated by cities in countries with populations no bigger than Canada. Germany is again the only large country to have a city in the top twenty; the UK's highest ranked city, London, ranks forty-first and the US's highest ranked city, San Francisco, ranks thirtieth (Mercer 2018).

Playing this out to the extreme, a well-regarded passport may begin to take on the characteristics of a 'positional good' – coined by the economist Thorstein Veblen for those instances when the demand for a good paradoxically rises as the price goes up, as with a Cy Twombly painting or a house in the Hamptons, New York.

Demand Attracts Supply

Far from receding in the wake of early criticism, supply has lunged forward to meet this demand. As we have seen, between thirty and forty countries now have active economic citizenship or residence programmes, and another sixty have provisions for one in law. Advanced economies, such as Australia, Canada, the UK and the US, have had immigrant investor programmes since the late 1980s and early 1990s. They also offer a route to citizenship in exchange for investments with specific conditions, though with more significant residency requirements.

Meanwhile, about half of EU member states, most of which were historically hostile to any immigration, now have a dedicated immigrant investor scheme. Also known as golden visa programmes, they give investors residency rights and access to visa-free travel across all twenty-six Euro-area countries. The cost and design of the programmes vary by country, but most involve upfront investment and residency requirements. The required investment ranges upwards from €35,000 (US$39,500) for Latvian residence to more than S$2.5m (US$1.83m) for fast track residency in Singapore (Kälin and Kochenov 2017). In most countries, the original investment can be withdrawn after some years.

Some nations demand a straight cash donation, others require investment in government bonds or the purchase of property. Several take a longer-term view of the potential economic benefits, offering citizenship to entrepreneurs who set up a local company and create a minimum number of jobs. 'It would give me great pride to let it be known that I am a New Zealand citizen,' said Peter Thiel in his application in 2011 (*Economist* 2017). A few days later, the New Zealand government said it granted Thiel citizenship due to his 'exceptional circumstances' (*Economist* 2017). Perhaps these circumstances could have been the understanding that he would promote New Zealand on the global stage, and provide introductions and contacts for New Zealand start-ups in Silicon Valley.

These programmes can be lucrative for the host country. Portugal's golden visa programme requires the purchase of a house for at least €500,000 (US$564,000) and a minimum residency requirement of only seven days in the first year (Expatica 2019). Visa holders gain access to live in Portugal and may travel freely in any one of the EU's member countries. This programme is thought to constitute one of the most important portions of Portugal's foreign direct investment income and also contributes to rising property prices.

As with football players, the market for rich and talented people is not one-dimensional. The extent to which countries are willing to compete for someone varies with the value of the applicant. For scientists, executives, doctors and the like, the perceived value can vary widely, depending on the needs at any time.

Figure 16.1: Choice

Source: Banx

Citizenship as a Competitive Advantage

Just as the flow of trade has grown and spread, so has the flow of talent. Much of the debate about immigration has been centred around keeping certain people out. Few would argue that a state is not a state if it can't control its borders. What is new, however, is that citizenship is becoming more fungible. Nations increasingly compete for the most desirable immigrants generally for two parameters – wealth and skill. Nations have come to realize that, as they become more desirable, they can effectively rent out or sell their 'social contract' to a growing pool of well-to-do, globally mobile people. Nobel laureate Gary Becker advocated that nations should sell rights to citizenship and let the market determine the price immigrants are willing to pay. Immigrants satisfying basic criteria and paying the highest would be admitted and proceeds could be shared among existing citizens or used to fund a nation's social contract (Becker 2005). A win–win outcome, according to Becker.

Sentiments about nationality remain complex and there will always be those who resent the increasing fungibility of citizenship. But circumstances have and continue to change, so the definition of national allegiance may become even more elastic. Globalization is creating a need for freer movement of people. And with it, political attitudes about citizenship have progressed. A new class of global citizens has emerged for whom multiple citizenship is becoming the norm.

At the end of the day, GDP equals people times productivity and, arguably, the people portion of the equation is the most reliable. So to increase its GDP, a country needs to increase its population. And we know that a bulk of growth over the past generation in most developed countries has been due to immigration.

At the working level, the more valuable the immigrant, the more choices he or she has. In an increasingly knowledge-based world, the nations which can attract and hold the most knowledgeable workers tend to be more successful. Many factors go into the decision a specialist in artificial intelligence will make about where to live, including facilities, stimulating peers (cluster factor), financial stability, security and quality of life. Historically, big countries, such as the US, the UK, France and Germany, have attracted most of these people. But a few small countries have become increasingly competitive in recent times. Lars Fruergaard Jørgensen, the CEO of Novo Nordisk, told me that nearly 60 per cent of researchers working in the Swiss and Danish pharmaceutical industry are foreigners. Companies like Novo Nordisk and Roche lead this sector not by cultivating indigenous skill, but by attracting the best in the world.

Other countries featured in *Too Small to Fail* also seem well positioned to compete for this new global contest for wealth and talent. They are among the most connected countries in the world, enjoy high standards of living, offer attractive social contracts and are increasingly sensitive to the need to be attractive in the market for top foreign talent and capital. They are also blessed with some of the world's most liveable cities.

Whatever happens, the result will be known publicly. Probably someone will establish statistics tracking the evolution of the price of citizenship in various recipient countries. Our money will be on the *TSTF* countries. A Chinese billionaire, who recently qualified for Portugal's golden visa programme, quipped to me, 'It's a bit like a modification of John Lennon's famous lyrics, "Imagine there's many countries to choose from. It isn't hard to do."'

I'm not sure if he noticed Lisbon was climbing the ranks among the most liveable cities, or if he read the advertisement in the airline magazine tantalizing him with 'Are YOU a Global Citizen? Let us help you become one.' But he is among them now.

(This chapter draws heavily on Judith Gold and Ahmed El-Ashram's *A Passport of Convenience*, which is an edited version of *Too Much of a Good Thing? Prudent Management of Inflows Under Economic Citizenship Programs*.)

References and Further Reading

Becker, G. 'Sell the Right to Immigrate'. *The Becker-Posner Blog*, 2005. https://www.becker-posner-blog.com/2005/02/sell-the-right-to-immigrate-becker.html.

El-Ashram, A. and J. Gold 'A Passport of Convenience'. *IMF*, 2015. https://www.imf.org/external/pubs/ft/fandd/2015/12/pdf/gold.pdf.

'Golden Visa Portugal: Requirements for a Portuguese golden visa'. *Expatica*, 2019. https://www.expatica.com/pt/moving/visas/golden-visa-portugal-requirements-for-a-portuguese-golden-visa-1042263/.

'How Peter Thiel became a New Zealander'. *The Economist*, 2017. https://www.economist.com/asia/2017/02/02/how-peter-thiel-became-a-new-zealander.

Huntington, S.P. *The Clash of Civilizations: And the Remaking of World Order* (London: The Free Press; Simon & Schuster, 2002).

Kälin, C. 'Opinion: The Rise of Multiple Citizenship'. *Henley&Partners*, no date. https://www.henleyglobal.com/industry-news-details/the-rise-of-multiple-citizenship/.

Kälin, C. and D. Kochenov. 'About the Index'. *Henley & Partners – Kochenov Quality of Nationality Index (QNI)*, 2017. https://www.nationalityindex.com/about.

'Quality of living City Ranking'. *Mercer*, 2018. https://mobilityexchange.mercer.com/Insights/quality-of-living-rankings.

Roy, E.A. 'New Zealand gave Peter Thiel citizenship after he spent just 12 days there'. *The Guardian*, 2017. https://www.theguardian.com/world/2017/jun/29/new-zealand-gave-peter-thiel-citizenship-after-spending-just-12-days-there.

The Global Liveability Report 2017, The Economist Intelligence Unit, 2017. https://pages.eiu.com/rs/753-RIQ-438/images/Liveability_Free_Summary_2017.pdf.

Valencia, M. 'Citizens of anywhere'. *1843 Magazine*, 2017. https://www.1843magazine.com/features/citizens-of-anywhere.

'Vienna tops Mercer's 20th Quality of Living ranking'. *Mercer*, 2018. https://www.mercer.com/newsroom/2018-quality-of-living-survey.html.

Conversations and Interviews

Christian Kälin, Dimitry Kochenov, Hans-Joerg Rudloff, Judith Gold, Lars Fruergaard Jørgensen, Reaz Jafri, Steven Pinker and Tina Turner.

17

Size of Nations

Why nations in the future will be smaller, nimbler and more cohesive

Small Can Be Better

Source: Banx

'Imagine there's no country. It isn't hard to do,' sang John Lennon once. Indeed, if you were to look out of the window of one of Elon Musk's Space X rocket ships in space, you would see no demarcations of national land borders. But this is just looking at the surface. Charles Tilly, a political scientist from Columbia, once said, 'War made the state and the state made war' (Tilly 1975). The taxonomy of political territories

283

as we know them today is like the rings of a thick oak tree – hidden and yet containing the vacillations of conquest and defeat. Places such as the Marne, Gallipoli, Stalingrad, Trafalgar and Valley Forge, even if no longer visible, have defined the controversial lines which both separate and bind modern societies and are indelibly etched into our historical memories.

This journey of conflicts has deeply entrenched our concept of nationhood, as well as our sense of identity and belonging. With nations come laws and social norms which govern our behaviour, social contracts which reflect our trade-offs between individual freedoms and collective rights and languages which facilitate how we communicate with one other.

Our modern political institutions have also been a result of conflict and struggle. Francis Fukuyama noted, 'Most people living in rich, stable, developed countries have no idea how Denmark itself got to be Denmark – something which is true for many Danes as well. The struggle to create modern political institutions was so long and so painful that people living in industrialized countries now suffer from a historical amnesia regarding how their societies came to that point in the first place' (Fukuyama 2012).

Throughout history, the size of a nation has determined its power. Smallness, to the extent anyone bothered to pay attention, has been associated with weakness, a limited capacity to act and even the ability to survive for long. While there is much discussion today about the future consequences of artificial intelligence, climate change, ageing populations or driverless cars, there is surprisingly little discussion about what nations might look like in the future. Nations – and nationalism – have taken considerable criticism of late, but they nevertheless continue to rank as the most important measure to define our sense of identity and belonging.

This chapter reviews the factors which have determined the size of nations and suggests that these parameters should be revised in the light of significant changes in technology, demographics and social cohesiveness. In closing, it argues that power, or at least competitiveness, is decoupling from size, which means being small may increasingly be an advantage for a nation's prosperity and its ability to adapt in a rapidly changing world.

* * *

The Decoupling of Size and Power

Throughout history, the size of a nation, both in terms of land and population, has been equated with power because it conferred three principal advantages which increased with scale. First, a large population allows defence costs to be amortized over more taxpayers thus lowering the per capita expense. Second, the richer resource endowment which tends to come with large geographical size reduces dependency on foreign imports and fuels the nation's industrial growth. Third, a bigger domestic market propels the economy by generating greater and more stable demand.

Much of wealth creation until the industrial revolution was a matter of conquest, plunder and colonialization, so size became a means to an end, legitimate or otherwise. The motivations of Alexander the Great, Julius Caesar, the Vikings, Napoleon, Hitler, Stalin or Victorian Britain may have differed in degree and era, but not in their primary objective.

However, at some point in each of these instances, aggressors encountered an unassailable resistance, which stopped the world from becoming 'as one – with nothing to kill or die for,' as John Lennon sang. The British empire under George V was the largest empire in history, yet at its peak, it controlled only 25 per cent of the world's population and even less farmable land. But that empire, like so many before it, soon began crumbling under its own weight.

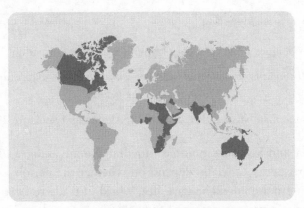

Figure 17.1: The British Empire

This map shows the countries controlled by the British empire at its peak in 1920, marking the apex of the 'bigger is better' mantra for nation formation.

Source: Wikimedia Commons

What determines a nation's size? Harvard's Alberto Alesina and Tufts' Enrico Spolaore's epochal work, *The Size of Nations*, argued that the size of nations has been historically determined by a trade-off between the benefits from scale and social cohesion. The time-tested advantages of scale include security; big nations tend to have more cost-effective militaries and are less likely to be attacked. Moreover, in a world of barriers to trade, larger countries have access to greater natural resources and larger markets. However, at some point, the costs of what they broadly dub 'heterogeneity' set in due to the political costs associated with increasing remoteness, the diversity of ethnicities and languages, clashing social norms or other bases for competing for public goods and policies which must be shared within a nation. At some stage, these factors offset the benefits of scale, and limit the expansion of nations, empires and other political unions.

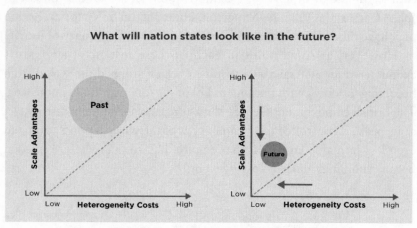

Figure 17.2: Changing Dynamics of State Formation

This graph shows how scale and heterogeneity will be less important for state formation in the future.

Source: Lambais and Breiding 2019; Alesina and Spolaore 2005

Alesina and Spolaore pointed out that the advantages of national size for prosperity crucially depend on whether the nation is closed or open to international exchanges. In a world of trade restrictions, large nations have a greater potential for growth since political boundaries determine the size of their market. However, these benefits are reduced or even eliminated by smaller nations through economic integration and globalization. Owing to the ubiquity of the internet, customer demand today is no longer limited to national borders and, thanks to declining transportation costs, companies can access vastly larger markets irrespective of their location. The cost of distance has collapsed, as we have already seen. Søren Skou, the CEO of A.P. Møller-Mærsk, confirms, 'It no longer matters whether you manufacture in Shanghai or St Louis' as far as transportation costs are concerned.

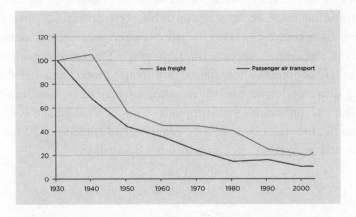

Figure 17.3: Declining Cost of Distance

This figure demonstrates how the cost of shipping sea freight and travelling by plane has declined over time.

Source: Minsch 2019

The internet is now the most important medium for distribution and sales for an enormous range of products. Amazon alone sells more than twelve million products and when Amazon Marketplace sellers are included in the total, the product count soars to over $353 million (Hufford 2018). Alibaba recorded $30 billion in sales within twenty-four hours during a one-day promotion (Kharpal 2018). To put this number in perspective, this exceeds what McDonalds generates in global annual revenue and is about Sainsbury's, the large UK grocery chain, turnover in a year. Spotify, the Swedish streaming music company founded in 2006, already has over 200 million monthly active users, which is twenty times the population of Sweden (Sanchez 2019). Spotify's most successful market, measured by per capita use, is Chile and it doesn't even have an employee there, let alone an office.

Of course, small nations are not the only ones to benefit from the globalization of trade. China, India, Korea and Japan have also become richer. America's most competitive companies earn more abroad than at home because people around the world want their products. Apple, the world's most valuable company, earns around 60 per cent of its revenues and more of its profits abroad (Thompson 2013).

While there may often be hard negotiations to ensure that international trade terms are equitable, few economic laws are as universally accepted as David Ricardo's axiom that international trade results in a win–win outcome for all nations. Yes, there are opponents and we will continue to hear the call for greater protectionism, especially during down cycles, or from those who, for various reasons, are losing out. But the inexorable tendency which has prevailed since Ricardo defined the theory of comparative advantage of trade in 1817 has been simple and compelling: 'It can hurt but it's worth it.'

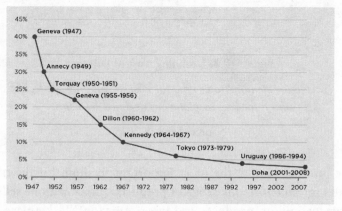

Figure 17.4: Reduction in Tariffs

This chart demonstrates how trade barriers have declined substantially over time.

Source: Minsch 2019

Like it or not, we live in a world where ideas, research, labour, manufacturing, financing and consumers have become more ubiquitous. Often, the components of a product cross borders several times through its production process. The iPhone has become the poster child of modern trade, where the idea was conceived in the US, the sourcing done in the US, China and Europe, the manufacturing in China and the distribution globally. The value of international trade in relation to world GDP has grown from 24 per cent in 1960 to over 71 per cent in 2017 (World Bank 2017). Trade has been growing at nearly triple the clip of domestic GDP, so those countries who are opening up are reaping the greatest benefits. It is difficult to imagine that anyone can truly put this genie back in the bottle.

While one may assume that there are benefits of scale when it comes to productivity per citizen, as our first chapter 'Fallacy of Scale' points out, there is no longer any correlation between size and relative productivity. Indeed, *TSTF* nations demonstrate a remarkable level of productivity for their size, vastly outperforming larger nations.

Furthermore, it is hard to see how even the biggest countries could leverage the former advantages of size into ever greater prosperity. For one thing, size and power no longer translate into territorial gains. Harvard's Stephen Walt points out that the US has spent trillions on military spending since the Vietnam war, but none of it has resulted in the expansion of the nation's territory by even one additional square kilometre. Nor has military success translated into political success. Far from being rewarding, the invading and occupying of other nations, such as Afghanistan, Iraq and Vietnam, have proven to be a massively pricey pain in the neck. To update Tilly's observation, 'States continue to make war, but war rarely makes states any longer.'

Size may even confer instability. Paul Kennedy of Yale argued in *The Rise and Fall of the Great Powers* that powerful nations are fundamentally unstable. The more states increase their power, the larger the proportion of their resources that they must devote time to maintain, which in turn leads to their fall. Kennedy cited the Roman, Spanish, Portuguese and British empires, as well as the USSR and others to support his thesis.

Thanks to the increasing cost of defence, smaller countries must rely on allegiances with a superpower for their protection, effectively paying rent in exchange for their protection rather than mounting their own costly defence systems. The US spends over two and a half times more than China and over nine times more than Russia on defence (Brown 2018). Smaller countries simply cannot compete unless, like North Korea, they are willing to sacrifice almost everything else. *TSTF* nations, if we exclude Israel, spend about half the amount on defence when compared to the global average, freeing up scarce tax money to invest in their social contracts, R&D and other benefits for citizens' well-being (World Bank 2017).

However, this doesn't come without problems. Donald Trump criticizes members of NATO and other countries for free-riding the US military or for not contributing their proper share. There may be some truth in this criticism, assuming the levels of expenditure are justified, particularly if one considers the expenses of Japan (0.9 per cent of GDP) and Germany (1.2 per cent of GDP) relative to their size (Brown 2018).

TSTF countries, however, are better at avoiding conflicts (and Mr Trump's attention). Our chapter on 'Modesty' shows how greater humility breeds fewer conflicts. Smaller countries understand the advantages of avoiding geopolitical rivalry. This requires achieving their goals not through confrontation, coercion or bribery but by negotiation.

The Global Peace Index, produced by the Institute for Economics and Peace, ranks nations' relative peacefulness by criteria such as homicide rates, prison populations and political conflicts. *TSTF* countries dominate the top rankings and the only country larger than Canada to feature in the top fifteen is Japan.

Far from initiating conflicts, *TSTF* countries try to alleviate them. A quick glance through the roster of past recipients of the Nobel Peace Prize shows the inverse relationship between nation size and the origin of the recipients. Henry Dunant, the founder of Switzerland's Red Cross organization, won the first Nobel Peace Prize in 1901.[22] Since then, the Swiss have won the prize thirteen more times; with their tiny population of 8.6 million, this puts them miles ahead of any other country on a per capita basis (Pariona 2017). Finland's Martti Ahtisaari won the prize for 'his great efforts, on several continents and over more than three decades, to resolve international conflicts' (Nobel Peace Prize 2008). Sweden's Alva Myrdal won the prize for 'her magnificent work in the disarmament negotiations of the United Nations' and Ireland's and Northern Ireland's John Hume and David Trimble, as our chapter on Ireland mentions, for 'their efforts to find a peaceful solution to the conflict in Northern Ireland' (Aarvik 1982; The Nobel Peace Prize 1998).[23]

Given that *TSTF* nations punch well above their weight in contributing to peace rather than conflict, their lower expenditure outlays on military would seem warranted.

---

22. Henry Dunant won the Nobel Peace Prize jointly with Frédéric Passy.

23. Alva Myrdal won the prize joint with Mexico's Alfonso García Robles.

The argument that a richer resource endowment contributes to a nation's prosperity has also become questionable. Studies show paradoxically that nations with an abundance of natural resources (such as oil, gold or industrial metals) tend to experience less economic growth, less democracy and worse development outcomes than countries with fewer natural resources in what is commonly termed as the 'the resource curse.'[24] Abundance of a natural resource can lead a country to focus its production means on a single industry, such as oil production, and neglect investment in other sectors. As a result, the nation becomes overly dependent on the price of the commodity, and overall productivity becomes volatile. Additionally, these countries are more susceptible to large scale government corruption, since lowly paid bureaucrats have considerable power and are tempted to accept bribes in exchange for granting drilling or mining rights, as seen in countries such as Nigeria, Angola and Venezuela.

Ironically, the absence of natural resources has motivated *TSTF* nations to overcome their deficiencies, making a virtue out of deprivation. Israel and the Netherlands have become global leaders in agricultural technology due to scarcity not plenty. Denmark leads the world in renewable wind energy and cloud storage thanks to its efforts to reduce dependency on oil after the oil crisis in the 1970s. Energy from water accounts for about 60 per cent of domestic electricity produced in Switzerland (Federal Council 2017). Land-constrained Singapore leads the world in urban planning across a range of parameters and is consistently ranked among the world's greenest nations even though it has no indigenous water. Despite, or because of, its island status, Singapore ranks among the most connected nations in the world through its leading airport and port at a time when connectivity offers a comparative national advantage.

In summary, several key trends in our era have severely compressed the 'Y' axis of Alesina and Spolaore's analysis. In the past generation, we have witnessed an extraordinary decoupling of power from size. Size has given way to competitiveness as the determining measure of a nation's well-being. It is a nation's ability to add value to raw materials, not dig them out of the ground, which matters today. A country's prosperity is

---

24. See, for example, Jeffrey A. Frankel's 'The Natural Resource Curse'.

increasingly determined by its ability to export superior products and attract top talent, besides its ability to respond and adapt to changing circumstances.

The Increasing Cost of Cohesion

Coincidental to the declining premium for size, many countries are now struggling with social cohesion. This trend applies to both small and large countries, but it seems especially challenging for the latter. Political upheavals, such as Brexit, the election of Trump and the surging right-wing movements in France, the Netherlands and Germany, suggest that societies are not as cohesive as they once were. There are a number of reasons for this; here is a survey of the most important.

Social cohesion was historically facilitated by institutions such as religion, family, community and employer. With their declining influence, societies are grappling to find other ways to encourage cohesion.

As our chapter 'Who Are We the People?' explains, there has been an appreciable movement towards 'me' and away from 'we'. It has been popular to celebrate diversity, but the consequence has been the proliferation of 'identity groups' formed by gender, generation, race and sexual preference, which atomise our lives and reduce our sense of shared values and belonging. As society becomes more polarized around identity groups, each side tends to take positions that please its most passionate members and, in the process, alienate others, splintering rather than uniting a nation.

Immigration also adds to social complexity. Around 13 per cent of the US population and 18.5 per cent of Sweden's population is now foreign born, which is almost three times the figures recorded in 1970 (*Economist* 2018). Around 25 per cent of the Swiss population is immigrants, four times the level of 1950, and nearly half of Singapore residents are foreign born (*Local* 2017; Yang et al. 2017). A society's ability to absorb, integrate and assimilate immigrants varies, but there is always a saturation point and the growing public backlash against immigration in many countries suggests that it may have been reached.

Some immigration is undoubtedly beneficial. However, the risk is that at some point, immigration detracts from the very thing which makes a nation attractive. Poor countries tend to have badly run institutions; rich countries have good ones, which explains in good part why they are rich. At some point these institutions and the common social norms which regulate so much of our behaviour become ineffective, undermining the attractiveness of the country.

Studies show that the cost of maintaining social cohesion increases disproportionately with each incremental immigrant and that there is an inverse relationship between social trust and heterogeneity. Kenneth Arrow, a Nobel laureate from Stanford, has shown that smaller, more homogenous societies are easier to govern and that democracy can become dysfunctional when an electorate becomes substantially more diverse and, as an almost inevitable result, more polarized (Arrow 2012). Indeed, John Howard, the former prime minister of Australia, told me that he felt part of Australia's extraordinary success over the past generation has been 'because we have a dominant culture that invites immigrants to assimilate'. The same could be said of other *TSTF* nations.[25]

Economic inequality by itself exacerbates the cost of social cohesion. The greater the difference between the haves and have-nots, the harder it is to achieve consensus on public policies. This also provides a greater temptation for politicians to seduce marginalized and civically uneducated voters by providing individual benefits such as public sector jobs, handouts or political favours in exchange for their votes.

Economic inequality and lack of cohesion also restrict a nation's ability to tax its citizens equitably. Redistribution of wealth is difficult in any society, but it works best when economic differences are moderate and there is an empathy accruing from common language, values, history

---

25. Some nations go to great lengths to assimilate new immigrants into their societies, but this is not without cost and complexity. People tend to associate with those of a similar background, who have similar social norms. As people congregate together, this sense of community can lead to the formation of ghettoes, with the risk that the nation serves as a multicultural host to colonies of immigrants. Singapore requires a cultural mix in its low-cost, subsidized housing to avoid this kind of ghetto formation. The mayor of Helsinki told me that they have measures to integrate immigrants, but lamented the challenges. Other nations, like Sweden and Denmark, have also struggled.

and sense of belonging, as in *TSTF* nations. Without these ingredients, citizens are inclined towards those self-centred tendencies which are the usual source of most political difficulties, such as tax evasion or benefits fraud. At the end of the day, society becomes divided between 'those who do' and 'those who mooch off those who do'.

Capitalism flourishes best in egalitarian societies with high degrees of cohesiveness and trust. Widespread distrust in a society imposes a kind of tax on all forms of economic activity, a tax which high-trust societies do not have to pay.

Imagine if a machine was able to generate social cohesion at a cost per unit. All nations are finding it more cumbersome, like a crowded airport security clearance, to process social cohesion. This decline in social cohesion and shortcomings in the political apparatus help explain the unprecedented dissatisfaction that many people feel towards their governments. In countries such as France, the US and the UK, trust in federal government is at an all time low. By comparison, in most *TSTF* countries, the level of trust within society and in their governments is considerably higher than the OECD average (*OECD* 2017). In Switzerland the percentage of those who trust the government is nearly 80 per cent, and in Singapore it is 65 per cent (Pew Research Centre 2017; Goh 2018).

Émile Durkheim argued that at some stage, anomie sets in: 'a condition in which society provides little moral guidance to individuals' (Gerber and Macionis 2010). It is a precarious state when the compass steering a nation's social behaviour malfunctions. Signs of this can be when shamelessness is marketed as a comparative advantage, as we have at times experienced with Donald Trump, or when discourse that has traditionally fallen with the sacred sweep of free speech suddenly become prohibited, as when the New York Times recently banned its use of political cartoons.

Towards Smaller, Nimbler, More Cohesive Nation States

'Democracy' derives from ancient Greek, meaning 'the power of the people'. It is the ability of a political system to intermediate a consensus across a variety of interest groups which determines its effectiveness. The difficulty, or cost of intermediation, rises in proportion to the number, ambiguity and breadth of interest groups, and the levels of inequality among them.

Smaller, more cohesive and egalitarian nations find it easier to craft and implement policy which gets to the root of a problem. Look at our chapters on how Australia eradicated atrocities from lax gun laws, how Finland reformed its primary education system and how Singapore implemented a novel healthcare system which achieves superior outcomes at a fraction of the costs faced by other nations. Or consider how Switzerland imposed limits on the amount of debt the government could impose on its citizens.

Size is not the only advantage. How a nation engineers its political system is also important in empowering citizens and enabling more effective policy formulation and implementation. The problem lies with the architecture of the system and not with the politician. Here are a few examples:

Each member of Congress in the US represents over 700,000 citizens; in the UK, it is 100,000 citizens per legislator (DeSilver 2018). This is less than 40,000 for most *TSTF* nations, the approximate number James Madison had in mind when he co-authored the *Federalist Papers* and helped conceive our modern-day system of res publica (DeSilver 2018). Most of the people I meet in Denmark, the Netherlands or Switzerland either know their representative personally, or feel they are one call away from someone who does if they wanted to voice a concern. People who feel they have some agency over government policy are more likely to pay attention and participate as citizens.

By contrast, nothing encourages resignation as effectively as when people feel they don't matter. Moreover, a legislator with countless and faceless constituents is likely to spend more time listening to special interest lobby groups in exchange for campaign contributions or follow a 'have I kept out of trouble today' course of public service. We are all held accountable if we choose an action which leads to bad results, but should we not also be held accountable for choosing to not do something? So argued Aristotle in his discourse on public engagement.

People are more likely to feel they belong when their interests are fairly represented. In 2017, Adam Bonica, a Stanford political scientist, found that legal professionals comprise only 0.4 per cent of citizens in the US but hold 39 per cent of the seats in the House and 56 per cent of the seats in the Senate.[26] By contrast, Bonica found that in Australia, Denmark, the Netherlands and Sweden, less than 15 per cent of politicians have a background in law. Bonica argued that a nation's inability to represent the diversity of society promotes inequality and leads to a more litigious approach when resolving conflicts.

More frequent litigation also shifts political responsibility and sovereignty away from the people towards the courts. The more courts rule upon, the less room there is for national decision making. The opposite of what Lincoln had in mind when he proclaimed 'government of the people, by the people, for the people.' There is growing concern in the US that nine Supreme Court judges decide over America's most portentous issues, rather than the majority of its legislature: Can gay people marry? Should abortion be legal? Does contributing money to political candidates count as speech? (*Economist* 2018).

This disturbing phenomenon can also be seen in Britain. Lord Sumption, among the most highly regarded former justices of the Supreme Court in the UK, argues that law is increasingly filling the void left by a decline in politics. In a series of *The Reith Lectures*, he warns that law 'now intrudes every corner of our lives, and is a corroding influence in our democracy.' Do we really need the 21,000 regulations currently imposed in Britain, plus another 12,000 by the EU—including one preventing us from recycling a teabag or children under eight from blowing up balloons? As a result, the number of lawyers per capita in Britain has increased nearly eight times in the past century. In 1911, there was one solicitor per 3,000 inhabitants; now, there is one per 400.

Law also has, in Sumption's view, an inherent bias towards individual rights. After all, it is mainly individual rather than collective grievances that serve as the impetus of new regulations. Is litigation—a process that is inherently authoritarian—always the right way to settle differences among citizens? Would not the sphere of public policy be more appropriate? Sumption confessed, 'Who am I to have, on account of

---

26. According to Justin Fox, the number of lawyers in the Senate and the House is actually declining steadily. For the first time in history, lawyers are in minority in the Senate. However, as Fox notes, 'Lawyers are of course still wildly overrepresented in politics relative to their overall numbers' and are 'wildly overrepresented in the US relative to other countries' (Fox 2019).

my position as a Supreme Court justice. A superior opinion on matters such as abortion or assisted suicide than the collective moral sentiments afforded by our political system?'

Hans Peter Frick, the former head of the legal department at Nestlé, among the most multinational companies in the world, told me there tends to be in inverse relationship between trust and legal costs among the nearly 200 nations Nestlé does business in.

For democratic structures to function and endure, they must listen to their citizens' voices, engage their participation, tolerate their protests and respond to their needs. It is dangerous when legal means are used to achieve political consensus as its legitimacy is fiat and coercion rather than collective choice. It is also hardly surprising that The Democracy Index, an index compiled by The Economist Intelligence Unit (EIU), ranks *TSTF* nations among the most democratic nations in the world.

Rank	Country	Score
1.	Norway	9.87
2.	Iceland	9.58
3.	Sweden	9.39
4.	New Zealand	9.26
5.	Denmark	9.22
=6	Ireland	9.15
	Canada	9.15
8.	Finland	9.14
9.	Australia	9.09
10.	Switzerland	9.03
11.	Netherlands	8.89
12.	Luxembourg	8.81

Figure 17.5: Democracy Index by Country 2018

TSTF nations rank among the most democratic nations in the world, according to The Economist Intelligence Unit's Democracy Index.

Source: *The Economist*

Most importantly, elected officials have the wrong incentives. Politicians everywhere are eager to get re-elected, spurring them to over-promise and under-deliver. They are also encouraged to accelerate the benefits of now and postpone the payment to later, as our chapter 'Critical but Not Urgent' shows in regard to important policy challenges such as climate change, excessive public debt and the financing of old age. Part of the success of *TSTF* nations can be explained culturally by the infamous 'marshmallow test' for children, demonstrating that the postponement of desire is better in the long run. The Swiss, for example, have voted against tax reductions and encouraged fiscal prudence. Not many countries would do that. These sorts of decisions are only possible if there is a prevailing sense that 'everyone is paddling this boat together, so it better float.' Elections in small nations also tend to focus more on issues rather than personalities and experience shows that consensus is more easily achieved on questions of facts than on personal matters.

Conclusion

If we are right in arguing that size has become unmoored from power; if we are right in saying that greater social cohesion results in more easily governable and economic efficient societies; if we are right to say that technology is causing the speed of change to accelerate at an unprecedented rate, then the future will favour smaller, nimbler and more cohesive societies.

To some extent, this is already occurring. Nations, a word stemming from the Latin 'natio', meaning birth, have increased from 74 in 1946 to 195 today. In 2017, 123 countries had fewer than five million inhabitants, 100 countries had fewer than 2.5 million and seventy-three fewer than 500,000. More than half of the countries are smaller than Switzerland, which has 8.4 million inhabitants (Spolaore, no date).

Historically, this has been a familiar pattern. Austria, Britain, Denmark, the Netherlands, Sweden, Russia and Turkey are just some examples of countries that formerly led vastly larger nations, but have downsized (or perhaps rightsized). Adapting to new circumstances has always been a catalyst for progress.

Why shouldn't Californians seek independence? To stretch the point somewhat, why couldn't the six million people living in the Miami conurbation join forces with Cubans and Puerto Ricans to create a Novo Havana as a proud vestige of the Spanish empire at its zenith? Liechtenstein, with a tiny population of 40,000, ranks among the most successful nations in the world with autonomous school, health and police systems. Hans Adam II, the reigning Prince of Liechtenstein, likens government to a utility company, which provides reliable, cost effective services to its citizens for a modest fee. Could we witness the formation of comparably sized nations? Or reframe governments along the lines Hans Adam II advocates?

The next generation will be critical, as societies confront a huge range of important issues such as climate change and ageing societies. A society's ability to respond to these challenges effectively will determine an increasing portion of its success. If smaller, nimbler and more cohesive societies confer competitive advantages, the scenarios described above may not be as far-fetched as they seem.

References and Further Reading

Aarvik, E. 'Award Ceremony Speech'. *Old.nobelprize.org*, 1982. http://old. nobelprize.org/nobel_prizes/peace/laureates/1982/presentation-speech.html.

Alesina, A. and E. Spolaore. *The Size of Nations* (Cambridge, MA: MIT Press, 2003).

Alesina, A. and R. Wacziarg. 'Openness, country size and government'. *Journal of Public Economies*, vol. 69, no. 3 (1998): pp. 305–21. https://doi. org/10.1016/S0047-2727(98)00010-3.

Alesina, A. et al. 'Is Europe an optimal political area?' *Brookings*, 2017. https:// www.brookings.edu/bpea-articles/is-europe-an-optimal-political-area/.

Aristotle. 'Book III'. *Aristotle: Nicomachean Ethics*. (Cambridge: Cambridge University Press, 2000). https://doi.org/10.1017/CBO9780511802058.007.

Arrow, K.J. *Social Choice and Individual Values*. 3rd ed. (New Haven; London: Yale University Press, 2012).

Boda, Z. and G. Medve-Bálint. 'Figure 3: Association between Institutional trust and per capita GDP (2010)'. *LSE*, 2012. https://blogs.lse.ac.uk/ europpblog/2012/08/21/institutional-trust-zsolt-boda/.

Bonica, A. 'Why Are There So Many Lawyers in Congress?' *SSRN*, 2017. https:// papers.ssrn.com/sol3/papers.cfm?abstract_id=2898140.

Brown, D. 'The 15 countries with the highest military budgets in 2017'. *Business Insider*, 2018. https://www.businessinsider.com/highest-military-budgets-countries-2018-5?r=US&IR=T

DeSilver, D.. 'U.S. population keeps growing, but House of Representatives is same size as in Taft era'. *Pew Research Center*, 2018. http://www. pewresearch.org/fact-tank/2018/05/31/u-s-population-keeps-growing-but-house-of-representatives-is-same-size-as-in-taft-era/.

'Energy – Facts and Figures'. *Discover Switzerland, The Federal Council*, 2017. https://www.eda.admin.ch/aboutswitzerland/en/home/wirtschaft/energie/energie---fakten-und-zahlen.html.

Fox, J. 'Maybe Washington Does Need More Lawyers'. *Bloomberg*, 2019. https://www.bloomberg.com/opinion/articles/2019-03-08/congress-might-need-more-lawyers.

Frankel, J.A. 'The Natural Resource Curse: A Survey of Diagnoses and Some Prescriptions'. *HKS Faculty Research Working Paper Series*, 2012. https://dash.harvard.edu/handle/1/8694932.

Fukuyama, F. *The Origins of Political Order: From Prehuman Times to the French Revolution* (London: Profile Books, 2011) .

Gerber, L.M. and J.J. Macionis. *Sociology*. 7th ed. (Toronto: Pearson Canada, 2010): p. 97.

Gino, G. et al. 'Globalization and Political Structure'. *NBER Working Paper No. 22046*, 2016. https://www.nber.org/papers/w22046.

'Global Peace Index 2018: Measuring Peace in a Complex World', *Institute for Economics & Peace*, 2018. http://visionofhumanity.org/app/uploads/2018/06/Global-Peace-Index-2018-2.pdf.

Goh, A. 'Singapore: Trust Slips Further'. *Edelman*, 2018. https://www.edelman.com/post/singapore-trust-slips-further.

'Governments need better ways to manage migration'. *The Economist*, 2018. https://www.economist.com/briefing/2018/08/25/governments-need-better-ways-to-manage-migration?fsrc=scn/tw/te/bl/ed/isdonaldtrumpabovethelaw.

'How America's Supreme Court became so politicised'. *The Economist*, 2018. https://www.economist.com/briefing/2018/09/15/how-americas-supreme-court-became-so-politicised.

Hufford, J. 'Amazon Statistics: Need To Know Numbers about Amazon [Infographic]'. *nchannel.com*, 2018. https://www.nchannel.com/blog/amazon-statistics/.

Kennedy, P. *The Rise and Fall of the Great Powers: Economic Change and Military Conflict from 1500–2000* (London: William Collins, 2017).

Kharpal, A. 'Alibaba sets new Singles Day record with more than $30.8 billion in sales in 24 hours'. *CNBC*, 2018. https://www.cnbc.com/2018/11/11/ alibaba-singles-day-2018-record-sales-on-largest-shopping-event-day.html.

Liechtenstein, Hans Adam II *'The State in the Third Millennium'* (Liechtenstein; van Eck Publishers)

'Martti Ahtisaari'. *Nobelpeaceprize.org*, 2008. https://www.nobelpeaceprize. org/Prize-winners/Prizewinner-documentation/Martti-Ahtisaari.

'Military expenditure (% of GDP)'. *The World Bank*, 2017. https://data. worldbank.org/indicator/MS.MIL.XPND.GD.ZS.

Pariona, A. 'Countries With the Most Nobel Peace Prize Recipients'. *World Atlas*, 2017. https://www.worldatlas.com/articles/countries-with-the-most-nobel-peace-prize-recipients.html.

'Public Trust in Government: 1958–2017'. *Pew Research Center*, 2017. http:// www.people-press.org/2017/12/14/public-trust-in-government-1958-2017/.

Putnam, R.D. *Bowling Alone: The Collapse and Revival of American Community* (New York; London: Simon & Schuster, 2000).

Rachman, G. 'Zero-Sum World'. *Financial Times*, 2010. https://www.ft.com/ content/bcfb2d80-dd62-11df-beb7-00144feabdc0.

Ricardo, D. *On the Principles of Political Economy and Taxation*. Reprint (Kitchener: Batoche Books, 2001). https://socialsciences.mcmaster.ca/econ/ ugcm/3ll3/ricardo/Principles.pdf.

Sanchez, D. 'Spotify Now Has 200 Million Monthly Active Users – But How Many Are Paying?'. *Digital Music News*, 2019. https://www. digitalmusicnews.com/2019/01/11/spotify-200-million-monthly-active-users/.

Spolaore, E. Handout from lecture, no date.

Sumption, J. 'Law's Expanding Empire'. *The Reith Lectures*, 2019. https://www. bbc.co.uk/sounds/play/m00057m8.

'The Nobel Peace Prize' *NobelPrize*, 1998. https://www.nobelprize.org/prizes/ peace/1998/summary/.

'There are now 2.1 million foreigners in Switzerland'. *The Local*, 2017. https://www.thelocal.ch/20170831/there-are-now-21-million-foreigners-in-switzerland.

Tilly, C. *The Formation of National States in Western Europe* (Princeton, N.J.: Princeton University Press, 1975).

'Trade (% of GDP'. *The World Bank*, 2017. https://data.worldbank.org/indicator/NE.TRD.GNFS.ZS.

'Trust in Government'. *Government at a Glance 2017*, OECD, 2017: pp. 214–15. https://doi.org/10.1787/gov_glance-2017-en.

Yang, H. et al. 'Immigration, Population, and Foreign Workforce in Singapore: An Overview of Trends, Policies, and Issues'. *Research and Practice in Humanities & Social Studies Education*, vol. 6, no. 1 (2017). https://www.hsseonline.edu.sg/journal/volume-6-issue-1-2017/immigration-population-and-foreign-workforce-singapore-overview-trends.

Conversations and Interviews

Hans Peter Frick, John Howard, Søren Skou and Stephen Walt.

Epilogue

The Future

Source: Sam Gross, 1996; Johanna Breiding, 2019

For all of human history, bigger has meant better. The size of a nation, both in terms of land and population, has been equated with power because it meant greater natural resources, larger armies, greater economic production and more stable demand. By contrast, small size has been associated with weakness, a limited capacity to act and a questionable ability to survive.

But now we know this isn't the case any more. *Too Small to Fail* shows that the tide is turning, and power – at least, economic power – is decoupling from size.

In a world of fast, cheap transport and low national barriers to trade, a vast international market is accessible to all nations, large or small, at magnitudes previously unimaginable. And in a world connected by the increasingly powerful internet, consumers revel in browsing through the biggest shopping arcade in history. Alibaba recorded $30 billion in sales within twenty-four hours during a recent one-day promotion, a figure higher than McDonalds' or Sainsbury's annual global revenue (Kharpal 2018).

TSTF nations are more competitive (according to rankings by IMD and others) and better prepared to face this situation than most G20 nations for many important reasons. Take your pick: superior primary education systems, less inequality, greater opportunity for upward mobility, more efficacy at intermediating political compromise and consensus. The list goes on.

These small, outperforming nations are successful in part due to geometry. The smaller the nation, the larger the average citizen's say (vote) in its affairs. Their smallness means they are immediately exposed to market changes and problems are usually recognized earlier than larger states. They must constantly rearrange themselves and innovate to remain competitive. There are fewer degrees of separation with fellow citizens, so contact is more frequent, information exchange more accurate and actions more visible. These factors foster a high-trust society which enhances economic efficiency.

With smaller size, it is also easier to disperse power rather than concentrate it, paradoxically leading to fewer systematic tremors. Nassim Nicholas Taleb describes Switzerland as 'the most stable country in the history of mankind, and probably the most boring' (Taleb 2008). He explains, 'Most decisions are made at the local level, which allows for distributed errors which don't adversely affect the wider system'. On the other hand, there may be a hint of truth in Leopold Kohr's statement in *Breakdown of Nations*: 'Great power attracts by its nature the strong rather than the wise, and tyrants rather than democrats' (Kohr 2001).

With change happening at an accelerating pace, success increasingly depends on embracing new circumstances rather than waiting for exogenous forces to exact their consequences. Thanks to their vulnerability, *TSTF* nations lack the sense of entitlement found in larger, established nations and are quicker to adapt to outside forces.

If our analysis is right, smaller, nimbler and more cohesive societies should continue to outperform and others will seek to emulate their success. It is thus likely that we will see more of these societies in the future. To some extent, this is already happening. In 1914, there were just over fifty internationally recognized states, mostly in Europe and the

Americas. Today, there are almost 200 states, and half the UN member nations have populations of less than eight million.

We started by saying that smallness is not sufficient. There are plenty of examples of unsuccessful small nations. Think of Haiti, Lebanon or Zimbabwe. Indeed, the impetus for this book was a course I took at Harvard University – Ricardo Hausmann's 'DEV-130: Why Are So Many Countries Poor, Volatile and Unequal?'

Much of the current debate focuses not on success but on failure. There is a shelf load of recent books discussing flawed states, including *Why Nations Fail* by Daron Acemoglu and James Robinson. Even among successful nations, there is a sense of dystopia. In *The Rise and Fall of American Growth*, Robert Gordon argues that progress is a thing of the past. *Has the West Lost it?* as well as 'Is Democracy Dying?' and 'What's Killing Liberalism?' continue in the same vein.

Have we not heard enough about failure?

Harvard's Steven Pinker reminds us, 'There are so many more ways for things to go wrong than to go right,' suggesting that success is not just more elusive, but far more valuable to explain than failure. Nations do not spontaneously organize themselves to achieve higher PISA rankings, file more patents and have greater confidence in their elected officials. Hence the first pillar of *TSTF* is based on optimism and a belief that the cardinal rule of progress is alive and well. We must find something which works better and learn from it.

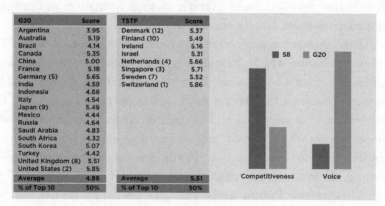

G20	Score	TSTF	Score
Argentina	3.95	Denmark (12)	5.37
Australia	5.19	Finland (10)	5.49
Brazil	4.14	Ireland	5.16
Canada	5.35	Israel	5.31
China	5.00	Netherlands (4)	5.66
France	5.18	Singapore (3)	5.71
Germany (5)	5.65	Sweden (7)	5.52
India	4.59	Switzerland (1)	5.86
Indonesia	4.68		
Italy	4.54		
Japan (9)	5.49		
Mexico	4.44		
Russia	4.64		
Saudi Arabia	4.83		
South Africa	4.32		
South Korea	5.07		
Turkey	4.42		
United Kingdom (8)	5.51		
United States (2)	5.85		
Average	**4.88**	**Average**	**5.51**
% of Top 10	**30%**	**% of Top 10**	**50%**

Figure 18.1: G20 Performance

TSTF nations have a higher average score in the global competitiveness rankings compared to the G20 countries, but less voice.

Source: World Economic Forum

To do so requires the courage to peek over the garden hedge. We all know the story of the old man who refuses to believe that the great world outside his village is any different from the one he has always known. Throughout history, little has held back progress more than this presumption. The increasing trend towards populism also leads countries to seek the solutions to problems internally, and thus compete with inertia. Yet lateral introspections are more likely to prompt social, political and economic reforms. The Federalist Papers, considered one of the most significant contributions to the field of political philosophy, and the most authoritative source for determining the original intent of the framers of the US Constitution, were an attempt to devise a form of government which could function sustainably without a king or a dictator. Hamilton, Jay and Madison surveyed the span of history and geography to find out what value could be learned from places such as ancient Greece and Rome, the Netherlands and France.

Similarly, Ludwig Erhard devised German post-war reforms, including the concept of a social market economy (soziale Marktwirtschaft) by studying what was working and not working in other countries. Germany is one of the few large nations which is firing on most, if not all, cylinders in large part because, as with *TSTF* nations, power is decentralized and its social contract more responsive. Lee Kuan Yew commissioned his talented and well-paid civil servants to find out what was working best globally and adapt it to Singapore's needs. Singapore may be the most successful example of state formation and prosperity in modern history, largely because of this approach.

There are many organizations such as the World Bank and the World Economic Forum which attempt to measure with great precision factors leading to a nation's success. They tend to look at a broad range of similar variables and measure them against peers and over time. These factors are then weighted and aggregated to form a composite score. Since they are the result of judgement x judgement x judgement they confer a false sense of precision. The differences can be quite staggering. Ireland, for instance, is ranked twenty-fourth in competitiveness by the World Economic Forum whilst IMD, which uses a similar approach, ranks it sixth.

Readers who accept this approach to analysis will be disappointed in *TSTF*. Our approach has been to treat nations as unique biological species, not spreadsheets. While we carefully studied Gini coefficients, PISA scores, patent applications and CO_2 emissions, we accept from the start that we cannot aspire to know the world with complete precision. What we have strived towards is a combination of analysis, interviews, experiences and anecdotes, as well as empirical measurements from many different perspectives. This approach has its obvious flaws, but it offers a more rounded idea of what makes these nations successful than the compilation of precise estimates of selected variables.

We have treated nations as unique species chosen for their differences rather than their similarities. Our attempt has been to show a broad range of successful cases. There are nations which are predominantly Catholic, Jewish, Lutheran, Calvinist-Zwingli and Confucian. Some are very old, dating back to medieval Europe. Denmark, the Netherlands and Sweden quit the 'bigger is better' game and downsized (rightsized) to a fraction of their former empires. Israel and Singapore are adolescents, having recently celebrated their fiftieth anniversaries. Ireland, a turnaround, has reinvented itself as arguably the most successful member of the European Union, at least as measured by the improvement of living standards of its citizens.

Approaches to social contracts vary considerably. The Nordics follow a 'tax and spend' approach, with the citizens outsourcing their social contracts as a means of freeing themselves to focus on their lives and careers. Switzerland espouses thrifty government intervention and greater self-reliance. Singapore assumes that citizens, like nations, have difficulty dealing with long term but important challenges such as pensions and health care. Their approach involves giving citizens a much-needed nudge.

Each of these nations are products of their own journeys, some longer and more varied than others. But each has been built bottom up and customized to their own circumstances. Professor Michael Hengartner, the energetic president of the University of Zurich, recently said that Singapore's system would be a disaster if implemented in Switzerland, and vice versa. He was speaking at a small dinner hosted for Kishore Mahbubani, the former president of the United Nations Security Council and Dean of the Lee Kuan Yew School, who agreed with him.

It is nevertheless encouraging to see that 'many roads lead to Rome.' The sheer breadth of successful variations should inspire hope for any nation stuck in a quagmire. Part of their journeys are common, as shown in the first section of this book. We found that citizens in *TSTF* countries tend to be better educated and more innovative, open-minded and cooperative. Their societies are more cohesive and inclusive due to a stronger emphasis on 'we' over 'me'. Their governments are better at dealing with slowly evolving yet important challenges like climate change, debt levels, pension obligations and healthcare provisions. We found that a sense of modesty is a big advantage in a world rife with envy and dependent on collegial collaboration. We even argue that a nation's approach to ownership can be valuable in preserving and passing on its industrial treasure to future generations. The skills and memories of advanced economies rely on clusters of competences of talented human beings intricately connected with one another. While less skilled parts of operations are prone to outsourcing, the most valued parts are less mobile, so should be cared for.

Notably, all the *TSTF* countries are democracies. They are simultaneously among the happiest countries in the world. This is hardly a coincidence. Where citizens are actively involved in the major decisions affecting their lives, the potential for widespread dissatisfaction and the tendency to blame the government is substantially reduced. With democracy in retreat in many places, *TSTF* is meant to be uplifting for freedom lovers.[27]

The second section of the book shows how *TSTF* countries have tackled problems with well thought-out policies and steadfast execution. Singapore achieves superior healthcare outcomes at a quarter of the costs of the US, in good part because consumers have skin in the game. Copenhagen has largely replaced cars with bicycles, resulting in less obesity, pollution and traffic congestion. Sweden spends five times more than the US on early childhood education and care so mothers have more freedom to work. The Dutch charge car buyers a fee to fund recycling as a way of encouraging responsible consumption. And Swiss citizens have inserted a 'debt brake' into their constitution to prevent their parliament from over-indebting the society.

---

27. 'Democracy in Crisis' by Freedom House, an American think tank, showed that for the twelfth consecutive year, countries which suffered democratic setbacks outnumbered those which registered gains.

1. Finland
2. Denmark
3. Norway
4. Iceland
5. Netherlands
6. Switzerland
7. Sweden
8. New Zealand
9. Canada
10. Austria

Figure 18.2: The World's Happiest Countries

The top ten happiest countries in the world have populations of less than forty million people.

Source: World Happiness Report 2019

All of these factors and policies help make *TSTF* countries fairer places to live. The Congressional Budget Office reports that the top 10 per cent of the US population owns 76 per cent of the wealth and the bottom 50 per cent controls only 1 per cent (Sahadi 2016). The same degree of division occurs in Britain and is even more pronounced in developing nations such as Brazil, India and Russia. In a world which is becoming increasingly polarized, *TSTF* nations have placed greater value on fostering inclusive growth and social mobility.

Capitalism flourishes best in egalitarian societies with high degrees of cohesiveness and trust, so nations with less inequality and a more comprehensive sense of 'we the people' perform better. Angus Deaton, the Nobel laureate from Princeton, put his finger on the nerve: 'People are quite tolerant of inequality, it is unfairness that bothers them.' Fairness occurs when political power is earned, not bought or conferred on the basis of privilege and economic reward comes from value creation rather than value extraction. *TSTF* nations succeed in large part because they are fairer places to live.

The litmus test for fairness in a society can be found in its underbelly. Life at the top tends to be good in most places. But how is life for the those on the lowest rungs? What is the extent of homelessness, incidence of crime and state of imprisonment? Here again, *TSTF* nations vastly outperform.

A New Order

TSTF is a call for a new order, one based on the recognition that the future will be very different from the world we live in today.

Technology is changing the way we work, shop and socialize. And yet, for all the talk about disruptive innovations, economic growth is largely stagnant. We are told that with new technologies, average citizens are empowered as never before, and yet large swaths of the population feels powerless and can no longer count on stable careers and a better life for their children. Pension obligations, materially underfunded today, will be ruinous tomorrow, as the number of years we live in retirement increases and the ratio of active workers to pensioners declines. Government debt levels in many nations have soared, as consumption has been accelerated and payment postponed on the expectation that future generations will bear the increased burden without receiving the benefits. This comes just at a time when social contracts should be adjusting to the increasing costs associated with 100 year lives.

Meanwhile, four trends are conspiring to make social cohesion more difficult and far more expensive to achieve. Traditionally cohesive institutions such as the family, marriage, military and religion have weakened. The difference between the 'haves' and 'have-nots' is growing, making it more difficult to achieve consensus on public policies. The proliferation of 'identity groups,' formed by gender, generation, race and sexual preference, is reducing our sense of shared values and belonging. Stagnating reproduction rates and a growing influx of immigrants adds to social complexity.

The world is also becoming more feminine. Women often have a superior aptitude for professions in a knowledge-based economy. According to one estimate, they stand to be the beneficiaries of a $22 trillion shift in assets because they will outlive their spouses, divorce or inherit (Fairley 2014). It is not an accident that almost all the gilets jaunes or those characterized in *Hillbilly Elegy* are middle-aged men, accustomed to manual labour, with meagre savings.

The onrush of change will further strain people's ability, especially the youth, to predict what skills they will need, what subject they should study and how their careers will evolve. One study predicts that 85 per cent of the jobs which will exist in 2030 haven't been conceived yet (Tencer 2017). An Oxford University study estimates that 47 per cent of US jobs could be replaced by robots and automated technology in less than two decades (Frey and Osborne 2013). These disruptions look programmed to happen faster and have a greater impact on much of the work force. Yes, the net effect is often positive and markets are self-healing, but over what time frame must they suffer? With an ageing work force, the prospect of recasting one's career at fifty-five, or even forty-five, is more daunting than a generation ago.

Wealth is supplanting wages as the determining metric of value. The majority of wealth in the developed world is now inherited and this portion is programmed to increase. This means that most of the world's wealth is owned by people who didn't work for it, which is already becoming a growing source of political conflict. The fairest societies are those in which people earn their wealth through meritocratic achievement rather than, in Warren Buffet's words, by being 'members of the lucky sperm club' (Thomas Jr. 2006).

In the face of these challenges and uncertainties, *TSTF* argues that individual enterprise alone will unlikely solve these problems, which means the burden must fall on the political system. Nations should thus be increasingly measured by their ability to intermediate political solutions and the quality and robustness of their social contracts. Yes, innovations and technological prowess are important, but they are not sufficient. Yossi Vardi, a founding father of Israel's form of Silicon Valley, summed it up to me: 'Society is a boat and if it sinks, the next big start-up like Google won't save it.'

Our survey reveals that social contracts in much of the free world were built for the last century and are woefully unprepared to face the challenges which await them in the near future. Government performance across the range of our basic needs, such as education, healthcare and savings, vary radically and in many cases are staggering under expectations with inadequate resources. Perhaps herein lies the next wave of progress.

TSTF countries have achieved superior social contracts by reframing the arguments. The traditional axis of debate has been between the left and the right. The right has argued that markets left to their own forces are the best method to allocate scarce resources – capital and labour. The left has traditionally argued that markets left alone produce vast inequalities and are prone to market failure.

Both are right.

TSTF nations are overwhelmingly pro-business, realizing that free enterprise and free trade are the twin engines which propel prosperity. They believe prosperity is more likely when effort is rewarded, but they are not naïve. While free markets work wonders in most areas, sometimes they go off the rails, as we have seen in banking, education, healthcare and the environment. Without interventions to prevent or limit market failures, consequences can range from damaging to catastrophic.

The belief in some nations is that anything the government touches turns into a mess. *TSTF* nations show us that the government and the private sector are not engaged in a zero-sum game or a tug of war between 'us' and 'them'. Instead, they are additive. Success requires more markets and a better government. They must co-exist and collaborate.

The Swiss state-owned railway runs better than any private railway system in the world. Singaporean and Finnish schools yield higher results than any private system of primary education and remind us that unequal societies are largely the result of unequal education systems. Ireland's IDA is head-and-shoulders above its competitors seeking to attract foreign investment. Zwolle, a small town in the Netherlands, is building roads from recycled plastic which should last twice as long as conventional roads, cost less and be more environmentally friendly. Denmark's concept of 'flexsecurity' is designed to enable its companies to have a high degree of freedom to lay off employees, while cushioning citizens from painful transitions in their career. All of these programmes are run by government officials for the benefit of their citizens.

Many of the challenges facing societies are agnostic to political boundaries, and the consequences of inaction will be meted out with no one spared. When it comes to climate change or the gutting of our oceans as a repository of plastic waste, we must take collective responsibility. These challenges are too big for any single nation to handle so the new order also requires a call for greater cross border collaboration, even if borders appear to be receding. The story of how Dutch communities work together to build dykes, enabling many of them to live below sea level, may be an apt example for the kind of collaboration and co-existence which societies require to survive and thrive in the future.

Getting to Denmark or Switzerland?

Why do some nations prosper and others not? What lurks at the bottom of the heart of a nation's behaviour? What determines its motivations, organizes its social relations, informs its ideologies and politics and regulates its conflicts? These vexing questions have fascinated and consumed the attention of experts in areas as diverse as anthropology, history, economics and political science.

In 2002, Lant Pritchett and Michael Woolcock wrote a paper entitled 'Getting to Denmark'.[28] They positioned Denmark as a stable, democratic and inclusive place, which all other countries should aspire to be like. In my last book, *Swiss Made*, I asked whether Switzerland was another possible model.

Getting to Denmark or Switzerland is easier said than done. At best, one nation's success can be a partial model for others. There are, however, elements which are worth considering. Why can't teachers be well paid and revered in all societies? Who would argue against the simple moral formula that effort and enterprise should lead to reward and that laziness should be shunned? Is the old Swiss adage of 'living within your means' pertinent today? And were they right to prevent their governments from living at the expense of future generations? Behind these questions are observations which go to the heart of *TSTF* nations and are available for any nation to consider or benchmark itself against.

TSTF nations are not successful because they have prevented change, or even found the optimal solution, but because they have found a way to cope with change. While *TSTF* nations are far from perfect, they grapple

---

28. 'Getting to Denmark' was the original title for 'Solutions When the Solution is the Problem: Arraying the Disarray in Development.'

more quickly, rigorously and honestly with some of the challenges facing us all. They are not utopias, but laboratories. As such, they may have arrived at the future first. Examining smaller, more adaptive and more cohesive countries may just give us the answers we need.

All nations start from different places. So, extrapolating judgements about them should be treated with caution. However, the primary generator of progress throughout history has been to find people making progress and to help spread that progress as widely as possible. Potatoes were indigenous to Peru but are now grown in many places. Not everyone had to invent the wheel—or the smartphone.

TSTF is an attempt to celebrate those things that work and invite others to evaluate them based on their own needs and circumstances. They may find that there are universal lessons to be learned from Singapore's healthcare system, Finland's approach to teaching and Switzerland's refusal to indebt future generations. If another nation is inspired by these success stories, *TSTF* will have achieved its purpose.

References and Further Reading

Acemoglu, D. and J.A. Robinson. *Why Nations Fail: The Origins of Power, Prosperity and Poverty* (London: Profile Books, 2013).

Breiding, R.J. *Swiss Made: The Untold Story behind Switzerland's Success* (London: Profile Books, 2012).

Fairley, J. 'Women to Benefit From $22 Trillion in Wealth Transfer by 2020'. *The Street*, 2014. https://www.thestreet.com/story/12956116/1/wealth-transfer-some-22-trillion-in-assets-to-shift-to-women-by-2020.html.

Frey, C.B. and M.A. Osborne. 'The Future of Employment: How Susceptible are Jobs to Computerisation?' *Oxford University*, 2013. https://www.oxfordmartin.ox.ac.uk/downloads/academic/The_Future_of_Employment.pdf.

Gordon, R.J. *The Rise and Fall of American Growth: The U.S. Standard of Living since the Civil War* (Princeton, N.J.: Princeton University Press, 2016).

'IMD World Competitiveness Rankings 2017 Results'. *IMD*, 2017. https://www.imd.org/wcc/world-competitiveness-center-rankings/competitiveness-2017-rankings-results/.

Kharpal, A. 'Alibaba sets new Singles Day record with more than $30.8 billion in sales in 24 hours'. *CNBC*, 2018. https://www.cnbc.com/2018/11/11/ alibaba-singles-day-2018-record-sales-on-largest-shopping-event-day.html.

Kohr, L. *The Breakdown of Nations* (Cambridge, UK: Green Books, 2001).

Mahbubani, K. *Has the West Lost It? A Provocation* (London: Allen Lane, 2018).

Pritchett, L. and M. Woolcock. 'Solutions When the Solution is the Problem: Arraying the Disarray in Development'. *World Development*, vol. 32, no. 2 (2004): pp. 191–212. https://doi.org/10.1016/j.worlddev.2003.08.009.

Sahadi, J. 'The richest 10% hold 76% of the wealth'. *CNN Money*, 2016. https://money.cnn.com/2016/08/18/pf/wealth-inequality/index.html.

Sala-i-Martin, X. and K. Schwab. 'The Global Competitiveness Report 2017-2018'. *The World Economic Forum*, 2017. http://www3.weforum.org/docs/GCR2017-2018/05FullReport/TheGlobalCompetitivenessReport2017–2018.pdf.

Taleb, N.N. *The Black Swan: The Impact of the Highly Improbable* (London: Penguin, 2008).

Tencer, D. '85% of Jobs That Will Exist in 2030 Haven't Been Invented Yet: Dell'. *Huffington Post*, 2017. https://www.huffingtonpost.ca/2017/07/14/85-of-jobs-that-will-exist-in-2030-haven-t-been-invented-yet-d_a_23030098/?guccounter=1&guce_referrer_us=aHR0cHM6Ly93d3cuZ29vZ2xlLmNvbS8&guce_referrer_cs=jvaxQcyE1O6EMlk7v43apg.

Thomas Jr., L. 'A $31 billion gift between friends'. *The New York Times*, 2006. https://www.nytimes.com/2006/06/27/business/27friends.html.

Conversations and Interviews

Angus Deaton, Ricardo Hausmann, Steven Pinker and Yossi Vardi.

Appendix

Selected List of High-Achieving Global Leaders from S8 Countries[29]

Denmark

A.P. Møller – Mærsk – Leader in container logistics

Chr. Hansen – Global leader in the production of probiotics, enzymes and natural colors

Demant – Leader in hearing and communication healthcare covering all areas of hearing

Grundfos – Global leader in pump technology to (re)move heat or cool water

Lego® – Leading manufacturer of interlocking plastic brick toys

Novo Nordisk – Global leader in the distribution and development of diabetes and hormone-related solutions

---

29 This list is not intended to be exhaustive but rather to showcase the breadth and scope of S8 companies' achievements in innovation and market performance across a wide swath of industries and sectors. I have preferentially chosen to highlight less-known examples of leaders in their respective fields. Therefore, this list does not include household names such as ABB, Carlsberg, Philips, Roche, Nestlé, Swatch, Unilever, UBS, etc.

Novozymes – Leading microbe and enzymes production and sales company for industrial applications

Vestas – Leading installer of wind turbines

Finland

KONE – Global leader in the elevator and escalator business

Metso – Worldwide supplier of equipment and services for the flow of natural resources

Slush – World's leading entrepreneurship movement and conference

Stora Enso – Pioneers in developing renewable eco-friendly products for various industries

Wärtsilä – Leading in smart technologies and lifecycle solutions for marine and energy markets

Ireland

Cosmo Pharmaceuticals – Global pharma company active in therapies for gastro-intestinal diseases

ICON – Global manager of clinical studies for the pharma, biotech and medical device industry

Kerry – Leading developer of nutritional and functional ingredients and taste solutions

Ryanair – Leading budget airline

Stripe – Leading software provider for online payments (founded by Irish entrepreneurs)

Israel

Check Point – Global leader in providing cybersecurity products and services

Frutarom – Leading provider of edible essences and fragrances for diverse applications

ISCAR – Supplier of precision carbide metal working tools

Mobile Eye – Leading provider of driverless-car technology

SodaStream – Leading producer of home water-carbonation and flavoring products

SolarEdge – Innovative provider of energy management solutions for photovoltaic systems

Netherlands

Acerta Pharma – Biotech company developing groundbreaking cancer drugs that recently became a 'unicorn'

Adyen – Leading provider of payment platform solutions

ASML – Leading provider of innovative lithography systems to the semiconductor industry

Inalfa Roof Systems – Leading manufacturer of sunroofs and open-roof systems for the automotive industry

NXP – Leading semiconductor manufacturer, supplying the automotive, industrial and mobile markets

Randstad – Global leader in the HR services industry

Royal Boskalis Westminster – Global leader in dredging contractor and marine services provider

Royal DSM – Global leader in nutrition, health and sustainable living solutions

TomTom – Leading developer of navigation technology, software and map development

Singapore

DBS Bank – Commercial and innovative bank in Asia holding three honors for best global bank

Grab – Leading provider of ride-sharing in Southeast Asia

Razer – Leading provider of gaming hardware, software and systems

Singapore Airlines – Leading company for passenger and cargo air transportation

Sweden

Munters – Leading provider of air treatment solutions for industrial applications

NIBE Industrier – Global leader in heating technology solutions

SOBI – Leader in treating rare diseases like hemophilia

Spotify – Global leader in providing music-streaming services

Switzerland

Barry Callebaut – Global leader in cocoa production

Bossard – Provider of world-class fastening technology

dormakaba – Leader in security and access solutions

EMS-Chemie – Globally active polymer and chemicals company

Endress+Hauser – Global leader in laboratory instrumentation and automation equipment

Firmenich – Largest privately owned company in the fragrance and flavor business

Givaudan – Global leader in flavours and fragrances

Logitech – Global leader in computer and mobile peripherals

Partners Group – Private markets investment manager for international institutional clientele

Pictet – Leader in private banking and global custody

Sensirion – Global leader in developing microsensors for the automotive market

Sika – Leading position in the area of specialty chemicals for buildings and automobiles

Sonova – Global leader in hearing-aid solutions

Stadler – Leading manufacturer of a broad variety of vehicles operating on rails

Straumann – Global leader in the manufacture of dental implants, prosthetics and biomaterials

Swiss Re – Leading reinsurance provider

VAT – Market leader in vacuum-valve technology

Index

Acknowledgements

This journey began while speaking with my daughter on holiday in Costa Rica. She was raised in Switzerland but went to college at Scripps University and Cal Arts and is an assistant professor at Williams College; so she spent most of her young adult life in the US. I grew up near Cape Canaveral during the Apollo project where my father worked, but spent much of my adult life in Switzerland. I had fond memories of the unity of purpose and remarkable esprit de corps that characterized American life at the time. As we lamented the disturbing decline in the sense of community and the rise of individualism, we began to ask ourselves why smaller nations – like Switzerland – seemed to offer a greater sense of social cohesion.

The project came to life after I gave a few preliminary lectures on the topic at Harvard, which seemed to resonate with students. Ricardo Hausmann, my former professor and head of Harvard's Centre for International Development, attended one of them and granted me a fellowship. Proposing the antithesis to his popular course 'DEV-130: Why Are So Many Countries Poor, Volatile and Unequal?' seemed like a 'mission impossible' so his consent speaks volumes about his intellectual integrity.

Harvard is a treasure chest of knowledge and talent, and I did my best to mine whatever was within my mind's grasp. I had the opportunity to go into the ring with the likes of Alberto Alesini, Peter Hall, Barbara Kellerman, David Laibson, Jenny Mansbridge, Steve Pinker, Dani Rodick, Ken Rogoff and Larry Summers. Each time, I emerged humbler and more knowledgeable than when I had gone in.

Years in the making, a book of this kind is always heavily dependent on the help and goodwill from a host of people and institutions. *TSTF* is written for a non-academic audience but nevertheless benefits from a number of academics who have spent a good part of their careers researching small nations and aspects of nation formation. These include John Campbell, John Hall, Peter Katzenstein, Tommy Koh, Ove K. Pedersen, David Skilling, Enrico Spolaore and Tobias Straumann. They have introduced me to so many aspects of history, culture, politics and socio economics, and for that I thank them.

Possibly the biggest contributors to this book have been the leaders of academia, industry and government from *TSTF* nations who made time for me to interview them. To an inordinate degree, my analytical and prospective assessments have been drawn and composed from their collective wisdom. Each of them, in different ways, have educated and influenced my views on aspects of their respective nations' history, economies, political systems, values and social norms. While I shall respect the privacy of my interviewees by not naming those who preferred not to be quoted, their patience, interest and support have been critical to the content of this book.

One of the compensating joys of working with small nations is that they have fewer degrees of separation, which makes it possible to meet scores of interesting people in the span of a few weeks. Early in the project, John Campbell from McGill University, an expert on small nations and one of the first people I interviewed, encouraged me to visit Denmark. 'Go there,' he said, 'they're lovely, accessible people and in a few weeks, you'll learn more than you will from studying a year in the library.' John was right.

I somehow managed to tug Ian Rodger, editor of my last book, out of retirement, and seeing his enthusiasm rise with each chapter provided me and our team with a shot in the arm. The editor–author relationship can be metaphysical. Ian Rodger spent a long and distinguished career with the *Financial Times* and covered more places and industries than I thought existed, ending up as international news editor. The finished text owes much to his critical comments on earlier drafts, which have long since been buried – some quietly, others after heated debate. It was these exchanges that helped me make sense of things when there was confusion. In other instances, they provided ripe and necessary moments of humour. Nobody except I knows the value of his countless comments and suggestions, or restorative bouts of humour – but it has been immense. Writing, like a sculpture, is significantly defined by what is removed.

I had a great deal of help from Bruce Mathers, who was a kind of pen-pal, exchanging provoking and valuable thoughts and criticisms every step of the way. He has never been less than wonderful. Iain Little, an old friend, is credited with having come up with the title 'Too Small to Fail.' Muireann Glenmullen was invaluable as an expert on Ireland, a valiant advocate for gender equality and occasional editor. Mineko Ikehashi was the first to read the fragile draft chapters and served as a litmus test on whether I should toss it out and go back to the drawing board or race across the finish line.

Maya Jones was a stalwart in the core team that made *TSTF* happen. She slaved over endless text revisions, provided valuable editorial input light years beyond her age, and was often the glue that held everything together.

Jeremy Banx, the renowned cartoonist, read each chapter diligently, and boosted our team's morale each time he submitted one of his amusing and insightful illustrations.

I owe a real debt to several people who helped us with specific nations or aspects of the book, including Gijs Braakman, Donald Carlow, Bjorn Edlund, Vikram Khanna, Johan de Koning, Guilherme Lambais, Shlomo Maital, Anders Magelund, Kfir Mizrachi, Frank Richter, Alp Rodopman, David Samuelsson, Max Sosland, Lilly Tahmasebi, Aloysius Chia Wei-Yan and Kevin Tan. I am very grateful to all of them.

Books are marathons, not races, and there is a massive delay between work and recognition; the occasional oasis of inspiration is essential to keep the caravan rolling. *Foreign Affairs* published an abridged version of our chapter on how Australia eradicated gun atrocities, so halfway across the dessert we received an encouraging nudge that the voyage may be worth crossing. The *Financial Times* published a short piece on my comparison of Switzerland and Catalonia, which achieved a similar effect.

A number of institutions joined our initiative and encouraged and supported me in this endeavour, thereby making this book and my Harvard fellowship possible. These include Realdania, The Wyss

Institute and Collegium Helveticum (University of Zurich and the ETH). From the outset, it was formally agreed that their support was not in any way linked to the outcome.

Special thanks also go to Sachin Sharma of HarperCollins India for making the publication possible.

There is no such thing as a definitive analysis of anything. Facts are nevertheless selected, weighed and interpreted differently. This book covers lots of nations and themes, so mistakes would have been made. Full responsibility for errors must be borne by the author. I hope those that remain are minor in impact and few in number.

The photograph on the cover jacket was shot at the Bodmerhaus by my daughter, Johanna Breiding. Built in 1640, the building has a rich history. During the earlier years, it hosted writers such as Goethe and Thomas Mann (his archives were housed here until June 2016). *Too Small to Fail* was conceived and largely written between here and Harvard University. Special thanks to Michael Hengartner, the President of the University of Zurich and newly appointed Chair of the ETH for having made my stay there possible.

I end with a special note of thanks to Mineko and my children, Nicolas, Joshua, and Johanna. This book is dedicated to them with love, gratitude and hope for a better and shared future.

About the Author

R. James Breiding is the author of *Swiss Made: The Untold Story behind Switzerland's Success* and co-author of *Wirtschaftwunder Schweiz*. *Swiss Made* has become the most authoritative work on Swiss achievements across the spectrum of industry and society. In 2014, it was selected by Pro Helvetia, the Swiss council for the arts, as the book that best conveys Swiss values and culture.

James is a graduate of IMD Lausanne and the Harvard Kennedy School. He has been selected as a fellow by Harvard University's Center for International Development in connection with his research on *Swiss Made* and *Too Small to Fail*. His work has appeared in *The Economist, The Financial Times, Foreign Affairs, The Wall Street Journal* and *The New York Times*, among other publications.

James has been awarded a fellowship at Collegium Helveticum, a research institute at the ETH and the University of Zurich. Formerly, he worked as a chartered accountant and senior manager at Price Waterhouse Coopers, a director at NM Rothschild & Sons and managing director at Templeton Investment. He founded, with the assistance of Sir John Templeton and other prominent investors, Naissance Capital, a Swiss boutique investment firm. He holds American and Swiss citizenships.